"My first thought ~~~~ Oh lord ~~~~~~~~~~~ ly read it. This one is worth the time – goo~

—Vint Cerf, Internet Pioneer

"A true business-oriented read, going deep into what social technologies are and why they are important from both a historical and future-oriented context. This book should be read by anyone wanting to understand just how important social media is in business. C-levels should carefully consider integrating social technologies into their overall strategies, managers need to know how improve their work processes and team-productivity through them and this book informs that journey."

—James Kent, Senior Solutions Consultant, Google

"With social media comes great responsibility. These networks are communities for building businesses and also for tearing them down. Ronan shows you how to inspire communities to build a meaningful and engaged brand in a new era of connected consumerism."

—Brian Solis, digital analyst; anthropologist; author of
What's the Future of Business (WTF)

"Many books detail why new technologies are changing business – Ronan Gruenbaum refreshingly shows us how organizations can embrace and adopt them."

—Erik Qualman, Pulitzer Prize Nominated Author

"Too many businesses – from start up to scale-up – misunderstand the importance of implementing social media correctly. And with thousands upon thousands of ill-informed blogs, articles, and frankly social-media-voodoo available on the web, the business world is ready for a simple and effective framework like SITCER to bring reality and experience to the forefront of our professional lives. This is a 'must-read'."

—Chris Howard, Mentor & Adviser, Techstars – the world's most
successful entrepreneur accelerator

"You will not find a more readable, more comprehensive or more commercially prag-matic guide to social technologies. Most useful to business readers, but lots of gems for individuals as well."

—Andrew Campbell, author of more than ten books including *Strategy
for the Corporate Level* (2014) and *Think Again* (2008)

"There are many books that talk about the 'what' of social media, but avoid the 'how'. Ronan tackles the latter head on with academic rigour. His framework highlights effec-tively how to integrate social technologies in any organization."

—Christer Holloman, author of *The Social Media MBA*

"In such a connected world, I find it ironic that the business world can be so discon-nected in terms of expectations, acceptance, and successful deployment of social technologies, both internally and for reaching current and potential customers. This book is an invaluable reference to help decision-makers understand the value of social technologies and create strategies for successful deployment."

—Garry Sagert, Director, University of Victoria Online

"Ronan Gruenbaum's book is a detailed primer covering all aspects of social technologies, and what businesses must consider as they are taken into the ultra-connected future. Recommended for anyone who needs to quickly understand how the world is changing, and who needs to familiarize themselves with the huge range of opportunities – including the pitfalls and gotchas their organizations may encounter along the way."

-Felix Velarde, digital marketing pioneer,
founder of Hyperinteractive, Head and Underwired

"Media is not new but the rules are and so are the implications especially when the work social is added. Social media requires a new framework and a fresh approach which is what Ronan delivers in this book. This book delivers a good balance between theory and practice and provides a framework to keep your thinking up to date and relevant."
-Tony Fish, Entrepreneur, Author and Investor

"Social media is changing our world. How can we turn social activity into revenue or even into a competitive advantage? Ronan Gruenbaum gives very tangible guidance with his framework: to strategize, to incentivize, to create trust, to champion, to engage, and to review. This book is a 'must-read' if you want to embrace the new opportunities."
-Lutz Finger, Director Data Science & Data Engineering, LinkedIn

"Social media is still under-utilized and feared; yet is a strategic differentiator/necessity. What are social technologies; how do you assess - and capture - their value in dynamic and recalcitrant organizations? Ronan's book provides a pithy, solid overview of frame-works for action - if you are working on strategy, business value - here's how to mobilize its value and make it work. It is useful both for the new economy and old."
-Katia Kerswell, social media engager on ISO's leadership programme
(and consumer policy team); Principal, Smadja and Associates
(director of the World Economic Forum); CEO,
the World Microfinance Forum Geneva

"Virtual is real, and social technologies at work are equal to real technologies in place in this supper-interconnected business world. If you do not yet agree, Ronan's book is the first and last book to challenge your 'business as usual'. By the time you get to the last page of this book, you will be thinking of your 'business as un-usual' with social technologies. Unusual is now everything!"
-Jeong Tae Kim, CEO, Merry Year Social Company;
advisory board member to the IICPSD of UNDP

"An indispensable guide to the rapidly developing world of social technologies – well-structured and well-written with many engaging examples and tips along the way."
-Jo Whitehead, Author of *What you Need To Know About Strategy*;
Director, Ashridge Strategic Management Centre

"This book provides a great overview of business aspects relevant for emergence of social technologies in everyday practices of modern companies. It shows that organi-zational effectiveness can benefit from new communication tools and concepts, which require careful planning and involvement of all relevant stakeholders for a successful implementation. Thereby, the key success factor is not the technology itself, but rather the way how people engage around social media and social technologies in order to meet their personal and business targets."

–Anes Hodzic, Managing Director, Robert Bosch, Car Multimedia

"Finally, a comprehensive survival guide for executives looking to not only understand but also implement social technology within their organizations."

–Jonathan Metrick, Founder, The Agility Project

"This provides a very comprehensive background and current status of social media. It is an eye-opener to where and how social technologies can bring value in any industry, even where you thought it would not matter. Well worth the time reading!"

–Janet Hoogstraate, MBA, PhD, Assoc. Prof., Director Biovation Park, Acturum Life Science AB, Södertälje, Sweden; Chairman, Stockholm Brain Institute, Stockholm, Sweden

"Ronan has laid out the benefits of the new age social technologies and how you can make your business (enterprise, projects, activities, etc.) more efficient by early and continued adoption of the guides he has outlined in this well-written book. I recommend this book to social leaders, business leaders, and entrepreneurs who want to succeed in the current internet age."

–Ucheoma Nwosu, Pipeline Projects Manager, Shell, Dubai

"With 14 global offices and often having engineers on the West and East coasts of the USA, in Europe, India, and Singapore all working on the same Life Science systems integration projects, we rely on using social technologies to deliver quality, manage stakeholders, share knowledge, and ensure consistency of practice. This book will help any organization in similar situations to implement social media and all social technologies to make their organizations work more efficiently, more collaboratively and producing more value."

–Conor Kane, VP & General Manager, Zenith Technologies, USA

PALGRAVE POCKET CONSULTANTS

Palgrave Pocket Consultants are concise, authoritative guides that provide actionable solutions to specific, high-level business problems that would otherwise drive you or your company to employ a consultant. Written for aspiring middle-to-senior managers working across business at any scale, they offer solutions to the most cutting-edge issues across modern business. Be your own expert and have the advice you need at your fingertips.

Available now:

ATTRACTING AND RETAINING TALENT
Tim Baker

MYTH-BUSTING CHINA'S NUMBERS
Matthew Crabbe

RISKY BUSINESS IN CHINA
Jeremy Gordon

THE NEW CHINESE TRAVELER
Gary Bowerman

THE WORKPLACE COMMUNITY
Ian Gee and Matthew Hanwell

PEOPLE DATA
Tine Huus

PUBLIC RELATIONS IN CHINA
David Wolf

Forthcoming titles:

CONVERSATIONS AT WORK
Tim Baker and Aubrey Warren

MANAGING ONLINE REPUTATION
Charlie Pownall

CRISIS MANAGEMENT
Alex Singleton

CREATING A RESILIENT WORKFORCE
Ivan Robertson and Cary Cooper

Series ISBN 9781137396792

Leveraging the Power and Managing Perils of Social Technologies in Business

Making Social Technologies Work

Ronan Gruenbaum

First published 2015 by
PALGRAVE MACMILLAN

Palgrave Macmillan in the UK is an imprint of Macmillan Publishers
Limited, registered in England, company number 785998, of Houndmills,
Basingstoke, Hampshire RG21 6XS.

Palgrave Macmillan in the US is a division of St Martin's Press LLC,
175 Fifth Avenue, New York, NY 10010.

Palgrave Macmillan is the global academic imprint of the above
companies and has companies and representatives throughout the world.

Palgrave® and Macmillan® are registered trademarks in the
United States, the United Kingdom, Europe and other countries.

ISBN 978–1–137–02481–7

This book is printed on paper suitable for recycling and made from
fully managed and sustained forest sources. Logging, pulping and
manufacturing processes are expected to conform to the
environmental regulations of the country of origin.

A catalogue record for this book is available from the British Library.

Library of Congress Cataloging-in-Publication Data

Gruenbaum, Ronan.
Making social technologies work : leveraging the power and managing perils of
social technologies in business / Ronan Gruenbaum.
pages cm
Summary: "This comprehensive and practical book looks at how to implement the
most effective social technologies in the organisation and how to manage and
sustain these successfully. Based on new research and a survey of practitioners
in the enterprise, the author provides a simple framework which makes the book
both a practical guide for managers, as well as an informative window into the
world of social technologies in business"— Provided by publisher.
ISBN 978–1–137–02481–7 (paperback)
1. Social media.   2. Internet marketing.   3. Business communication.
4. Organizational change.   I. Title.
HF5415.1265.G78 2015
658.8'72—dc23   2015012357

Typeset by MPS Limited, Chennai, India.

For Magda, Lucas, Ann, and Tom

Contents

Part 2 Why it Matters

Part 3 How to Do it

Part 4 The Future's Bright...

List of Figures

About the Author

Ronan Gruenbaum is Professor of Marketing and Technology and Associate Dean at the London postgraduate campus of Hult International Business School. Previously, Associate at Ashridge Business School, he has over fifteen years of corporate experience in e-commerce, digital marketing, mobile technologies, online learning, and social media. In addition to teaching on MBA and executive education programs Ronan has spoken extensively on the role of social technologies in business education at conferences for industry organisations AACSB, EFMD, CEEMAN, ECBE, and ABS. He is the author of the chapter "When the Classroom is no Longer a Room" in *The Future of Learning: Insights and Innovations from Executive Development* (2010, Palgrave Macmillan).

Ronan blogs at www.TechnoWaffle.com and Tweets as @SealTree.

Acknowledgments

Thanks must go first to everyone at Palgrave Macmillan for their unending patience. Unlike the great technophile and author Douglas Adams, I don't like deadlines and I hate the whooshing noise they make as they go by even more. The whooshing sound ended up being like a hurricane with so many deadlines passing by since I first agreed to write this book. Particular thanks to those who have had the misfortune of having to chase me repeatedly and guide the focus of the book: Stephen Partridge, Josephine Taylor, and Eleanor Davey-Corrigan.

Thanks must go to everyone who took part in the primary research, both through the surveys and the extensive interviews. In some cases they spoke to me about practices within their organizations without the permission of said organization. For this reason, all their comments and quotes in the book have been anonymized. But they are all real.

Thanks to Gartner for permission to discuss the details of Gartner's Technology Hype Cycle and thanks to Nic Mitham at Kzero.co.uk for permission to use their graphics and information on Virtual Worlds.

Figure 16.2 is reprinted with the permission of The Free Press, a Division of Simon & Schuster, Inc., from Everett M. Rogers, *Diffusion of Innovations*, 5th edition by Everett M. Rogers. Copyright © 1995, 2003. Copyright (c) 1962, 1971, 1983 by The Free Press. All rights reserved.

Figure 19.1 is used by permission from Geoffrey A. Moore *Crossing the Chasm*, 3rd edition. Copyright © 1991, 1999, 2002, 2014 by Geoffrey A. Moore.

I have endeavored to correctly reference and cite all sources used, but if there are any mistakes or omissions, my apologies.

Every effort has been made to trace rights holders, but if any have been inadvertently overlooked the author would be pleased to make the necessary arrangements at the first opportunity.

Thanks for the support from my colleagues at Hult International Business School and to the hundreds of students who, through different class projects, conducted a lot of primary research from which I was able to draw examples of what works and what does not. Thanks to my ex-colleagues at Ashridge Business School, for supporting me through the original research and pointing me in various directions of further study.

Finally, thanks to my wife, Magda, for her unending support and for listening to the whirling whooshing sounds of those deadlines over such a long time.

Preface

I originally thought of writing this book in 2005 when I first became aware of social media, then still in its infancy, unknown by most, ignored by some, and assumed to have no place in business. I expected someone to write a book on how to successfully implement social technologies in the workplace a long time ago, but all the books I saw talked about the successful uses of social media, often focusing on one particular platform or another, and none of them seemed to address the question of *how* an organization, of any size or type, might be able to overcome the inherent obstacles that exist in implementing any change, let alone a technological change such as this that exists thanks to the large numbers of ordinary people, employees, customers, and stakeholders who have bought into it. Social technologies have not, in general, grown thanks to decisions by the executive boards of the Fortune 500.

The number of platforms and tools proliferated to such an extent that it then seemed to me more relevant to talk about social technologies, rather than social media. Some of the tools being used were not "media" – they were not simply means of communications – but were perhaps better explained by the moniker of "Web 2.0" (all terms will be explained further in the main body of the book). That is to say that they had grown and developed thanks to the increasing use of multiple authors or creators. The ability for individuals to build products and services out of nothing, to create businesses and organizations with no up-front financing, and to disrupt the status quo with their innovations is something new. If you, the reader, can accept that your organization might not have the best minds in the world to solve a particular task, it might not truly understand its customers, that the leaders are fallible, or that great ideas can come from anywhere, not just the head of strategy, then you are closer to understanding the huge potential social technologies can offer you. If, like many, such acknowledgments for you equate to admissions of weakness and are, therefore, an anathema to the concept of business, then you will struggle to embrace the change. It is worth remembering the old adage that the only constant is change.

A few years ago I conducted some research into who had successfully implemented social media and what they considered to be the keys to their success. I also asked those who had tried and failed to implement social media, to see why they believe the experiment had been abandoned. In addition I spoke to those who had not attempted to implement any type of social media. Time, workload, and procrastination on my part meant that this book, which I had originally hoped to be finished several years ago, is not now as cutting edge as I had intended. Nonetheless, my work with organizations, with business students, with executive education, and through the industry press tells me that there are still a huge number of people who view social technologies as, "you know, for kids." And even the "kids" don't always get it, as hundreds of post-graduate business school students remind me every year.

This book is aimed at everyone. Those who still struggle to see the advantages of social technologies are strongly urged to read Part 1, if nothing else, to see the case studies and examples of how different organizations have benefitted from the various tools and platforms.

Those who are familiar with innovation and change will be interested in Part 2, which discusses the academic and business research that has already taken place over the past seven or more decades. This will also help those who need to present a case to their board or manager on why innovation is always resisted at the beginning, demonstrating the importance of the right communication methods and giving some answers to provide when the board starts listing obstacles and reasons why the innovation won't work with that particular organization.

Part 3 is the framework itself, intended as an instruction manual that can be taken by an individual and used to introduce the social technologies into the organization. Like many frameworks in business literature, everything will seem obvious and straightforward when you see it, but sometimes we need to see things clearly written out to remember to tick all the relevant boxes and not try to cut corners along the way. Cutting corners sometimes works, but it will more often than not involve hitting curbs and crashing into walls, leaving casualties in its wake and ensuring the next people who try to drive through any change are forbidden from even turning at that spot for fear of further accidents (if you will forgive the continued, mangled, metaphor).

Finally, Part 4 is about the future: Its aim is to help readers remember that one should not embrace and implement innovation now and then bury one's head in the sand when newer technologies come along in five, ten, or twenty years. As the text explains, the pace of innovation and the speed of technological development are increasing. The dreams of science-fiction are becoming science-prediction ("sci-pre" anyone?) and the unexpected couplings of disparate technologies often supersede the imaginations of sci-fi writers.

Nostalgia isn't what it used to be.[1] Things never are. Any attempt to only hold on to the technologies we know and use comfortably would keep us in the dark-ages. The future is not what we make of it. The future will happen and we will be a part of it. We can choose to stick our heads in the sand and pretend it will all go quietly away, that "our customers don't like it" and that "that's not the way we do things around here," but of course that won't happen. The future will carry on growing relentlessly. Our competitors, suppliers, and customers will embrace it. Our families, our children, and, eventually, our grandchildren will go through an existence that is inconceivable to us – imagine what your great, great grandparents would have made of the technologies we enjoy every day, the lifestyles we have become accustomed to.

Embrace the future. It can be bright. It will hopefully be fun. But regardless, it will *be*. It is up to us to change.

Ronan Gruenbaum
London, 2015

Part **1**

What is it?

What is it?

chapter 1

What are Social Technologies?

In the beginning there was order, not chaos. Everyone knew what was what and there was a clear direction of information flow from the top to the bottom. Large organizations such as the BBC, ABC, *Financial Times*, *The Wall Street Journal*, or *Le Figaro* would broadcast to millions through TV, radio, and newspapers. Within organizations strategies, directions, and dictats would be decided from on high and passed down to the worker bees. The only way information could flow up the organization was through forming special interest groups, such as trades unions. Businesses were run, more or less, like the military, with a clear hierarchy where one level would obey orders from their "superiors" without questioning them or suggesting modifications. The division of labor means that not only were people expected to perform one specific task, but that it was assumed they would be unable to do anything else.

This paradigm, of top-down control and dissemination of information, existed throughout society, from political movements to the arts and media; from education to shopping. The "little people" did not have the power, and those at the top controlled things to maintain the status quo.

Now there is chaos, not order, and organizations are stuck with the dilemma of trying to ignore what is happening and pretend that there is still order, or accept the fact that there has been a significant paradigm shift (please forgive the cliché!), that the barriers to entry have fallen, allowing entire industries to develop through the disparate and scattered individuals who would never have previously been able to unite towards a common goal.

This book will help any organization embrace the chaos, keeping a wary eye on the pitfalls and potholes it will encounter on the way.

New technologies, *social technologies*, of which social media and Web 2.0 are probably the best known examples, have completely changed society, how we live, how we work, how we do business, and, of course, how we communicate.

Anyone can do anything and organizations both large and small need to be aware of the threats to their businesses, as well as embrace the new technologies and explore the opportunities that they can offer those who have the courage to change, to experiment, to be bold, and to prepare for the future.

There have, over the past decade, been dozens of books detailing how these technologies are changing businesses and industries, but there seems to be a lack of direction on *how* an organization can embrace and adopt the new technologies.

Those who are well versed in what social technologies are might choose to skip through to Part 2, but the mini-case studies included in Part 1 will hopefully spark the imagination on how your organization can succeed and join the twenty-first century. No strategic analysis today can ignore the influence and effect of social technologies. Take the "4Cs"– the company, the competition, the customers, and the context.[1] The company can be far more efficient and innovative if it explores how to make best use of its human resources and, where appropriate, outsource through crowdsourcing. The competition will no doubt be in a similar situation, so the organization that is not engaging will be left behind. The customers are all using social technologies and utilizing the new opportunities to shop directly from suppliers, publish, help each other, complain as a group, or influence new product development. The context in this situation refers not just to the existence of social technologies but to their effect on the geo-political landscape, where privacy, data protection, security, ethics, crime, espionage, and freedom of expression are all influenced by, and fundamentally changed by, social technologies.

It is not, therefore, a case of needing to be aware of these new systems, but a business imperative to engage and implement them within the organization.

All of this we can, for the sake of this argument, include under the umbrella label of "old media" not because all examples were in the media industry, but because the media they used – the channels of communication (both internal and external) – contrasts with what became known in business as "new media." In 1990, Sir Tim Berners-Lee invented the world-wide web following his work at the nuclear research organization CERN. The networks that existed before this, and which led to the development of the internet as we now know it, were focused on peer-to-peer communication but only between academic and military institutions. Peer-to-peer communication existed for a long time before that, through such things as phone calls, letters, bulletin boards, and face-to-face meetings. The birth of the world-wide web promised a great new space where everyone could speak to everyone; and through forums and chat rooms that did occur to a certain extent. The new platform allowed access to information at an unprecedented level with new business opportunities for reaching new audiences and selling products and services online. The websites for the BBC, CNN, Yahoo!, and most other companies were, however, little more than newspapers, journals, and brochures in an online space. Individuals were able to set up websites and publish to the world, but to do so required some programming skills (or the resources to hire a developer) and, therefore, still remained the preserve of the few. The now defunct Geocities is a notable exception to this rule and many non-techies got their first taste of content creation through such tools.

Sites such as Craigslist and eBay showed how simple platforms could, however, enable the great unwashed to get online and make money from it through selling both second-hand and first-hand goods – in some cases making a living out of it.

The internet was, therefore, still characterized by the paradigm of a *one-to-many* communication with most internet usage focused on accessing sites owned by large organizations to consume content or buy products online. Some now choose to refer to that period of the development of the internet as Web 1.0, to differentiate it from the new buzz-word Web 2.0, which was reportedly first used towards the end of the 1990s[2] but only took its current meaning in 2003 when coined by Tim O'Reilly of O'Reilly Media who organized the first Web 2.0 Summit in 2004.

In 2005, O'Reilly said "Web 2.0 is about systems that harness collective intelligence"[3] and he defined the core competencies of Web 2.0 as:

- Services, not packaged software, with cost-effective scalability.
- Control over unique, hard-to-recreate data sources that get richer as more people use them.
- Trusting users as co-developers.
- Harnessing collective intelligence.
- Leveraging the long tail through customer self-service.
- Software above the level of a single device.
- Lightweight user interfaces, development models, AND business models.

This definition has stood the test of time and could be applied to the broader set of *social technologies*. There is now more power in the hands of the users, using online services rather than traditional purchased software, tapping into the "wisdom of crowds" by making use of the extra data they bring and making everything easy for normal users, not just being the preserve of the technically minded.

The terms "social media" and "Web 2.0" are essentially synonyms. "Enterprise 2.0" was a term coined by Andrew McAfee of Harvard Business School in a MIT *Sloan Review* article where he defined it as "those platforms that companies can buy or build in order to make visible the practices and outputs of their knowledge workers."[4] He later defined Enterprise 2.0 as "the use of emergent social software platforms by organizations in pursuit of their goals".[5] By "emergent social software platforms" (ESSPs), McAfee refers to all tools (such as the publicly available sites Facebook and YouTube) where the digital environments allow users to connect and collaborate online and where the software allows people's interactions to become visible over time through links and tags.

According to McAfee, ESSPs share common technical features (which he calls *SLATES* for the acronym), such that they are searchable, they link to each other, they allow for anyone to post, they can be tagged for easier search and horizontal navigation (which shall be discussed more in Chapter 6), they enable content to be repurposed or the tool to be reinvented, and they allow for users to know when new content is published. The following terms are used throughout the book and are all examples of social technologies and all contain the *SLATES* features.

Crowdsourcing

The outsourcing of a project or task to members of the general public (the "crowd").

Crowdfunding

The public, the crowd, funding projects (entrepreneurial, artistic or "causes") with small investments and usually no equity in return.

Blogging

Online journals, now also used as easy-to-create personal websites.

Microblogging

Small messages that are "broadcast" to followers of that account (such as Twitter).

Folksonomies/Tagging/Social Bookmarks

The labeling of content by users that makes it easier to find.

Wikis

Websites (or online platforms) that can be edited by any user.

Podcasts

Audio and video content distributed online, often created by non-professionals.

Social Networks

Platforms that allow users to keep in touch and interact with their friends, colleagues and contacts.

Widgets/Apps

Small programs that usually do just one function on a website, a desktop, or a mobile device.

Internet of Things (IoT)

When technologies are social, where everything is connected and sharing information so that the technologies can "decide" what action to take without us needing to give any input.

Location-based services

Such as Foursquare that allow users to "check-in" to physical locations to show others where they are.

Mashups

Combining technologies to achieve a new functionality.

Virtual Worlds (VWs)

Three-dimensional graphical online environments that allow users to interact with each other through their online personas, known as "avatars."

Gamification

The use of features of games to motivate greater engagement with a product or service.

Whilst this list is not exhaustive – new platforms are being produced every week that seem to provide new connectivity that challenges once more how people interact – it covers the most important and most common tools.

Many readers will no doubt know all of the above vocabulary, a number will know some, and there are those who will only have a cursory passing knowledge of what the terms actually mean and include.

The terms *social media*, *Web 2.0* and *Enterprise 2.0* are, therefore, used interchangeably here to refer to any of the following tools used for business purposes, be they internally or externally focused. Part of the reason for this is that while McAfee suggests Enterprise 2.0 revolves around using internal platforms, it ignores much benefit that can be gained by using the same types of tools externally. Furthermore, those in business are often unsure of terms like "Enterprise 2.0," whilst others feel that "social media" refers only to social tools that have no place in an organization.

Social media, however, suggests media – means of communication, publication platforms, connection through social networks. It does not necessarily include the concepts such as crowdsourcing, mashups, maker communities, or hackathons, which, rather than being separate developments, are all part of the same mindset that allows social media to exist and thrive. That is why it is better to think of these innovations as *social technologies* – innovations that have grown through the combined efforts of many and, often, can only operate with the input of the crowd. For these reasons, "social technologies" will be used here on in: It includes software and hardware; public and private platforms; for both social and business use.

Social technologies are so-called because they are not a part of the old paradigm where a system is designed, created, and implemented with little or no input by the end-user; where potential benefits of combining data or giving more people access to it are ignored; where the system is as the system does, because that is what has been decided.

Having taught this topic to MBA and Masters students as well as executive education participants with ages ranging from early twenties upwards, it is clear that any assumptions made about generational differences in understanding of the nuances and potential of the technology are misleading. Some enthusiastic proponents of social technologies are in their fifties and beyond – whilst there are those starting out on their careers who consider Facebook a waste of time and have not considered the potential both for themselves and their organizations.

Consequently, whilst some readers may wish to skip this section, all are strongly encouraged to read it to get a better idea of how the tools are being used now in different organizations, both well and badly.

Social Technologies are...

... all of the above and as explained in the remaining chapters of Part 1. They are all technologies that only work because the people, the crowd, provide the input, create the content, give feedback, accumulate data, and collaborate. Some of them, such as virtual worlds, might not be truly embraced for some years to come – until, for example, every business person has 3D goggles and gloves and can interact with the virtual world in a more natural way, rather than through the archaic qwerty keyboard. Gartner defines social technologies as "Any technology that facilitates social interactions and is enabled by a communications capability, such as the Internet or a mobile device. Examples are social software (e.g., wikis, blogs, social networks) and communication capabilities (e.g., Web conferencing) that are targeted at and enable social interactions."[6] There are other uses of the term social technologies (see that social "technology" Wikipedia for an explanation of the other uses of "social technology"[7]).

The questions we will explore in the chapters that follow are:

- How can the social technologies described here be effectively implemented in the workplace?
- Why have so many tried and failed to jump on this particular bandwagon?
- And is it worth it?

The answer to that final question has, I hope, already been answered. One can exist without using social technologies. Organizations, both in the public and private sector, can carry on as they always have done. But any organization that does not keep one eye on new technologies is doomed to fail in the end. *Encyclopædia Britannica* almost went out of business in the 1990s because it failed to see the importance of the CD-rom and how a new competitor, Microsoft's Encarta, was suddenly more relevant.[8]

2 chapter

Crowdsourcing

Definition and Description

The *Crowd* refers to the general public. *The great unwashed*. All the people who are not working directly for you or on your project or in your area. James Surowiecki, in his 2004 book *The Wisdom of Crowds*, argued that the collective intelligence of a large group is often more accurate or more useful than that of individuals or small groups. This concept was first noted by Sir Francis Galton a century previously. Amongst other achievements, Galton founded Differential Psychology and developed statistical concepts such as correlation and regression. The concept that the mean of a large group of people is more likely to be the right response rather than any one individual in that group should be obvious to anyone familiar with the traditional bell-curve in Figure 2.1 showing a normal distribution, where most responses of a study would be within one standard deviation of the mean, with a few *outliers* on either side being very high or very low. Most people are more or less the same height, but there are exceptions. Most exams produce a large number of "average" students with a few excellent results at the top end and a few who fail at the bottom.

Galton found at a county fair that the median of 800 guesses of an ox's dressed weight were within 0.8 per cent of the actual weight.[1] It was later pointed out in a letter to *Nature* that the sample population at

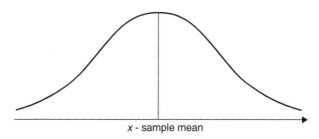

x - sample mean

FIGURE 2.1 **Normal distribution bell curve**

the country fair were used to and even trained in guessing weights of animals and that, therefore, the median (the midpoint of guesses from highest to lowest) of those guesses was a *voxexpertorum*[2] or educated guess rather than a *voxpopuli* (the opinions of the majority). Galton later showed that the *mean* of the guesses (the average) was only 0.08 per cent off from the actual weight. The implication of this was that it is better to take the average of a large number of opinions, rather than any one opinion, or even those of a small group. Self-evidently, the opinions from a large group of experts would be even better.

The reason for discussing the "crowd" so early here is that it goes to the root of all social technologies. It talks about the *many* rather than the *one*. Whilst one expert is still valued, social technology allows the *many* to publish, share opinions, and, to a certain extent, also be valued as experts in their field. It also enables multitudes to collaborate online and for those combined efforts to have a value that is more than the sum of the parts. Wikipedia would not be possible with just one author or even a small group of expert authors. As Wikipedia itself states "It is unlikely for any single reader to read all of Wikipedia's new content,"[3] but by empowering the general public to edit each other's entries, to literally be editors on Wikipedia, all entries are peer-reviewed – that is – both written by and edited by the general public. This has enabled the website to have over fifty times more words than *Encyclopædia Britannica*,[4] although this, in itself, does not of course make Wikipedia more important or more reliable.

There tend to be two main reasons why organizations are wary of allowing documents to be created or edited by multiple, often unknown, hands: firstly, why should someone trust the content created by persons unknown, and secondly, related to this, how can one ensure the content is not vandalized? Both arguments are easily answered.

The idea of having the crowd editing and approving Wikipedia is precisely that with a large number of users, errors, unsubstantiated comment, and malicious content will be corrected by other users. I, when studying law, corrected factual errors about specific cases on Wikipedia by comparing them with the official published reports of the cases. In recent years Wikipedia has also instigated a process of monitors to help identify suspect content.

First of all, as to the reliability of Wikipedia, an article in *Nature* in 2005[5] compared forty-two articles for accuracy on a range of scientific subjects from *Encyclopædia Britannica* and Wikipedia. *Encyclopædia Britannica*, growing from three original volumes in 1771 to thirty-two volumes in 2005 (its final print edition was 2010 – in 2012 it announced it would no longer publish print versions) was found to have an average of 2.9 errors per article compared to Wikipedia's 3.9 (these were "factual errors, omissions and misleading statements"). Whilst this showed *Encyclopædia Britannica* to be more accurate, on average, than Wikipedia, the study found that there were no articles in *Encyclopædia Britannica* that were completely error free, whilst Wikipedia had four such articles.

The study was refuted by *Encyclopædia Britannica*[6] but *Nature* then reasserted its accuracy and relevance[7]. What surprised all, including those at Wikipedia, was how reliable unpaid volunteer contributors could be – who were then able to correct the errors found in the *Nature* article more or less immediately.

Secondly, whilst Wikipedia has formalized its approvals process and has more moderators protecting articles and with greater powers to revert to previous entries, the principle behind why wikis work is still relevant for any kind of wiki – and that is that even though there will always be small groups of individuals who maliciously might seek to put false content on a wiki (or who might post inaccuracies by accident) there are far more users who are interested in ensuring the content is accurate and reliable and it is the weight of those contributors that ensures errors *made* by the crowd are *corrected* by the crowd.

Regardless of the objective accuracy of Wikipedia, however, it is – as with most encyclopedic entries – a collection of secondary resources and, as such, a good place to start research, providing an overview of a subject, but a bad place to finish at.

Business Applications

Crowdsourcing is a type of mass collaboration where an organization *outsources* a particular task to the *crowd*. The idea is a simple one: Can any organization be sure that the best ideas will come from its own employees?

There are plenty of examples of businesses that have benefitted from crowdsourcing and yet many in business continue to believe it is for the preserve of small businesses, or tech industries, or entertainment… and not for "real" business.

"Wikinomics" is the term used by Don Tapscott and Anthony Williams in their book of the same name to describe the business cases of crowdsourcing.[8] They describe how the gold mining company Goldcorp was struggling to find new seams of gold on their land. They decided, therefore, to offer a prize of $575,000 to anyone who could locate seams that the company had not previously identified and uploaded all their research data relating to Goldcorp's land for the crowd to study. Over fifty new seams were located that Goldcorp had not previously considered, with over 80 per cent of them having abundant quantities of gold. Perhaps more relevant to the doubters is how the company's value rose from $100 million to $9 billion.

Eli Lilly, when their best-selling Prozac was reaching the end of its patent and generic alternatives would soon swallow the pharma company's profits, launched Innocentive as a platform to help bring solution providers (the crowd) together with problem holders (companies who are unable to solve a particular issue).[9] *Nature*,[10] teamed up with Innocentive to help promote the challenges and source new solvers. Prizes offered ranged from $5,000 to $1,000,000 with only written proposals required for many of the challenges (recognizing that most solvers are unlikely to have access to laboratories for rigorous experimentation). In early 2012, Innocentive launched Brainstorm as a way to create ideas through the crowd (as opposed to seeking proper solutions) where the best ideas are rewarded.

IdeaStorm is a similar platform set up by Dell following the reputation for poor customer service they garnered in the mid-2000s. Procter & Gamble invites outside developers with promising product, technology, business model, method, trademark, package, or design ideas to submit their proposals for a chance to strike the next game-changing deal with the corporation through its P&G Connect + Develop program. Kraft foods have a platform to encourage the public to innovate with them. General Mills, one of the world's largest food manufacturers, has also requested ideas for innovation from users and customers through challenges such as: "*Label friendly yeast and mold inhibitors.*"[11]

Nokia's Beta Labs is aimed at "creating new and exciting things," whilst Airbus sought collaboration on the design of the wings on the A380 – which reduced the overall lead time on wing production by forty-one weeks (36 per cent).[12]

Crowdsourcing is not just for the preserve of large companies with big budgets to offer as prizes and rewards. Amazon's Mechanical Turk site[13] allows anyone with an internet connection to sign up to completing simple repetitive tasks online for organizations. Their tagline "Artificial Artificial Intelligence" explains how many services that the general public might think are conducted through high powerful machines are in fact done by humans.

The maker and hacker cultural phenomena are extensions of crowdsourcing but where individuals collaborate to repurpose existing objects or software or combine different ones to achieve something new.

The difference with crowdsourcing is that there is no large organization motivating people with the promise of prize money for successful solutions – makers and hackers try and build things for the fun of doing it. Hackathons will often take place over a short period of time, such as forty-eight hours, where teams of coders and developers will compete against each other to find a solution to a particular problem (it does not, as "hacking" usually implies, involve unauthorized access to another's computer or data). Hackerspaces have the same philosophy but without the competition or deadline. Makers are more than DIY enthusiasts and whilst the "Maker Faire" events suggest the focus is on arts and crafts, there is a strong emphasis on participants pulling electronic components apart to combine them in different ways.

Geeklist,[14] billing itself as "The first social network for developers and the tech community," launched #hack4good events where coders collaborated (and competed) to "build and launch projects for social good."[15] In the same vein, the Hult Prize[16] is the world's largest student competition for social good, where solutions to a specific problem are crowdsourced from teams at top universities and business schools.[17]

The philosophy behind crowdsourcing and hacking is the red thread that goes through this entire text: Your organization possibly, or even probably, does not have the best people capable of solving a range of given problems and only by collaborating with people both within and outside the organization are the optimal solutions likely to be found.

One positive and negative side to crowdsourcing is its potential to be harnessed for nefarious ends. TOR, or "The Onion Router," which allows users to surf the internet anonymously (and, therefore, immune to the spying eyes of regimes that prefer censorship to freedom of expression) has had a bounty of $65,000 placed on it by the Russian government to anyone who is able to hack the platform.[18]

Risks of Implementation

There are three main risks when embracing crowdsourcing. First of all, there is the danger of accidental or malicious damage (to the product, idea, or organization) caused by strangers, or even competitors, sabotaging good intentions. Secondly, there is the problem of quality control – leaving Wikipedia to be self-edited by the masses worked for a while but eventually a new layer of monitoring was introduced in order to have checks and control over what was produced... just in case it wasn't actually any good! Thirdly, there is the danger that no one will engage. Many organizations seem to have dipped their corporate toes in the "social" waters and, on seeing a lack of quality or an absence of engagement, decided it wasn't for them – when in fact it is more likely to be the case that they had not properly considered *how* to implement social technologies.

chapter 3

Crowdfunding

Definition and Description

An extension of crowdsourcing is *crowdfunding*, where individuals can give money to a particular project to help launch it, rather than relying on traditional bank loans and angel investors.

Business Applications

These projects might be the launch of a new product, for which funds are required to create prototypes that can then be used to obtain further funding through more traditional channels. They have included arts projects, from recording music, to filming documentaries, to mounting and touring stage productions. They can include charitable causes – usually to help a specific person achieve a particular goal. Some of the platforms, such as Kickstarter, probably the best known, do not allow causes to raise money. In fact, they have a strict list of projects that are not permitted on their crowdfunding platform, including automotive products, baby products, bath and beauty products, cosmetics, electronic surveillance equipment (although many other types of electronic gadgets are allowed), exercise and fitness products, home improvement products, and pet supplies.[1]

It is easy to see why some projects, such as alcohol, drugs, and weapons, might be prohibited. It is less obvious why users are unable to raise funds for scholarships or international charities. There are, however, many other crowdfunding sites, some which explicitly allow cause-funding (such as Indiegogo[2]),and others which focus only on funding arts projects, such as wefund.com[3] or pleasefund.us,[4] or are specifically for certain countries, for example, the UK's PeopleFund.it.[5] The UK's crowdcube.com[6] enables potential investors and start-ups to get connected by allowing budding businesses to offer equity in return for the investment. This differs significantly from the typical model where there is no contract and any money provided by funders is completely at the control of the recipients to do with what they wish. If they choose not to proceed with the project, they are able to keep the money with nothing more than the wrath of online funders to tend with.

A third type of crowdfunding is where anyone can become a lender and help fund growth and development in the third world through micro-finance initiatives on platforms such as Kiva[7] and Kubaru,[8] investing as little as £10 as a loan. Those who tend towards risk aversion with their investments might be interested to know that borrowers have paid back loans with a 99 per cent success rate.[9]

Risks of Implementation

The idea of individuals spread across the world giving you money with no promise of any return, as happens on many of the platforms, suggests that any organization should try their hand at crowdfunding. On the most basic level it is what the local church might do to raise funds for the new roof – calling for donations amongst its congregation. With the online crowdfunding sites, the congregation is the world and the new roof might be a product or even just an idea. However, the church congregation will rarely claim ownership of part of the roof in return for the donation.

This is usually the case with crowdfunding – people give money because they think it's a good idea and they want to encourage innovation, or to show that they are at the cutting edge of entrepreneurship, or possibly to get the first generation of the product being developed. If the organization then successfully acquires further funding from venture capital, or is bought by a larger company, there is the danger that the crowdfunders will be against the idea of "their" company "selling out."

Oculus VR, the start-up creating 3D headsets for use in virtual environments (discussed further below), suffered a media backlash from their early funders when they were purchased by Facebook for $2 billion.[10] People who had donated from $25 upwards and received t-shirts or products felt that they should also have benefitted from the Facebook purchase. Losing the trust of the early-adopter community in this way could be dangerous when the product in question is so niche at this stage.

Conversely, if one chooses to do crowdfunding where the funders are offered equity in the company for their contributions, this might affect the attractiveness of the company to venture capital funds later on who would rather deal with the founders and not need to worry about thousands of shareholders.

Regulations (such as the JOBS Act in the USA) are also likely to damage the potential of crowdfunding making it harder and less attractive for both start-ups and investors.

chapter 4

Blogging

Definition and Description

"Blogs" or "web logs" were originally intended as online journals that anyone could set up with no programming knowledge, posting new entries through a WYSIWYG[1] editor. They are not just text entries, however, but can include photos, videos, and audio recordings and have now been around for so long that they are very much part of mainstream media, but are still an unknown force to many in business.

Blogging software and platforms have improved so much that they are now used to create websites and can even allow individuals to develop their own e-commerce platforms (for example, through Wordpress). The "blogosphere" refers to the collection of all blogs on the internet – currently estimated to number several hundred million.

It is easy for detractors to ignore blogs and assume that they are of no value, disregarding not only the wealth of topics available but also the quality of writing on many of them and the experience and seniority of the authors. Opinions expressed in newspapers tend to receive far more respect due to the medium, rather than the quality of the opinion or the background of the writer. The very nature of the internet and social media in particular means that if everyone can be an author, how do you sort the wheat from the chaff? Newspapers, for all their faults, provide a platform that tells the reader "these are experts in their field" – whether that is true or not. The problem for online publications is getting that recommendation or endorsement to the valuable content. "It's not information overload" said Clay Shirky[2] in 2008, "It's filter failure," meaning that we need to improve the way we find information.

Social technologies can provide this filter, based on recommendations, both personal and public. If a friend tells you that book *A* is a really good read and you trust your friend's judgment on books, you are likely to notice that recommendation and possibly even buy or seek out the book.

So how do you decide to trust recommendations that are by complete strangers? One recommendation is no longer enough, unless it comes from a recognized "expert" on the subject. But what is an "expert"? Someone who says they are an expert? Someone who is rated by others as an expert (who knows if those raters know what they are talking about – after all, in the land of the blind the one-eyed man is the decorator) or someone who is rated by those rated by others as an expert?

If the person is in the public eye, this often lends weight to their opinion, regardless of their experience or education on the subject. Reality TV shows and the fashion for celebrity gossip have given anyone in the public eye a platform to espouse on any subject they care to. An eBay seller with 200,000 positive feedbacks is likely to be more trusted as a safe place to buy than an eBay seller with fifty positive feedbacks. It doesn't mean the person is more trustworthy – but when one doesn't know where to go one goes where most people go. There is a safety in numbers.

When dozens, hundreds or thousands of people agree, that mass of opinions will be elevated from random stranger to trusted crowd.

Of course this might be a good way of trusting a seller on eBay. It might be a good way to choose a book on Amazon (a book with a hundred four-star reviews might get your attention more than one with just two five-star reviews), but should you trust the opinion of someone just because they have large numbers of followers on Twitter? At the time of writing, of the top fifty accounts on Twitter with the most followers (all over twelve million each) only two are not in entertainment (Barack Obama and Bill Gates). The current leader, with over sixty-six million followers, is Katy Perry, ten million more than Obama's fifty-six million.[3] Does that mean Katy Perry is a better authority on subjects? Or Justin Bieber (in second place)?

The belief that thousands or even millions of people cannot be wrong is being further confused by a new phenomenon: Crowdturfing, the creation of a fake grassroots public opinion through crowdsourcing sites in countries such as China. Studies undertaken in 2011 at the University of California, Santa Barbara[4] and the University of Victoria[5] have shown how over a million dollars is being spent every month on crowdturfing, paying a few cents for comments and other responses that favor particular brands on social networking sites. When labor is cheap, opinion and consensus can be bought.

So whilst large numbers of people endorsing a particular product might suggest it is worthy of attention, popularity is not a reliable indicator of quality or relevance – and therein lies the problem. Receiving millions of endorsements from the general public does not necessarily make the filter any better. Other criteria must come in to play and those criteria – which are still being decided – will probably use a combination of personal connection to the endorsers and numbers of endorsers.

If you want to start following blogs, how do you know whose blog to follow? And why? The easiest way to start with blogs, as indeed with all social media, is to think of pet subjects – be they areas of expertise in the workplace or personal interests or hobbies. So this might range from customer relationship management (CRM) usage (if you are a data manager or marketer), for example, to cup-cake decorating; from politics in the Caucuses to the trials and tribulations of having a toddler. Google searches will produce a range of results that are based on, amongst other things, popularity. What set the Google search algorithm apart from the competition (Yahoo!, MSN, Altavista, Lycos, Ask Jeeves, etc.) at the turn of the millennium was how it relied not just on the website itself, but also on how others linked to the site from their own websites; essentially endorsing the first site as an expert on the terms used to create those links. There are "official" lists of good blogs on a range of subjects but, once again, they are merely acting as filters. This will be fine for many, but may not be ideal for your particular tastes.

A colleague, for example, was researching capitalism and theology for her PhD. There are, as one might imagine, a limited number of websites and blogs dedicated to this niche area, so she decided to start a blog about her research with the aim of sharing her findings and insight and, hopefully, connecting with the handful of people worldwide focusing on the same area. The blog has proved extremely successful for her, connecting with those like-minded academics and leading to some people attending conferences where she is speaking simply to talk to her afterwards about things they read on her blog. That blog, however, is unlikely to ever appear on a list of "must-read" blogs. Popularity is no sign of quality and a lack of "official" endorsement is no indication that the blog is of no interest.

Blogs are easy to set up, easy to write, and easy to follow. They are not, however, easy to maintain – which is why there are so many millions of blogs that have been abandoned. Many people have something to say – but often do not have things they want to say on a regular basis. Many find the time commitment required to write regular blog entries is too much of a burden. This author, never short of an opinion, finds it difficult to dedicate time to updating his blog when there are so many other, more urgent, issues that require his attention (doing, in short, the day job).Often the best ideas for a post, or a comment on issues of the day, come when one is in the bath or driving to work or walking down the road – not times when one can easily take out a keyboard and start typing. Mobile apps to allow easy blog updating can be difficult to use to write anything more than a couple of sentences. Dictation software is improving by leaps and bounds every year but who wants to start talking loudly into their mobile while on the train (although, admittedly, that has not stopped thousands of people doing just that to tell their loved ones that they are "on the train").

Different types of blogging platforms allow different types of content to be posted – it doesn't have to be text. Tumblr and Pinterest, could be described as "visual blogs" because they allow users to collect images on themes. Audioboom enables users to record voice entries or mini-podcasts that can be posted as blogs entries. Some of the biggest or most popular blogs have since become businesses in their own right. The *Huffington Post*, *BuzzFeed*, *The Verge*, *Mashable!*, and *Gawker*, for example, (the top five in Technoratti's Top 100 blogs[6]) all started as blogs.

There are, of course, plenty of blogs by those who are recognized as experts "offline" also, for being authors, journalists, academics, politicians, or industry leaders. Blogs can serve not only to increase the personal brand, but also drive conversations and debates about specific topics. Andrew McAfee's blog, for example, focuses almost uniquely on Enterprise 2.0 and boasts dozens of comments from readers on most entries. Jeff Jarvis, Professor of Journalism at CUNY, podcaster, and technology pundit, has also garnered a big following.

Jarvis was an early adopter of blogging and had thousands of followers by 2005 when a minor issue of poor customer service became a major example of a company ignoring the power of social media. Jarvis had bought a Dell laptop and had a problem with it. That, of course, would not be much in itself. However, the failure of Dell's customer services to respond to him and the fact that Jarvis wrote several high-profile blog posts about the failings of Dell meant that Jarvis was no longer one person complaining in an empty room. He became the focal point in what he called "Dell Hell"[7] for unhappy Dell customers across the USA, if not the world, to vent their fury about Dell's products and customer service. Jarvis entitled his post "Dell lies, Dell sucks" and wrote about the issue also in the UK newspaper *The Guardian*.[8] On his blog he said that Dell had failed the test and that "the age of *caveat emptor* is over. Now the time has come when it's the seller who must beware. *Caveat venditor*."[9] Unfortunately for buyers, there are still many sellers who ignore this warning. This book is aimed at helping to understand the imperative of waking up to social technologies, but every so often for a long time to come we will see yet new examples of companies that gave bad customer service and ignored the power of the individual.

Influencers

According to Webster and Wind,[10] there are six separate roles in the *decision making unit*, or *buying center* – those involved in the decision to purchase a product or service. Their "ibuild" framework differentiates between the *initiator*, the *buyer*, the *user*, the *influencer*, the *lodge-keeper*, and the *decision maker*. For organizations, those roles might be entire departments – the buyer might be the procurement department and the lodgekeeper (the one who might refuse the purchase) might be the finance department, for example. In a household, one person (such as a parent) might occupy various roles with a child being the *user*. An important role, made more visible through the growth of social media, is that of the *influencer*. The influencer might be a magazine comparison guide to the latest gadgets. It might be the cool crowd in the hippest clubs.It might be a celebrity. It could be a trusted friend. It can be the *crowd* (reliable or not as that may be, as indicted above). The influencer is the one who says "don't buy that, buy this."

Crowdturfing aside, there is an important role for influencers in the buying process and brands ignore them at their peril. Dell did just that, and paid the price. As with many organizations at the time (and lots who still maintain that stance), they had a "look don't touch" policy with blogs and, rather than seeing them for what they were (free customer feedback which could influence others), failed to realize the significance of what their customers were telling them.

Dell didn't just ignore one unhappy customer, they ignored one with a large following. The ripples of Jarvis' blog reached across the blogosphere and Dell's name became synonymous with poor customer service and a backward attitude to social media.

Dell then found an ex-employee blogging about how to get good deals from the company and asked for the blog to be removed. A reasonable response, some might think, if an ex-employee is distributing confidential information. The blogosphere, however, did not take kindly to the company's heavy-handed tactics and it was forced to apologize for being overzealous and withdrew its request to have the blog taken down.

Dell then started its own blog – "Direct2Dell"– having learnt the lesson post-Jarvis that they needed an informal channel of communication with their customers. However, the blog was widely criticized by bloggers as being little more than a corporate mouthpiece. The response, on the blog, was "Real people are here and we're listening. […] Thanks for the feedback guys. We'll keep working to get it right."[11]

However, a year after Dell Hell, the company suffered another PR disaster when a laptop exploded at a conference in Japan due to a faulty battery. Again, one minor incident, which would probably have been quickly forgotten if the event hadn't been captured on film by a conference delegate and posted on the tech website The Inquirer.[12] A few more batteries were reported to have exploded and when one caught fire in the Yahoo! HQ, Dell's product recall of four million batteries was communicated in Direct2Dell but this did little to help improve the reputation of the company, despite companies such as Apple also needing to recall 1.8 million of the same Sony batteries.[13] However, the company created an FAQ section and found their community of customers was helping each other with the information, taking the pressure of their call centers.

Dell was one of the first victims of social media, but in 2007, through the creation of their blog and a website for customers to share product ideas "Ideastorm," they had successfully learnt those lessons and become the example of how organizations should embrace social media.

Their Twitter "Social Media Listening Command Center" was set up shortly afterwards to monitor and *engage* with customers talking about Dell,[14] their outlet feeds on Twitter (@DellOutlet and @DellOutletUK) had generated $3 million of sales between 2007 and 2009 with total revenues earned through Twitter amounting to $6.5 million at that time.[15] They were also training 350 employees per week in social media best practice.

Hindsight is always 20:20 and it is easy to see the mistakes Dell made when they ignored Jarvis. The point, however, is not to think about how organizations should have a corporate blog (not all organizations would benefit from one) nor how they should monitor their customers' blogs and ensure good customer service, although, of course, they should.

The point is that new technologies will always come along. That's part of what it means to be "new". New channels of communication and new ways for customers, employees, investors, journalists, suppliers, and the authorities to communicate will also come along every so often. Can you be sure – hand on heart – that your organization will adapt to the new ways your stakeholders may choose to communicate with? Is it monitoring Twitter? Is it monitoring all the different social networks (there's so much more than Facebook)? What about virtual worlds? Are there videos on YouTube about your company? Are there opportunities to engage with your customers or suppliers better through mobile? Does your PR department or agency only talk to newspapers?

The Pareto rule, or 80:20 rule, has been further refined for the internet and the creation and consumption of content. One rule of thumb suggests the new ratio is 1:9:90 – where 1 per cent of the users actually create content (write blog posts, record and upload videos, share photographs, etc.); 9 per cent comment on that content and engage; and the other 90 per cent simply observe and consume.[16]

Forrester's Bernoff and Li's 2008 book entitled *Groundswell: Winning in a World Transformed by Social Technologies*[17] identified six groups of internet and social media users, which they later grew to seven:[18] *Creators, conversationalists, critics, collectors, joiners, spectators,* and *inactives.*[19] The percentages change according to age, gender, and location but as one might expect, the *creators* – those who write blogs, record videos, and so on, are a small minority, with most of the others engaging in different levels of interaction. The *inactives* are those who don't even read other people's blog posts or watch their videos. From Forrester's research, Germany seems to have the highest level of inactives and across all geographies the older demographics tend to engage less.

This is important for two reasons. Firstly, not every organization will get benefit from engaging with social technologies – as with all marketing, it is essential to understand your customers, what they do, what their behaviors are, and how you might reach them – segmentation is easy online and not spending time doing it is wasting resources and potentially alienating neutral members of your target group through ill-fitting messages. Secondly, careful targeting of *creators* – the influencers of the social media world – will reap dividends in getting the message through to the others.

Perhaps a useful addition to the above categories would be that of the *sharers* – people who find content on the internet and share it with their social networks – obviously a crucial step in helping content reach a wider audience.

The same unequal usage across the population applies to the use of social media for knowledge sharing and knowledge management. Not everyone in your organization will engage with a group blog, wiki, or forum. Most will, at best, read what others have posted – and possibly ignore the existence of the blog, wiki, or forum altogether. That is not to say that the blog, wiki, or forum has no value. The diffusion of information through any community, as with the diffusion of innovations (as we shall see later), is complex and the *inactives* of today might be the *spectators* of tomorrow, and one day even *creators*. Equally, they might learn of information on the blog, wiki, or forum through friends and colleagues who are more active.

Business Applications

Much has been written, as one would expect, about good and bad blogging practice (there are, also unsurprisingly, blogs dedicated to the subject), with recommendations ranging from not engaging with your customers, stakeholders, or readers, to doing oversell on the content and from making the blog only about you, the writer, to not focusing enough on a subject. As with all methods of communication one should of course remember that it all depends. Some successful blogs break all the rules, whilst others that have only marginal readership tick all the boxes. Blogs should not be considered solely as a method of communicating with customers – as a marketing tool. Their potential for internal communications, project management, and knowledge sharing is huge – and largely untapped.

The largest opportunity for organizations is, unsurprisingly, the corporate use of blogs. Blogs can be used internally to share information amongst a team or to cascade information down from the leadership across the organization. The important thing to remember is that the tone should always be informal. If a blog is little more than a press release, then it gives no added value over reading that press release on the main company website. It should be clear that blogs are written by people, not a corporate machine; and that when readers post comments and engage in conversations on blogs, they are talking to real people in the organization.

So why should your organization have a channel with an informal tone in addition to the existing, formal, corporate PR one? In an age of many-to-many communications, many of the *many* are no longer satisfied by organizations that continue to pander to the old paradigm of one-to-many communications and simply preach at their customers, stakeholders, or users through PR speak. Depending on the type of industry and the sorts of customers it has, an organization can use its blog as a PR tool to get their formal messages out; rather than posting press-releases on a website which are often difficult to find and frequently aimed purely at journalists and old-media channels. The "marketing" blogs can be used in a variety of ways. Volkswagen (VW) promote and discuss viral marketing; General Electric (GE) creates emotional attachment through its branding;[20] Google uses their official blog to announce new products and investor relations; and a large number of organizations aim to show their thought leadership and level of expertise through blogs. Others aim to drive customer engagement and loyalty, direct sales and problem solving,[21] and, as with some of the blogs referenced here, to build a reputation for expertise in a subject area.

An organization might have a range of formal blogs ("formal" to indicate that they are sanctioned and/or branded by the organization and not the writer's personal blog) to post news and information to different internal and external audiences, such as DisneyParks[22] or SouthWest Airlines[23] or the McDonald's blog on their corporate social responsibility strategy and operations.[24] As with all marketing and communications, segmentation of the audience is essential to ensure messages are targeted and there is less danger of them losing interest through irrelevant communications.

Marriott on the Move[25] is the blog written by executive chairman and chairman of the board of the hotel chain Bill Marriott, and seems to be aimed at both loyal customers and employees. Posts are written from a personal perspective and discuss everything from his father's work ethic and his own childhood through to the company's latest marketing campaigns. The idea for Marriott's blog came not from him but from his head of global communications, Kathleen Matthews.[26] This in itself is not a bad thing. Nor is the fact that he dictates his blog entries that are then transcribed by an assistant. Not every corporate leader will be aware of new technology or how to use it, but that is not to say that they will not embrace it when shown the potential benefits. However, when Marriott admitted in June 2008 that his PR people sometimes write the blog, there was a lot of criticism.[27] The concept of authenticity in leadership is never so important as when communicating directly with your employees, stakeholders, or customers. Having said that, the comments on the blog from readers suggest that the general public, the target audience of the blog, find sufficient authenticity in the blog's voice that they leave positive comments and in the first eighteen months of the blog, $5 million was generated in reservations through the site.[28]

Marriott is not the only high-profile blogger in business[29] and there are plenty of other C-level executives with successful blogs, such as those from Royal Carribean,[30] Forrester,[31] Reuters,[32] or Saatchi & Saatchi,[33] to name but a few. Jonathan Schwartz, former CEO of Sun, was an early adopter of blogs, although his official Sun blog was deleted following his 2010 resignation.[34]

In a time when the leaders of companies need to be in the public eye, blogs help give some personality to the anonymous suit. Of course blogs are not ideal for all leaders and whilst the initiative to start a corporate blog might come from someone else (as with the Marriott on the Move blog) the intended blogger should only embark on it if they are dedicated to keeping it up-to-date and being a personal voice-piece. If the CEO is neither enamored with the idea nor suitably verbose to blog, other high-profile people in the organization could take on the role. The important factor is that they are keen to do it themselves.

Ironically, whilst writing these words, I received an update from LinkedIn to a post by Richard Branson, CEO of Virgin Group, entitled "Why aren't more business leaders online?"[35] He quoted a newly-published IBM Study[36] that showed only 1 of 1709 CEOs had their own blog and only 16 per cent currently use social media to interact with customers, although they expect this to increase by over 250 per cent during the next three to five years.

If none of the leadership is interested in blogging, it is a wasted opportunity but does not mean that the organization cannot have "corporate blogs." Some corporate blogs are actually run by the employees, such as Johnson & Johnson's JNJ BTW blog that states:[37] "Everyone else is talking about our company, so why can't we? There are more than 120,000 people who work for Johnson & Johnson and its operating companies. I'm one of them, and through JNJ BTW, I will try to find a voice that often gets lost in formal communications."[38]

Nokia Conversations[39] is the corporate blog from Nokia with global staff able to post and share news with colleagues and the general public.

Various government bodies' country leaders from around the world also have official blogs, such as the US White House[40] or the Prime Minister of Australia.[41] Although early-adopters, the UK's Prime Minister's Office[42] has morphed from being an informal blog to becoming a website for the office with only the News Stories section being a pseudo-blog (in that it is a list of informal press releases). Many other UK government department websites, including blogs, were closed in 2010 and 2011 in an effort to cut costs.[43] There are still plenty of informal uses of blogs and other social media by the UK government and guidelines were published in 2012 on how civil servants should use social media.[44]

The flexibility of blogs as a tool means that they are used for a variety of tasks. With many geographically diverse and virtual teams still sending emails to each other (and the confusion inherent in that system knowing whether or not one is reading the latest update or email from all members) an alternative to managing projects is for members of the team to all be editors of the same blog and update it such that any reader will instantly know the latest update and the status of the project by reading the most recent entry. Bell Canada's use of blogs for project management was discussed in CIO.com as far back as 2007.[45]

As with Dell's example earlier, blogs can be used for updating customers with important information and can be used to enhance the customer relationship. They can of course also be used to complement traditional advertising or PR campaigns and help create an emotional attachment to a particular brand. Research by IBM in 2011[46] showed that businesses must be careful not to think blogs are a one-stop shop for all communications and marketing needs. The top two reasons consumers interact with brands through social sites are to find out about discounts and to make purchases, but businesses mistakenly believe it is to learn about new products and for general information.

There is a constant stream of information from business publications and online consultancies about the importance of blogging and social media in general for marketing purposes. Hubspot's "The 2012 State of Inbound Marketing"[47] report shows that 25 per cent of organizations believe blogs to be "critical" to their business, with only 19 per cent believing them not to be of any use. Blogs were believed to be by far the most important of all social media channels, although this figure is no doubt due, at least in part, to two important reasons. Firstly – and coincidentally one of the main motivations for writing this book – noticing how little most business people understood social technologies. Secondly blogs are a channel that can be completely controlled by the organization – whilst Hubspot's report in 2010[48] showed that companies that blog generate 67 per cent more B2B leads than those that do not, rising to 88 per cent more leads for B2C businesses.

The surprising result from the above studies, however, is that small organizations, who are more likely to focus on marketing strategies with lower costs, tend to embrace blogs far less than large organizations who already have a range of corporate communications platforms. The important thing to remember is that blogs are not the preserve of the marketing departments and, ideally, should be separate from them. Authentic voices from real people are more likely to garner a loyal following than regurgitated PR-speak. Of course blogs are also a key tool for sharing knowledge within organizations of all sizes.

Whilst the above statistics show that blogging is useful, if not essential, to lead generation in both B2C and B2B markets, the reason why blogs are useful is not always immediately apparent. Blogs play an important role in search engine optimization (SEO). SEO, however, is often the preserve of the most technically minded in a marketing department or regularly left completely to the IT department to manage. It is worth spending a few words on explaining what it is, why it is important, and why non-marketers and non-techies need to understand its importance as they can and do influence it.

Search Engine Optimization

Imagine your organization invests thousands or even millions of dollars (or whatever your currency is) on an amazing new billboard campaign, that involves static posters combined with video that engages with the passer-by and even tailors the message specifically to that person, as suggested by the 2002 Steven Spielberg film *Minority Report*. It could be the most amazing, cutting-edge campaign ever devised and would have a predicted return on investment (ROI) that redefines what can be achieved by outdoor marketing.

Would you then site the interactive billboard in the middle of a dense forest where the only possibility a potential customer would have of seeing the billboard is if they were completely lost while on a hiking trip in the wilderness? Of course not. Yet that is what many organizations are doing with their websites. With almost 650 million different websites (according to the Netcraft Web Server Survey at the time of writing[49]), many organizations forget that they need to consider the map and road signs to guide customers through the digital forest when building an online presence. In the case of websites, the map and road signs are search engines, such as Google, Bing, Yandex (in Russia), or Baidu (in China) – although many more exist.

Whilst each search engine will have a different algorithm to decide which sites appear at the top of their search results for a particular query – and they will change the algorithms regularly to improve results and avoid the system being abused by spammers, there are some basic principles which all search engines now seem to follow. First of all, there is website structure and programming – making sure the right codes are used for headers, that site-maps are included, there is consistent navigation, and that the web crawlers or spiders[i] can enter the site and read the content (not possible, for example, with most sites or content built with Adobe® Flash®). These issues are usually left with the IT or web-design departments but not all coders and programmers are aware of the requirements of SEO.

Secondly, the content of the website is important. Does a page on a particular topic or product that you want customers to find have titles and content that include the terms the users are likely to search on? Content needs to be readable by humans but also include synonyms so that different search queries will hopefully find that particular page as the most relevant on that topic. Images, furthermore, should be labeled in the code (using "alt tags"), which not only is a requirement for making the site readable to those with vision impairment and reliant on screen-reading software, but also helps the spiders to see that the images are also relevant on the topic in question. The content used in meta data (particularly the "meta title") is also important here. Again, this usually requires liaising with IT departments to ensure each page has distinct metadata.

Also relevant to the content issue is the frequency with which content is updated. A website that is frequently updated will appear to the search engines as more "alive" and, therefore, relevant. Many websites are to all intents and purposes dead and are consequently downgraded in their search rankings accordingly. Another point here is to make sure that the pages are easy to find from other points of the website both through the main navigation and menu bars, as well as through direct links to other sections and the inclusion of site-maps.

---

[i] Web crawlers or spiders are pieces of code used by search engines that go, like mini-robots, from one website to another reporting back on all the different links within a website, both internal and external facing.

Finally, and perhaps most importantly, is the question of popularity. Google pioneered the idea that the best way to identify if a page or website is relevant for a particular search query is to see what the crowd think. The crowd – in this case the collection of all other websites (including blogs) on the internet – will link to other websites when they want to refer visitors to another site as an expert on a particular subject. That "expertise" might be simply a good place to buy product *A*, or it might be an article about issue *B* or where further information about topic *C* can be found. If a lot of websites, that is, a lot of people (because websites are created by people), link to another website *X*, they are giving that website a vote of relevance. The more people who link to website *X*, clearly the more popular it is. When search engine spiders identify these links and they are collated, those popularity links help the search engine to decide that website *X* is more relevant because it has been voted as such by real people (who create websites).

There are far more nuances to this process that need not be explained here. However, there is another issue with links that help the search engines determine exactly what it is that the people think website *X* is relevant for. "Anchor texts" are <u>the words in a website that have an embedded link</u>. They are usually underlined and in blue (although this depends on the coding of the website and the settings on the user's particular browser). In this paragraph, if it were posted online, the underlined text (the link) would be read by the spiders as showing that website *X* (the website I have linked to) is relevant on the subject "the words in a website that have an embedded link." That text is the anchor text. Using good anchor text that indicates the subject of the intended link (i.e. the content of the destination webpage) is essential to accessibility – as with "alt tags" on images – to make sure screen-reading software can let a visually impaired reader know where a link will take them if clicked.

To show how important the anchor text is, it is worth considering two anomalies. The first is a result of thousands of websites offering a PDF to download. To help users who do not have software capable of opening or reading PDFs, a link to download the free Adobe® Reader usually appears by the link for the PDF with the anchor text: "To download Adobe Acrobat Reader, <u>click here</u>." Thousands upon thousands of websites linking to the same page (the Adobe Reader download page) with the anchor text "click here" has made the page come first in Google's results for the search query "click here."

The second example, used for good and bad (depending on your politics), has been when thousands of people from a particular community deliberately create misleading anchor texts. Examples range from US President George W Bush appearing top in 2003 for the term "miserable failure"[50] to the Church of Scientology's official site appearing in top position for the search on "dangerous cult,"[51] the latter reportedly through a consorted effort by online hacker group Anonymous. *Wired* magazine's website hosts a wiki from 2008 with instructions on how to run such a campaign.[52]

The reason for talking about SEO here is to explain the hidden value of blogs within a general online marketing strategy. If blogs are created within the corporate web domains (i.e. they are a sub-domain with the main "corporate.com" website) they will help show frequently updated content, which the spiders like. Furthermore, if the blog contains content that is of interest to others (and if it does not, why is it being written?), this will encourage readers to link to the blog and, by extension, improve the link equity of the corporate website. Links from other social media sites, such as Facebook or Twitter, are often ignored by search engine spiders (or blocked by the social media sites themselves) and, therefore, have a less obvious effect on SEO, although they are still useful for raising brand awareness.

If a corporate blog is created on a separate and independent domain (e.g. "blog.com" rather than "corporate.com") it will help raise brand awareness but can also help build link equity by driving traffic to the main corporate website. The advantages of this, however, are negligible compared to the accumulative benefits of links from users.

Risks of Implementation

There are two sides to blogs; the author(s) and the readers. The biggest obstacle to having a successful blog is not updating it regularly with engaging attractive content. It doesn't seem to matter how specialized that content is, so long as it is written with authenticity by someone who knows their subject. The problem is writing the content, and most blogs die, or remain unupdated, making them unattractive to both human readers and bots. There is nothing worse (OK, there are many things worse... but you understand the point I hope) than finding a blog for an organization or by an author or on a topic of particular interest to you and then seeing that it hasn't been updated for two years. I have been guilty of this with my own blog – paid work gets in the way and makes it impossible to find the time to update my personal blog. It must, therefore, be the responsibility of someone in the organization to make sure the corporate blog is regularly updated – even if that simply makes them "Chief Nagging Officer."

The biggest obstacle to having a successful blog is not updating it regularly with engaging attractive content

The other main risk is that the blog, which takes effort to set up well and keep updated, is simply not read. This is, unfortunately, a very "chicken and egg" scenario. One could spend thousands on detailed market research on potential readers of a blog before setting it up, but I suspect the market research wouldn't be very accurate. You will only know if a blog gets readers by setting it up, updating it regularly, and ensuring the content is engaging. The feature of the internet that never fails to surprise me is how there is always someone, somewhere, interested in what you have to say.

chapter 5

Microblogging

Definition and Description

Microblogs are, in effect, small blogs. They allow anyone to broadcast short messages to update one's followers to what one is doing, what is happening, or to alert them, similarly to RSS Feeds, to new events. Messages sent through Twitter, probably the most famous microblogging platform, are referred to as "Tweets" and are limited to 140 characters in length, because they originally used mobile SMS systems to transmit the messages.

Microblogs have grown, however, to include photos, audio, and video – and range from the general interest Tumblr.com to the specialist Dribbble.com (for designers). There are a number of platforms offering a version of text-based microblogging for the enterprise, such as Yammer.com and ShareTronix.com, or the open-source Status. net that can be adapted for any private use.

Given the ease with which users can create Tweets (or other short messages) Twitter is often cited as a good example of the reinvention of an innovation. The original platform was very basic and only allowed for messages to be posted. The creation of tags (see Folksonomies

Twitter is often cited as a good example of the reinvention of an innovation

in Chapter 6), using the hashtag symbol (#) and the ability to re-Tweet someone else's messages (forwarding them to your own followers), for example, were functionalities created by the users and adopted *en masse*.

Twitter "clients" are third-party applications that have been created to provide different levels of functionality and the ability to Tweet from different platforms or, for example, include short links within the message that directs users to another webpage. The fact that Twitter allowed third-party developers to create clients to interact with the Twitter platform from the beginning is seen to be a crucial feature of the exponential growth of Twitter, enabling users to personalize the experience in a myriad of ways.

Just as social media is a *many-to-many* communication, microblogging, probably more than blogging itself – perhaps due to the lower writing requirements – allows the many to broadcast on any subject they wish to all their followers… the many. This is the benefit and the curse of Twitter. Whilst there are millions of people using it for useful knowledge sharing, comment, and debate; many use it to share the banal of their daily lives, such as describing their emotional state or the fact that they've just had a hot caffeinated beverage of higher or lower than average quality.

Business Applications

Despite the "banal," however, Twitter has benefited more than any other platform from being mobile. In addition to having a web-based interface and various third-party clients to manage a variety of accounts (such as through Hootsuite or Tweedeck), Twitter, by its very nature, is suitable for communicating whilst on the go. Messages can be uploaded to Twitter via SMS messages or through apps for the smartphone. This means that the "many" can communicate anywhere, any place, and at any time.

A well-documented[1] example of this is how Sarah Lacy, a technology journalist for *BusinessWeek* in 2008, interviewed Facebook founder Mark Zuckerberg at a keynote event at the South by Southwest music and technology conference in Austin, Texas (commonly known as SXSW). The audience was mostly made up of young technologists, or geeks, who did not like Lacy's interview style and told her so during the interview. Much has been written on how the interview went wrong.[2,3,4] However, rather than this simply being a disappointing event within a specialist industry conference and quickly forgotten, the audience were tech-savvy and early adopters of Twitter (which was launched at the same conference two years previously). Many in the audience Tweeted their opinions of the conference, which were read by technology reporters and enthusiasts around the world, so that Twitter was alight with conversations, comment, and criticism about the interview *as it was happening*.[5] Two years previously that would not have been possible and without videos on YouTube[6] for others to dissect the interview after the fact, it is unlikely that so much would have been written by so many about it (at time of writing, Google produced over 22,000 results on the search query "sarah lacy mark zuckerberg interview sxsw 2008."[7] However, reflecting Oscar Wilde's opinion that "The only thing worse than being talked about is not being talked about," Lacy does not seem to have suffered professionally, continuing to be a columnist for *BusinessWeek* and *TechCrunch* for several years and co-launching Pandodaily.com, dedicated to providing news on Silicon Valley.

Since then many event organizers have quickly understood how audiences can be engaged through Twitter, with the "Art of Digital" event at Saddlers Wells in London[8] in 2009, the audience's Tweets were projected onto a screen behind the panel discussion, such that two discussions were taking place simultaneously. It was clear from the reactions of the audience that the Twitter conversation often captured more of their attention than the panel of distinguished speakers. Whilst some may complain that this is distracting people from the serious points being made, this would be missing the point: Everyone now is able to share their opinion on any topic and, whilst popular opinion may not be right, it should certainly not be ignored. That is to say, it is worth emphasizing the fact that Twitter is a communications and broadcast tool available to all and that, as with any media monitoring service, brands need to monitor Twitter. This will be covered in more detail later on, but one should assume that any group of customers, employees, or stakeholders has access to broadcast to their network and that, in some cases, those networks will count in the tens of thousands or more (Twitterholic.com shows the 1000th most popular person on Twitter at time of writing had almost two million followers).

The use of Twitter as a communications and broadcast tool came to a fore in 2007 in the protests against Burma's military regime. Whilst foreign journalists were kept out of the country and unable to report on the civil unrest, citizen journalists broadcast text, audio, and video over the internet[9] through blogs, forums, and email. However, when the government shut down the country's only two internet service providers (ISPs), protestors were able to continue to get messages out using Twitter, which worked on the mobile phone SMS system, before the government shut down the phone networks too.[10] Twitter (along with Facebook) was also an essential communications channel for those involved in the various protests and revolutions that made up the Arab Spring of 2011,[11] using tags (see the section on Folksonomies/Tagging later) to group related messages for the general public to find easily. The hashtags used on Twitter, for example, included #Cairo for those involved in the Tahrir Square protests in Egypt and #Mousavi for those discussing the disputed Iranian election in Tehran in 2009.

Astute marketers have latched on to hashtags as a means of engaging with customers on a specific topic (e.g. UK opticians Specsavers Tweeted their tagline "Should have gone to Specsavers..." along with the hashtag #Korea following the South Korean flag being incorrectly raised during a women's football team match between North Korea and Columbia at Hampden Park, Glasgow during the London Olympics 2012.[12] Conceivably some North Koreans might have thought the Tweet belittles any disrespect to their flag they may feel... but no such complaints were registered.

Risks of Implementation

Marketers and business people in general should be careful, however, about using hashtags on topical subjects. US designer Kenneth Cole suffered a media backlash in February 2011 when he hijacked the Tahrir Square protests with a Tweet saying "Millions are in uproar in #Cairo. Rumor is they heard our new spring collection is now available online at http://bit.ly/KCairo – KC"[13]. The Tweet only lasted two hours before being removed but not before a fake @KennethColePR account was set up with parodies of such Tweets.

The UK homeware chain, Habitat, left an intern in charge of the Twitter feed who had a good grasp of how hashtags work, but not on how Twitter users dislike brands spamming them. A series of Tweets were sent out including the hashtags for trending topics on that day, including *#mms*, *#Apple* and *#True Blood*. This in itself would only irritate users, but what brought the mistake to the eyes of national media[14] was the use of *#Mousavi*, aimed at rallying supporters of the Iranian protestors. Habitat removed the offending Tweets quickly and underwent a three-month long self-imposed Twitter silence.

Twitter can be used for direct advertising, with promoted Tweets appearing at the top of Twitter streams or at the top of trending topics, but the many-to-many form of communication that is Twitter has meant that this does not always work as intended. McDonald's launched a campaign promoting two topics in January 2012: *#meetthefarmers* to showcase the suppliers, and *#McDStories* for customers and workers to share what the company means to them. The *#McDStories* tag was quickly usurped with protests and complaints by disgruntled customers and the company was forced to pull the campaign within two hours of launching.[15] The ease with which the crowd can communicate on Twitter is no doubt the reason it has become a great force for communication and also a great danger for brands. Dell, as described in Chapter 4, understands the importance of monitoring the Twitterverse and of using Twitter as a business development or sales channel (with @DellOutlet) – but there are still, at this late stage of social media's development, large numbers of organizations that ignore the potential and the dangers of Twitter.

Some brands have attempted to tap into the influence of celebrities by paying them to Tweet about the brand. In January 2012, Snickers, the chocolate brand, paid a range of British celebrities including Rio

Ferdinand and Katie Price to post five Tweets within one hour, the first four of which were uncharacteristic of that particular celebrity (such as discussing quantitative easing or the GDP of China in the case of Katie Price) before posting a fifth tweet saying "You're not you when you're hungry @SnickersUK *#hungry #spon*."[16,17] Two complaints were made to the UK's Advertising Standards Authority (ASA) that the ads were not obviously identifiable as a marketing communication,[18] but the ASA did not uphold the complaints and believed the *#spon* tag on the final Tweet was enough to show that all five were sponsored.

The message for marketers is that Twitter can be used to speak directly to the target audience through promoted Tweets, to engage the existing customer base as a community, or to reach specific users through influencers or celebrities.

How one engages an existing customer base seems to be remarkably confusing for new marketers who appear to be surprised that, despite creating a twitter account and diligently posting on-target messages with suitable regularity, they still have few followers and have completely failed to engage the community. They felt that if they built the channel, the audience would come. The audience, of course, stayed where it was and carried on doing what it wanted. And that is what the social media marketer needs to do – go to the audience and do what it (the audience) wants. If the target audience is discussing the merits of a rival's products, it won't take kindly to being spammed by your organization about your product, or having the rival's products being criticized. If your products are being attacked on twitter, you would do well to not become defensive (as most of us are inclined to do in private, if not our professional lives) but instead to listen and take the feedback as free market research.

Social media is about transparency – it is difficult to hide anything for long so it is better to air your own laundry first before someone else does. It is better, surely, to know of a problem sooner rather than later, and to then explain to the complainers that you are working to fix it. Communities will form and engage about any topic and their messages cannot, therefore, be controlled.

Ensuring one is on top of any such complaints from customers and other stakeholders requires social media monitoring. It is surprising, therefore, how few organizations employ media monitoring services that also deal with social media, but prefer to focus only on old media. Many online services exist to help companies monitor a range of platforms, and for small and medium enterprises (SMEs) there are many free services that work well – a quick search on "social media monitoring tools" will produce a range of lists for recommended, free services.

Twitter can also be used, as we have seen, by a community as a decentralized communications system. Such uses do not need to be the preserve of protestors but are relevant to all stakeholders of an organization. One of the best uses of microblogging is using closed groups for managing projects and knowledge sharing. Just as for blogs, as explained above, it is easier to view headlines (Tweets) of updates once or twice a day, potentially with links to more information (e.g. on a blog) if it is required, so that members of the group can instantly see the status of other members of the team, including any problems that have arisen, without needing to wade through dozens of emails that have been replied to at different times by different people and have consequently split off into separate conversations.

The free enterprise tool Yammer is a combination of a microblogging tool and a social network, with users able to post short messages as subject lines, leading to longer posts (involving text, images, and attachments as well as other features) that readers can then directly reply to. The replies can also be replied to, allowing clarity in conversations that can instantly be seen on the same page at the same time. There are white-label providers of similar systems that can be implemented within an organization's intranet and offer yet further personalization options.

Twitter, Facebook, and Google+ can be used in this way by setting up private groups. With so many options available, it is surprising that over a trillion emails are sent each year[19] and corporate users are sending and receiving over 110 emails each day on average,[20] with business emails amounting to eighty-nine billion per day.[21] A McKinsey report in 2012[22] found that knowledge workers spent up to a third of the day on email and that social media could be better used to reduce the time used on group communications. A BBC report quoted by McKinsey described how the French firm Atos had banned internal email use for its 80,000 employees.[23]

Twitter has also become, for many, the first source of news, being updated long before traditional news outlets broadcast,[24] and of course this includes news related to organizations and brands as well as any type of news that might appear in a newspaper.

Microblogging, in short, has many positive uses for organizations. It also presents potential dangers to an organization's reputation and brand. What most organizations still need to do is realize that new technologies are not just marketing tools or the preserve of the IS&T departments. Knowledge sharing and knowledge management is something that all managers and, indeed, employees should be concerned about. Efficient use of employee time to ensure the rapid exchange of news and avoid the growth of email traffic will save time and money and will lend itself to improved team performance.

As we shall see when we discuss how to successfully implement social technologies in an organization, decisions on using such tools do not need to come from the executive team or the technical experts. They are, in fact, more likely to be adopted if they do come from the needs of a team and are aimed at meeting those needs.

chapter 6

Folksonomies/Tagging

Definition and Description

As described in Chapter 4, Clay Shirky ascribes the problems we face with increasing amounts of information to "filter failure." The filters can come through recommendations but it is how those recommendations are passed from one person to another that could present another logistical problem.

Technology, fortunately, is able to help here by collating recommendations from a group and delivering an easy-to-read indication of how good, or bad, a particular product or piece of content is. The most obvious example is the star ratings used by many e-commerce sites that have already been discussed. These are, in essence, user-generated recommendations at their most basic level – by rating something on a scale of one to five or one to ten.

If the users generated labels, or "tags," for the content, it would give a qualitative element to the quantitative rating system by allowing users to explain what they think a piece of content is about or who might find a particular product useful. The term "Folksonomy," coined in 2004,[1] is used to describe such user-generated classification and categorization, differentiating itself from the *taxonomy* of traditional classification systems such as the Dewey Decimal System used in libraries around the world.

For example, if one followed the original categorization of the Dewey Decimal System, should a book about the implementation of social media for marketing, knowledge management and sharing, stakeholder engagement, and social interaction be classified under 001 (Computer Science, information & general works: Knowledge); 070 (Computer Science, information & general works: News media, journalism & publishing); 302 (Social Sciences: Social interaction); 370 (Education: Higher Education); 600 (Technology: Technology); 604 (Technology: Special Topics); 607 (Technology: Education, research, related topics); 652 (Management & Auxiliary Services: Processes of Written Communication); or 658 (Management & Auxiliary Services: General Management)? The answer is all of them, but traditional taxonomies don't allow this.

Physical storage has traditionally benefitted from a strict taxonomy, allowing librarians, warehouse managers, and filing clerks to quickly locate a particular book, item, or file. Most websites operate on the same system, with individual web pages being located within a sub-menu of the central website navigation. To go to a page on a similar subject, however, one might need to go back up the different menus to the home page, and then drill down through the other menu to locate the page in question.

Electronic systems enable content of any kind to be classified in all manner of ways, such that users can navigate horizontally through a website to see all pages on a related topic without being concerned within which menu, or classification, they sit. The classifications are possible by adding tags, or labels, to the content in question. Tag clouds show the range of tags used for a particular item and are ranked by size according to the most commonly used tag – allowing users to quickly identify what the most popular tags are and, therefore, what most people believe the content to be relevant for.

The hashtags used on Twitter (and adopted on Google+ and other platforms) work in exactly the same way, allowing individual Tweets to be labeled on a particular topic and, therefore, efficiently searchable. Photographs and other images can be tagged showing the content of the image. Images, more than text, benefit immeasurably from this tagging, which humans are still able to do far quicker and more accurately than image processing software.

Business Applications

The benefits of folksonomies, or tagging, for knowledge management should be obvious. When a piece of content (be it an organization policy, report, procedure, guidelines, creative, designs, or even employees themselves) is labeled by users, it will be easier to find.

For example, this book could be tagged with the following labels and, therefore, rather than being restricted by the classification under the Dewey Decimal System as above, it would be findable by users on any of those terms, according to the exact use of the content they are looking for:

- social media,
- knowledge management,
- digital marketing,
- stakeholder engagement,
- technology for education, knowledge sharing,
- Enterprise 2.0,
- social networks,
- intranet,
- tagging,
- folksonomies,
- categorization,
- blogging,
- microblogging,
- Twitter,
- Yammer,
- Jive,
- Convo,
- Google+,
- Facebook,
- virtual worlds,

- podcasts,
- widgets,
- apps,
- wikis.

An extension of this is the growth of social bookmarking. Rather than keeping one's internet favorites or bookmarks on a specific computer (and not, therefore, being able to access them from another computer), various services (such as Del.icio.us or Google Bookmarks) started allowing users to bookmark internet sites through an online service several years ago. Most browsers now offer the opportunity to access your favorites through any device, but not all offer the option of sharing the bookmarks with contacts and friends or with the general public. If people then search for tags (or terms) on those bookmarking sites they will see the websites that are bookmarked the most often, or (depending on the settings) the bookmarks that the original user thinks are worth visiting. The popularity index of Google's search algorithm does the same thing across all websites on the internet. The difference here is that individuals can say they like particular websites (without having to link to them through their own website).

Users can also share websites they like or think others would find useful – or search websites that large numbers of people recommend. Several websites allow this, such as, Digg.com, Stumbleupon.com, and Reddit.com.

This means social bookmarks could be used, therefore, within teams to ensure that all relevant websites, pages, and documents are shared across the team, instantly updated and relevant, through being editable by all members of the team. Organizations might have, in the past, had a central repository of information needed for a particular group, such as a set of books, files, or directories on a main shelf in the office that everyone could access as necessary. Social bookmarks allow organizations to do the same thing (department by department, team by team) for online resources – but they rarely seem to, preferring at best a static page on an intranet with popular or useful links. The links are often out of date and often don't include all the resources a new recruit might need to access.

In addition to making documents, knowledge, content, and products easier to find by employees, colleagues, customers, and others, the fact that everyone is involved in the categorizing process ensures both that the categories are relevant to all (with the caveat, of course, that they have participated in the process – that they tag the content when given the opportunity and understand the importance of it) but there is also a cost saving in not needing dedicated documentation specialists to label and categorize everything.

Risks of Implementation

They might need to take an overview. Some tags, for example, might prove to be spam or abuse and not relevant at all. However, the best systems take this into account and allow the other users, the crowd, to flag something as inappropriate or offensive. It is easy to create simple filters on whatever platform is being used to ensure expletives and other offensive words are blocked.

chapter 1

Wikis

Definition and Description

Despite what many think, a wiki is not Wikipedia. However, Wikipedia is an example of a Wiki. According to Wikipedia in 2008, a wiki is "a website that allows the easy creation and editing of any number of interlinked web pages via a web browser using a simplified mark-up language or a WYSIWYG text editor."[1] The fact that Wikipedia, the free online encyclopedia written by members of the global public, the crowd, is so easy to edit explains why the definition at the time of writing the first draft of this book had changed to "A wiki is a website which allows its users to add, modify, or delete its content via a web browser usually using a simplified markup language or a rich-text editor,"[2] and by the final draft it was "A wiki is a web application which allows collaborative modification, extension or deletion of its content and structure.[3]"

It is highly possible that the definition will have been updated once again by the time this is read by you, dear reader.

The term wiki, according to another public wiki, Wiktionary (an online dictionary and sister site to Wikipedia), originates from 1995 and is "Abbreviated from WikiWikiWeb, from Hawaiian wikiwiki ('quick') + English web."[4]

Business Applications

Much has been written about the advantages of knowledge sharing and management within organizations through using wikis in the work-place[5] so we won't spend much time here doing the same, suffice to say that the same ethos that is applied to Wikipedia using the wisdom of the crowd to create a rich online encyclopedia can be used internally to generate policy documents, best practices, instruction manuals, or any other piece of content that would benefit from the input of stakeholders from across a department, division, region, or entire organization.

The alternative, the paradigm that still exists in many organizations, is that documents (in Microsoft Word, typically), are sent to various recipients via email, with notes added to and changes *tracked* on the Word document, with each revision adding further layers of multi-colored addenda and the problem of version control, with different participants adding notes or changes to different versions. Wikis allow all those stakeholders to edit and comment on the same document in one common place and all know that the document they are working on is always the latest and only version. Most wiki software now allows users to go back and review previous versions, a safety mechanism for when radical edits are (possibly accidentally) saved.

Many document sharing systems work in similar ways: Microsoft Sharepoint, IBM's LotusNotes, or Google Docs are formal systems that allow multiple users to share and edit the same document, often with multiple users editing the document simultaneously.

Collaborative spaces are nothing new. Notice boards have been around in organizations and public communities for decades. Everyone can post comments, news, or ads that anyone can read. Boards would often be created around specific topics with universities typically having dozens of boards, each one dedicated to a specific extracurricular club or interest. Electronic Bulletin-Board Systems (BBS) were created in 1978[6] and allowed users to connect to central boards via dial-up modems and post messages, questions, and comments that others could respond to days or weeks later.

Wikis can be created by small teams, for example, to collaborate on group projects at school or work and, as described above, can involve bespoke systems for an entire organization or for the world at large. As described in Chapter 2 on crowdsourcing, the accuracy of a wiki can exceed that of formal academic literature.

Wikipedia.org and Wiktionary.org are part of the Wikimedia Foundation,[7] which also incorporates a range of other public wikis aimed at improving access to knowledge, from Wikiquotes.org (a repository of famous sayings and quotations) and Wikibooks.org (for textbooks) to Wikisource. org (a library) and Wikiversity.org (providing learning resources).

The purpose of listing these sites is not to promote them nor endorse them, but to emphasize the body of work that can be accomplished when people are trusted and given free access to improve things.

Risks of Implementation

Wikileaks.org, another famous – or perhaps infamous – site aimed at bringing "important news and information to the public"[8] is not related to the Wikimedia Foundation but also shows how the general public are able to make a difference when given the tools to easily, and anonymously, leak information about their organizations or governments that would otherwise be kept secret, so that journalists and other news organizations can expose illegal and unethical practices. An early example was how Rudolf Elmer, the former COO of Bank Julius Baer in the Cayman Islands, exposed the bank's offshore structure for tax avoidance[9] in 2008, which is mentioned here to remind readers that if an organization wants to avoid social media (be that internally or externally facing) on grounds of confidential information being at risk, the information is already, always at risk. If an employee or other interested party wishes to expose the organization publicly, they will find a way. In the old days it was through an indiscrete word in a journalist's ear over a drink. Photocopying and miniature cameras allowed whole documents to be leaked. Sensitive information is no more nor less secure through having an internal knowledge sharing system. What will make more of a difference is ensuring policies and procedures have been defined and explained to employees beforehand.

McAfee, in his 2009 book,[10] goes to great lengths to explain how he sought evidence of Enterprise 2.0 disasters from conference attendees and CIOs for several years with none actually having occurred. Most of the fears around security seem to be related to IT departments concerned with compliance and being sued over inaccurate information on the wiki.[11]

The ethos behind wikis, as with crowdsourcing, is the same as that behind open source software, where computer code is worked on and improved by many different, independent minds with a view to the code being as good as it can and for others to then build on it with future improvements. It is the antithesis of proprietary software for which users must purchase licenses (i.e. buy the program) and endure any limitations that software might have. There are currently over sixty different open source licenses available[12] and hundreds of free applications replicating the functionality of proprietary software in every area, from productivity to security and from communications to financial tools.[13]

When Elon Musk, who made his fortune with PayPal and founded Tesla Motors "to accelerate the advent of sustainable transport" through high-performance electric cars, explained that Tesla would not pursue infringements of their patents by those who "in good faith" want to use Tesla technology, he was, in effect, making the technologies open source. He said in the blog post "Tesla, other companies making electric cars, and the world would all benefit from a common, rapidly-evolving technology platform."[14] It is unlikely other patent-heavy organizations will follow suit, but it is worth considering how different the world would be. Would those organizations currently suing all competitors for patent infringements (achieving nothing other than holiday homes for their lawyers) really suffer if they made their patents available to all? They might, potentially, lose a short-term competitive advantage, but wouldn't they also then be able to benefit from the technology of others, thereby allowing innovation to feed innovation and ensuring advancement of the technology at the fastest speed possible – to the benefit of all? Maybe not, but I remain hopeful that it would. Tesla want to increase the development of innovation in the electric car market, thereby improving their own viability – more electric car manufacturers would mean more electric cars on the roads, leading to more recharging points in public places, ensuring more people were more comfortable buying electric cars, thereby feeding the industry to build more and develop better.

Open source works on the same idea.

8

Podcasts

Definition and Description

For these purposes, let us assume that any audio and video content delivered through the internet is a podcast, although strictly speaking podcasts are downloadable episodes as part of a series that can be subscribed to. But YouTube, with over a hundred hours of content uploaded every minute of every day[1] (and all the other video streaming services, such as Blip.tv, Vimeo, or Veoh), is relevant here as the content is created by the crowd, for the crowd. Anyone with a video camera or a mobile phone can become a content producer and many have managed to make a living out of their home-produced content (sometimes very, very good livings – running to hundreds of thousands of dollars annually[2]).

The technology available to create and post videos from domestic video cameras and even mobile phones has also allowed individuals and organizations to stream video content live from anywhere in the world. LiveStream and Ustream are just two streaming services that only require a webcam for anyone to be able to broadcast, for free, to anyone in the world (premium services are available for those who want a more personalized, bespoke experience). Bambuser allows live streaming from a mobile phone, truly changing the possibilities of *citizen journalism* such that it is not just text and images provided by the general public on events as they happen, but also live broadcasts.

Business Applications

This has enabled anyone within an organization to make a video, be it to communicate to employees, customers, or any other stakeholder. Demonstrations of products can be done without resorting to high-cost equipment, production facilities or broadcast networks. Videos can be used to advertise and showcase product ranges directly on an organization's website. "How-to" and training videos can be produced for employees (as an audio-visual extension of the text-based knowledge management tools mentioned already) as well as for customers and the general public, reducing the need for customer service agents to field as many calls on these matters. IKEA, the Swedish furniture manufacturer and retailer whose assembly instructions for their flat-pack furniture have often confused customers, have produced videos that show how to put items together in more detail.[3] Many other organizations have been producing such videos for many years.

In addition to training videos for employees and customers, educational uses of podcasts allow lectures, seminars, and tutorials to take place virtually, with the participants in different locations and time zones. This can be used for delivering distance learning and catch-up material, or, if we extend the concept of podcasts, to facilitate video conferencing over the internet (using free and premium systems such as Skype, Google+, WebEx, or GoToMeeting, for example).

Newspapers and journals are able to enter the world of broadcast media, with traditional newspapers now providing videos of events on their websites and podcasts of news and opinion (both audio and video) – turning, in effect, text-based journalists into radio broadcasters. The following is a list of some UK and US podcasts that discuss business, technology, digital, and media that I have found useful... being able to keep up-to-date with latest changes in business areas that

I, personally, am interested in. There's some comedy too, because there's nothing better than having a laugh on the Monday morning commute to work:

- Click[4] (radio broadcast on technology available as a podcast from the BBC World Service).
- Digital Marketing Podcast[5] (from training and consulting agency, Target Internet).
- Freakonomics[6] (from one of the co-authors of the eponymous book, Stephen Dubner – with the best accompanying music selection of any podcast).
- Friday Night Comedy[7] (regular radio comedy from BBC Radio 4).
- *HBR* Ideacast[8] (interviews with authors and thinkers by *Harvard Business Review*).
- Internet Marketing Podcast[9] (from SEO agency Site Visibility).
- MediaTalk[10] (media podcast from *The Guardian* newspaper).
- TechWeekly[11] (technology podcast from *The Guardian* newspaper).
- TED[12] (presentations by innovators of all types from TED conferences).
- This Week in Google[13] (internet, the cloud, and Google-focused podcast from Twit.tv).
- Wired Podcast[14] (from the UK edition of technology magazine *Wired*).
- Zen Monthly[15] (technology updates from Zen Internet Ltd.).

Of course, this is a personal list (possibly out of date by the time this book is read) and is not intended to endorse any of the podcast producers, but simply to illustrate how podcasts have helped this humble writer keep up-to-date with news, innovations, and trends on the core areas of professional interest whilst walking to work or driving. A quick search for "best business podcasts" will provide links to articles by various publications listing podcasts on a range of business topics and many organizations have created dedicated channels, such as Cisco's CSR channel on YouTube,[16] to disseminate information on particular policies or practices.

Risks of Implementation

Sites such as YouTube can, as well as helping brands reach their audiences in new ways, also be platforms upon which brands can be damaged even more than through blogs and Tweets. Domino's, the pizza chain, suffered in 2009 when two employees filmed themselves creating pizzas that were not using the company's recipes or ingredients.[17] In the same year, United Airlines suffered a social media backlash for refusing to compensate a passenger, Dave Carroll, for a guitar damaged by the company. He wrote a song and filmed a short video, which went on to get over fourteen million views on YouTube and spawn a book by Carroll. Whilst causality is difficult to show, it is worth reflecting that the airline's stock lost 10 per cent in value, or $180 million during this period.[18] Nestlé was the focus of a successful campaign by Greenpeace to get the food manufacturer to stop buying palm oil for chocolate bars from Sinar Mas, a supplier reported to be destroying the rainforest in its attempts to harvest the palm oil.[19] A video of a FedEx employee throwing a customer's package over a fence (and breaking it), was caught on camera and was seen by over five million people within five days, prompting the company to use the same medium two days later on 21 December 2011 to apologize and deal with concerns about the employee's behavior.[20]

As with all social media, audio-visual content such as podcasting offers great opportunities for all organizations to engage stakeholders in a more personal way. Its ubiquity and ease of use also means it poses a significant threat to organizations that commit an innocent or isolated mistake. What would once be contained and of little significance, can now be seen globally and held up as an example of the organization's practices, rather than a one-off.

Social Networks

Definition and Description

"Social networks" is a term that is often, incorrectly, synonymous with social media. It is merely one type of social media, arguably the most popular type given that the term can cover a wide range of sites. A social network is quite simply a list of all one's contacts, friends, and/or family in an online community arranged around a particular topic and where individuals can share thoughts, ideas, and other content. That topic might be "socializing," such as with Facebook.com, Renren.com (in China), or Vkontakte.com – now known as vk.com – (for Russia); "business," as with LinkedIn.com or Xing.com (in Germany); "conferences," with Lanyrd.com; "music" (Soundcloud.com); or even "sexual preferences" (Fetlife.com). Users are usually able to gain introductions to their contacts' contacts, and other "no tie" connections, as McAfee called it.

Messages can be posted on the social networks that are visible to one's direct contacts or, depending on the settings, everyone. Small programs, or "apps," created by third parties (the "crowd" of developers) can be often used on the platforms and messages can be spread virally.

A list of social networks can be found on Wikipedia[1] and is worth explor- ing to see the range of interests that have a dedicated social network. There are, it should be stressed, many more social networks that are available and not listed there, including those built on the Ning.com platform for specialist groups, such as professionals interested in the use of multi-user virtual environments (see Chapter 14 on virtual worlds) in the "Association of Virtual Worlds"[2] or those in London's arts sector interested in the new possibilities that digital offers through "Art of Digital London."[3]

Network Effects

Social networks are, furthermore, an easy illustration of how "network effects" bring benefits to all members of that network (as first described by Theodore Vail in the nineteenth century). There is little value in creating a social network of one person. With whom will they share their thoughts, knowledge, photos, or best practice? I first joined Facebook in 2006, shortly after it was made available to those who were not connected to specific universities, to explore possible uses for the organization I worked for at the time. During most of that time there were only two friends or relatives I knew who were also connected. It took several years for most other friends and relatives to join and start using it, with some of my late-Gen X social group still avoiding Facebook, citing no time and lack of interest (and many friends now, eight years later, still vowing to not get sucked in). Metcalfe's law suggests that the value of a network is proportional to the square of the number of users and, whilst originally referring to telecommunications networks where users were, in fact, connected devices, there is an intuitive truth in this. However, defining "value" is worthy of more discussion than there is space for here and does not suggest that Facebook, with over a billion users, is of more value to an organization (or an individual) than a smaller subject-specific network as just described.

Nonetheless, the "law" (which Metcalfe and others amended to suggest that the value of social networks is equal to the number of users multiplied by the log of that number – which is perhaps being a little too pedantic)[4] helps explain the mechanism for reaching and passing the critical mass necessary for a new technology to take off, as will be discussed later on.

There is, however, a point at which the value of the network can diminish as more people connect to it when, for example, there are so many users producing so much information that coherent messages are drowned out by the noise. This is one of the biggest problems with Twitter. If you follow more than a few dozen people (and most of us do) then even if they only post once per day, we will usually miss the vast majority of messages. So how can we find out what messages are worth seeing? Is it just the ones that have been re-Tweeted or "Liked" more than any others? As already discussed, probably not. Mark Zuckerberg, founder of Facebook, apparently missed a post announcing the birth of his niece because a co-worker's birthday ranked higher in the Facebook news feed (he promptly had the ranking algorithm adjusted).[5]

What is a Network?

The exact definition of what constitutes a social network and what does not is also much harder now that many sites allow the user interaction and communication one associates with social networks (sending messages, online chat) in what is otherwise a normal website with user-generated content. Sites focused on sharing user-generated content such as Flickr.com, for photography, YouTube.com, for videos, and Slideshare.com, for PowerPoint presentations, also allow users to have profiles and to post messages or comment on and rate the content shown.

Social networks can be open as well as closed. Arguably, closed networks which allow members of a closed community to communicate with one another are more likely to provide real value to the members as interactions are limited to the topic in question (the business) and the closed nature of the community should allow a freer expression of opinions and ideas with no fear of them being disseminated to the wider, general public. That is not to say the opinions and ideas will not be republished, or leaked, to the general public, but the fact that the network is closed, or private, will help satisfy the fears of some.

Business Applications

The most obvious enterprise social network is that of an organization's intranet or people finder. Before the internet and all office personnel having individual access to local networks or the world-wide web, organizations produced print copies of internal phone directories, showing names, job titles, departments and contact details for all workers. The development of intranets did not automatically encourage the growth of internal social networks beyond the basic people-finders of the paper-based years. Individuals were often not required to put further information about their jobs and specializations on the systems and the people-finders remained as online versions of offline directories.

The social network should, however, be at the core of any attempt by organizations to manage and share knowledge. If there is a healthy culture of sharing knowledge within an organization such that the explicit knowledge, that which is written down and recorded, is easily searchable, then one might not, it would seem, need to communicate with the expert in question: one only needs to search the database to find what one needs to complete the task or project.

However, there are times, as former US Secretary of Defense Donald Rumsfeld said: "as we know, there are known knowns; there are things we know we know. We also know there are known unknowns; that is to say we know there are some things we do not know. But there are also unknown unknowns – the ones we don't know we don't know."[6]

When we don't know what we don't know, sometimes all we do know is that we need to talk to an expert. Some knowledge will always remain tacit (unrecorded, but kept in the brain of the beholder) precisely because a new scenario involves nuances that had not been previously thought of. The first step in being able to identify tacit knowledge that needs codifying is understanding who the experts are and then engaging with them. An internal social network where employees were obliged to list their areas of specialization should not be a threat to them (a common obstacle to getting people to share their expertise being the very fact that once shared, it cannot be unshared and the employee might feel that they are no longer essential for the organization). An internal social network that allowed personal employee profiles where information about the employee's background, previous experience, studies, projects and areas of interest should make any reader instantly aware of what they might want to ask that person about. In this era of portfolio careers and the end of the concept of a "job for life," or even a career for life, it should be obvious that one's colleagues (particularly those with whom we do not share water-cooler moments but who still might be sat in the same building or even on the same floor) have a past that we do not know about and that, therefore, are a *known unknown*.

Sadly many organizations, and the people who sail in them, still only view a person by their current job title and assume that is the sum of their abilities and knowledge. The knowledge might be fluency in a particular language, experience of (or contacts within) a particular organization, experience of developing a particular system or tackling a project in particular conditions.

Social networks are, therefore, best when doing what the term suggests and connecting people who might not otherwise know of each other's existence.

There are, however, multiple uses of public social networks that benefit organizations. The billion-plus network that is Facebook has long been a target for marketers to try and capture the audiences there and many have succeeded in connecting with their fans (as followers are known on Facebook) with, at the time of writing, Coca Cola® the leading brand on Facebook with over eighty-three million fans, followed by Red Bull on forty-three million and Converse on forty million, whilst KFC and Sunsilk had enjoyed the fastest growth at the time of writing.[7]

It is worth remembering that the Coca Cola page, which states in the "About" section "The Coca-Cola Facebook Page is a collection of your stories showing how people from around the world have helped make Coke into what it is today," was started not by the company, but by a fan.[8]

Organizations now have the dilemma, particularly when they are smaller enterprises, as to what platform should they drive their target audiences to. As with any website design, the first thing the designer, or organization, needs to consider is: What is the website for? What purpose does it serve? Brands such as Coca Cola, Red Bull and Converse are aimed at younger demographics and will endeavor to extend the brand presence with that audience through the online experience. If the brand is about fun, then the online experience needs to be fun. If the brand is about excitement, then the online experience also needs to suggest that.

A brand's target audience, however, is not necessarily the typical user of their website. Whilst Coca Cola, to focus once again on that brand, is the most recognized brand in the world,[9] its main corporate website (CocaCola.com) is not aimed at the target audience but at other stakeholders, such as investors, journalists and job-seekers. If an organization wishes to connect with its audience, should it try and bring the audience to them (that is, to their website) or go to where the audience already is online (such as on a social network)? Some brands have tried to drag their audiences kicking and screaming to the main websites with the promise of special features, offers or exclusive content. The audience has to be very loyal to the brand to spend the energy in going to the brand website and is ideal for communities of hard-core fans but is less suitable when trying to engage with the wider public, tapping into one's fans' friends and helping the fans become brand ambassadors. In those cases, it will be more effective to go where the audience is (and, importantly, where the ambivalent customers are, where the friends' friends are) and leverage the network of that platform to reach new people.

it will be more effective to go where the audience is and leverage the network of that platform

The question is not whether Facebook (or any other social network) will replace a brand's website, but if it is more suitable for engaging with particular audiences and stakeholders then it might well need to be created as a separate channel to reach those audiences. By the same token, one cannot assume that Facebook is the best vehicle with which to reach online audiences in every country. Facebook's ubiquity ignores the fact that other platforms are used in different countries and even in the USA and the UK it is often easier to reach specialist audiences through other networks.

Whilst Facebook has finally overtaken Google's Orkut in its strongholds of Brazil and India, it has created a two-tiered social network landscape with Facebook being the network of choice for the more affluent and more connected layers of society in Brazil, whilst Indians will go where their friends are and wherever is deemed "trendy." In Germany, where Xing.com is the main network for professionals, the platforms SchülerVZ, StudiVZ and MeinVZ were aimed at accompanying German networkers from school through university to the workplace (although SchülerVZ has now closed). Russians prefer to use their homegrown vk.com (formerly Vkontakte.ru) and odnoklassniki.ru, whilst China has Renren.com, QZone.qq.com, Kaixin001.com, 51.com and TencentQQ with a combined user-base of over 1.5 billion active users.

In Taiwan, whilst Facebook penetration has grown by 7000 per cent in the two years since a Chinese language version was launched, for a long time it was – according to one of my Taiwanese students – the preserve of "good looking young people who like posting photos of themselves." "Normal" people tend to prefer the anonymity offered both through not needing to post photos nor use real names on Bulletin-Board Systems (BBS) – old-school forums such as PTT and PTT2 where 10 per cent of internet users communicate on a wide range of subject-specific topics with a "gossip" forum operating as a pseudo Wikileaks for journalists.

Identifying the target audience for the communication in question is, of course, essential. Once the target audience is identified, the organization can study their habits and behaviors and then work out which platform is the best channel to connect to them with. The use of the term "target audience" though typical in marketing, should not be misunderstood either to suggest that we are only thinking of current and potential customers. The *target audience*, for these purposes, also refers to investors, journalists, job-seekers, employees, retirees, suppliers, NGOs and any other party with an interest, or stake, in the activities of the organization.

Many organizations have begun to use Facebook to manage their recruitment process. One Indian IT consultancy had 1000 applicants for the fifty vacancies on its graduate scheme. By connecting the applicants with each other in a Facebook group, the applicants were able to discuss the recruitment process, help each other and make friendships that were cemented at times when meeting offline. The benefits of this were that when the fifty offers were finally made by the organization, all fifty applicants accepted the offer (in previous years many would have accepted other positions by that time). Furthermore, all fifty turned up to start the job on the first day and all fifty were still there three months later thanks to having already created a supportive community amongst themselves, which helped them feel that they belonged even before they were offered a place. In previous years the drop-out rate due to people feeling that they didn't "fit in" lead to high costs for the organization who had to return to the recruitment process.

Others have used their fanbase on Facebook to test new products or gain feedback on website redesigns. UK bank FirstDirect, part of HSBC, attracted "fans" through targeted ads on Facebook that said "FirstDirect: Want to have a hand in how our products and services develop? Like our page to stay up to date with the FirstDirect Lab Tests." This had over twenty-nine thousand likes at time of writing and customer feedback on the website was already being incorporated into site updates, which are communicated back to the fans through their Facebook page.[10]

Risks of Implementation

There are many other ways organizations can use social networks for business and many social networks. They are channels of communication, but the crucial difference is that, as with all social media, the direction of communication is two way. Organizations need to *engage* in conversations with their audiences. Pharmaceutical companies, for example, restricted from marketing medicines to the public, have to find new ways of getting their target audiences, be they medical practitioners or sufferers of the ailment in question, and must listen to the conversations taking place by the communities that have self-formed around diseases. Only then will they know how the general public choose to communicate on the topic and, importantly, better understand the issues they face.

It is surprising how often organizations still view Facebook, and other social networks, as a drain on resources and a way for employees to waste time rather than as an opportunity to reach the customer base, employees or other stakeholders.

Of course there are many ways in which an organization can fail in their use of social networks, most of which revolve around people feeling that the organization is inappropriately "invading" their personal online space. Even if an individual "likes" an organization's page on Facebook, for example, the organization must be careful not to publish too many messages that will appear, or clog-up, that person's timeline. They will want, perhaps, to hear about special offers, or possibly when a new line of products is available, but not necessarily the fact that the organization has won an award or has a change of leadership. There are messages that are best suited to press releases for journalists, and messages that are best suited for customers. Are there campaigns that the organization can run, however, that will encourage them to spread the brand message to their contacts? A competition, for example, with a suitably attractive prize or a funny video might extend the reach of the brand. But be careful who decides what "funny" is!

chapter 10

Widgets/Apps

Definition and Description

Widgets are small programs (or interactive virtual tools) that are "bolted on" to existing applications and will generally do one function, such as displaying data from a particular application on the desktop. Apps are small programs for mobile devices (generally) that differ from mainstream applications in that they are usually only intended to do one particular function rather than cover every possible requirement of an office productivity suite, for example. As apps become more mainstream, however, they are also growing in complexity and the apps available on tablets (such as the iPad, Windows, or Android tablets) are often replicating the full-blown applications of desktop computing. Widgets have migrated to mobiles and once again give desktop access to particular functions of an app, such as showing a stream of updates from social media.

The reason these are social technologies is two-fold. First of all, apps for mobile devices, are usually distributed through dedicated online app stores according to the operating system of the device (Apple's iOS, Google's Android, Microsoft's Windows, etc.) and are promoted by users virally, sharing favorite apps and rating them. These user-generated recommendations have driven many start-up apps to achieve large numbers of downloads (which puts the apps at the top of the leader board of app downloads, thereby driving further downloads). Secondly, the distribution network of the app stores has allowed any amateur programmer to create a simple product (app) and monetize it by either making it free to download (and earning revenue from ads built in to the app or from in-app purchases) or charging for the download itself.

Penultimate, for example, a hand-written note-taking app for the iPhone and later the iPad, was developed by an individual coder but quickly became the fourth highest selling iPad app before eventually being bought by Evernote.[1] Another example is Pocket God, a game that has been downloaded over six million times at a cost of 99 cents in the four years since its release.[2]

Such app entrepreneurs, or "appreneurs,"[3] have become rich by tapping into two business models, the Long Tail and Freemium, highlighted in books by editor-in-chief of *Wired* magazine in the USA, Chris Anderson.[4,5]

In summary, the Long Tail refers to the niche markets available through the online catalogues, e-commerce, and digital downloads. Rather than only focusing on the few most popular products and selling them in large quantities, the Long Tail is when there are far more product lines (hundreds of thousands or millions) but only a handful of sales of each line. Despite limited sales of individual product lines, however, the total revenues can add up to be a significant source of revenue. App development also follows the Long Tail in that a few apps are created by large software companies, but most of the hundreds of thousands of apps are created by individuals or small teams and start-ups working on a shoestring – not all of them getting rich from the development but many of them making extra money from it.

Freemium is the business model that most app developers operate under: Offering two versions of the app, a free one and a premium one with a cost ranging from a few cents to a few dollars. The free version will either be a basic, no-frills version of the premium app – encouraging users to pay to access more advanced settings and features – or will contain ads that, thanks to the large numbers of downloads, are still capable of generating income for the developer. The premium versions are sometimes the same as the free ones but users pay to not have intrusive ads in their app.

Business Applications

There are two important points organizations should consider with regards to apps. Firstly, that their customers, whether B2C or B2B, might wish to have access to information, products, or services on mobile devices and apps are more user-friendly ways to access online services than through mobile websites. Secondly, that the pool of app developers worldwide means that creating apps for internal or external stakeholders does not necessarily involve a significant financial burden, as the development would almost definitely benefit from being outsourced.

There are complex apps that need considerable development to access multiple databases simultaneously – and have a correspondingly high cost – but they are not the norm. Large organizations will want to consider having multiple apps for different audiences. GlaxoSmithKline, for example, has dozens of apps, mostly aimed at employees although some, such as the Piri Pollen app, is a branded tool for hay-fever sufferers to get pollen forecasts and set reminders to take their medication. Of course users can choose to purchase different brands of antihistamine but as the app also shows the nearest stores and allows online purchases, it helps bind the user to the brand. Shell, by the same token, have a handful of apps aimed at consumers (including one for investors – whom they are not allowed to contact directly) but ten times as many apps for employees, including one to help filling-station managers and another to share the output of their scenario planning team with the rest of the organization.

Risks of Implementation

The biggest risk to organizations, to paraphrase Google's Chair Eric Schmidt, is that, "If you don't have a mobile strategy, you don't have a future strategy." However, any organization thinking that it might want to look at developing an app should first think, as with all channels of communication, about who their audience is – what are their needs, wants and behaviors. If that audience is the company workforce, then it should be segmented (e.g. by region, by department, and by focus or sector) and the app-development team needs to talk to the audience and find out what it currently does, what tools it needs to do the job better and what synergies might be obtained by combining information or processes from other departments or audiences.

The app-development team would need to include people who take a user-centered focus and specialists who work on the user-experience (or the user-interface) – if the app is not intuitive it will not gain traction. That focus could be on something as simple as ensuring the app includes high-quality photographs of the products, something that helped AirBnB improve the overall app experience and encouraged property owners to upgrade their listing on the platform.

chapter 11

Internet of Things

Definition and Description

The Internet of Things (IoT) is used to describe a future where all man-ner of objects are interconnected using the internet. This could include anything from the much talked-of fridge that knows when you are out of milk and orders anew, or fruit that can indicate when and where it was picked, before when it should be consumed, and if it has actually started to go off, to medicines that can only be used by certain people, cars that can send usage information to a mobile app, or thermostats that know when people are not at home and can adjust the heating accordingly – thereby reducing waste.

Kevin Ashton, one of the first to talk of the IoT, said in 2009: "If we had computers that knew everything there was to know about things – using data they gathered without any help from us – we would be able to track and count everything, and greatly reduce waste, loss and cost. We would know when things needed replacing, repairing or recalling, and whether they were fresh or past their best."[1]

The fridge, car, and thermostats that are interconnected already exist – some with more commercial success than others. I am waiting, for example, for the mug that will tell me when my tea is exactly the right temperature to drink – not so hot it scalds my tongue, but not so cold it is no longer enjoyable. And of course it should know it's me and the temperature I like, rather than my friend who has an asbestos mouth and can virtually drink the tea straight after the boiling water has been applied.

Business Applications

The business applications of IoT are obvious, surely? As Ashton said, if costs can be cut through reducing waste (both in materials and labor costs), through repairing before the breakdown occurs, through ensuring cars that are not road-worthy do not actually go on the roads, through helping organizations with their supply chain, inventory, and shipping needs, then the benefits to organizations are huge. It could mean that every organization ran on the "lean" principle – each one making efficient use of all its resources and manpower, thereby improving cash flow and helping companies avoid failing when there is an economic downturn. The environment is likely to benefit from not only a reduction in wastage but also ensuring the right materials can be appropriately recycled or reused and don't end up in landfill.

We already have smart TVs that allow us to surf the web and watch streamed content on the big screen. These can be operated by apps on our mobile phones – which also, in turn, are connected to our wearable fitness devices to track exercise, our transport hubs, our social networks, as well as giving us the ability to track the devices when they are stolen. We have near field communication (NFC) chips – and the simpler radio-frequency identification ones (RFID)in mobile phones, bank cards, and transport cards (such as London's oyster card) allowing contactless payment and removing the need to renew travelcards.

Risks of Implementation

The biggest risk with IoT seems to be the same fear that affects all new technology involving the networked systems – namely security and privacy. For IoT to work data needs to be transferred between millions of devices (Gartner expects there to be twenty-six billion connected units by 2020[2]), which, of course, means that the data needs to be held in databases, ushering in an era of much larger "big data" crunching than is currently seen.

There is a concern, however, that the data could either be stolen or used by organizations for purposes it was not originally intended (which of us, after all, reads the entire "Terms and Conditions" of any service we currently sign up to online?). There is another concern that, if all the objects in our lives are controlled by information obtained through the internet, how can we be sure that the objects will not be hacked by criminals? Is it possible, for example, for thermostats to be hijacked and held to ransom – householders will only have heating in the depths of winter if they pay a "fee" to a third party? Of course, as with new technology, all these risks are real. It is possible for someone to hack a device and, if they see large enough potential rewards, it is likely that many will try. Also, however, the risks are easily mitigated by using industry-standard security protection – viruses, for example, tend not to be a problem for most computer users now because most are sure to have a reliable anti-virus system installed.

chapter 12

Location, Location, Location

Definition and Description

Social technologies have done a bit of a U-turn over the past few years. The beginnings of social media and embracing the crowd meant that individuals and organizations were able to reach large numbers of people spread throughout the world. It understood that the best people for a particular task, or the target audience for a particular product, might not be in your neighborhood but could be, quite literally, on the other side of the planet. This is the new era of "Glocial Media," where social media can have global reach but needs to also be focused on a local scale. As mentioned in Chapter 9, if organizations wish to use social media to reach customers in Russia, for example, they would do better to use vk.com rather than Facebook; StudiVZ, MeinVZ, or Xing in Germany; or Bulletin-Board Systems (BBS) such as PTT and PTT2 in Taiwan.

There is, of course, another side to "local" and that is "location." The connectivity of mobile devices now allows users to get hyper-local recommendations and search results based not on their country, nor their city, but on their neighborhood.

Business Applications

The possibilities for small organizations should be obvious and are already being exploited – if someone searches for "pizza" in a specific area, they could be sent discount vouchers for a particular restaurant. Equally, if a loyal customer is near a brand's shop or premises, they might be welcomed and offered a special deal. In the same way that local cinemas, in days of old (certainly in the UK), used to show low-budget ads for local bistros and businesses, those same businesses are now able to tap into location data with their advertising (Google Adwords has allowed geo-location targeting for many years). Away from search, however, more and more apps now have the ability to detect the user's location. Again there are many who are concerned about privacy and security and who do not want to use the location-based services. Brands and organizations that wish to embrace the opportunities with location need to be aware of the potential for that data to be abused.

Nonetheless, there are ample opportunities for organizations to use location-based apps and marketing. The leading platform at the time of writing, Swarm (part of Foursquare), allows users to become "mayor" of a location if they check-in more times than anyone else within a given period of time. Businesses have often offered discounts (such as a free coffee) to the mayors of their establishments as a way of rewarding loyalty and tapping into a self-forming community of regular customers. Being "mayor" is nothing but a badge in the gamified system that encourages users to check-in promiscuously to win obscure badges and become mayor of the most locations or beat their friends to the top of the leader-board with points gained for each check-in.

The element that makes Foursquare (and its ilk) more than a game is the ability of locations or venues (businesses, bars, restaurants, shops) to create special offers that are visible to those who check-in and the offering local recommendations based on previous check-ins. However, despite Foursquare (and Swarm), at the time of writing, having over thirty million users and over three billion check-ins (millions done on a daily basis), and although there are over a million businesses on the system, most organizations are oblivious to the potential of marketing with location-based services and rewarding their most loyal customers or offering specific incentives when there are events in the area and a large potential audience. Checking-in on location-focused apps is still the preserve of geeks (specialists in the field – or early adopters – rather than the general public) and the search abilities of Google will always make the recom- mendations service of apps like Foursquare rather redundant to most. However, as we shall see in Chapter 16 and beyond, the biggest problem is how to improve adoption beyond the early users.

the biggest problem is
how to improve adoption
beyond the early users

The point, therefore, is twofold. First of all, that organizations should be aware of new businesses, new apps, and new functionalities as, even if the apps are relatively short-lived, they may be a valuable engagement and marketing channel for a couple of years. Secondly, the personalization and location features of mobile mean that any organization with a physical local presence should be able to find a way to engage with their local customers and stakeholders and provide customized products, services, or discounts for them.

Risks of Implementation

There is, now, a strange dichotomy in this glocial media, if you will, in that when the internet started, it allowed everyone to communicate on a global scale, keep in touch with friends, family, and colleagues wherever they were located, and find new contacts, customers, or con- tent anywhere in the world, whereas now the new connectivity allows everyone to segment their friends, family, colleagues, and customers by geography, connect to those closest, find personalized local recommen- dations, and find content that is pertinent only to the local community. This combination of the global, local, and social media has not, how- ever, been embraced by most organizations who have not accepted the global marketplace and the use of social technologies to engage with customers and employees the world over, or conversely, organizations who focus on internationalization and ignore the specificities of the local markets.

The more information we have about our stakeholders, be they customers, employees, investors, or others, the more we can segment them and ensure that we create specific messages to meet the interests of those segments, using the most appropriate channels that will drive the messages home. Managing all the information to correctly segment the audiences is no easy task and using location data about customers when they are not expecting it, or sending the wrong information to stakeholders due to not segmenting properly, will alienate those customers or stakeholders. Get it right, however, and they will feel that they are having a permanent, personalized service.

chapter 13

Mashups

Definition and Description

The concept of the mashup (or mash-up) is not new. The term comes from the music industry where examples of two different musical styles would be combined to create a new work, such as DJ Danger Mouse's famed *Grey Album*, which combined The Beatles' *White Album* and Jay Z's *Black Album*.

In tech terms, a mashup is when two or more independent datasets are combined to create a new service. A typical example of this might be how (real) estate agents' websites now combine their database of properties for sale or rent with a mapping service (such as Google Maps) so that potential purchasers can quickly see the location of the properties in question.

Business Applications

As with many innovations, it is so obvious it is a wonder how people sought and bought property before. Many mashups use cartographic data, tapping into the location-based services mentioned in Chapter 12, but enterprise resource planning (ERP) systems are to all intents and purposes large-scale mashups, combining data from across an organization to help managers better understand the status, flows, and bottlenecks of the company's production process, and so on.

As with widgets and apps, many mashups are created by individuals outside the organization who see a possible service that the company in question had not provided. *The Guardian's* "Free our Data" campaign in the UK over recent years[1] aims to have all data held by the public sector (such as the highly detailed Ordnance Survey maps, Transport for London service updates, or crime statistics by area), which, therefore, belongs to the country, to be made openly available so that developers can find new ways to combine it and make it more accessible to the general public. This is not to say that private and corporate organizations should release data when it is sensitive or when it would breach data protection, but giving developers access to data, particularly for online services, can help strengthen and spread the brand. Twitter, for example, released its API (Application Programming Interface – the door through which external programs or apps can access data within a proprietary service). This seeded a myriad of start-ups that did everything: From providing more user-friendly Twitter clients, to combining Tweets with a map showing the location of the user; from statistics of one's Twitter usage to posting updates to Twitter on what music is being listened to; from identifying what photos are being taken or where someone is, for example, to showing Tweets together that rhyme to form the "Longest Poem in the World."[2]

Non-tech organizations could also benefit from exploring mashups, but they might need someone from outside to see how disparate areas of the business could be linked together, or combined with data from government or other sources. For example, at the very least, I would expect a corporate website to show me store locations on a map (and it shocks me how many still do not) but why not show transport information too, local car parks (and spaces available along with expected costs), public transport routes and timetables, along with real-time status updates? Why not also show how busy the store is at a given time, so that people with mobility issues or, for example, those with small children, are able to postpone their visit until the store is quieter?

Once again this all comes down to knowing your customer – or stakeholder. Knowing what their needs are and giving them, where possible, tools that will meet those needs. A leading luxury retailer, for example, produced a digital magazine of the latest fashion trends and had a separate e-commerce platform. However, they had not connected the magazine to the e-commerce site so that users reading the magazine could click on an item they liked and purchase it directly. This is obvious, or should be obvious, to anyone who has worked in the digital realm. So how is it possible that the well-paid and experienced people responsible for the magazine and the e-commerce site had not thought of connecting them up? It is, I suppose, why there will always be work for contractors and consultants. It is possibly a result also of political empire-building within organizations, with managers trying to protect their online fiefdoms and the traffic that comes to it.

Risks of Implementation

Senior management, therefore, would do well to think about how metrics and KPIs (key performance indicators) might currently be set in a way that discourages collaboration across different departments. If, for example, the analytics show users from the digital magazine staying on the site for less time than before, this should not be a negative if they can be seen to be going to the e-commerce site and, ideally, their future purchases tracked to see at which point the magazine might have influenced or encouraged the decision-making process.

There is no risk to company data being made available – the organization needs only make accessible such data as it is comfortable to release. This might mean, for example, anonymizing data or aggregating it so that individuals cannot be identified. When combining data with third-party datasets, one only needs to be sure that the third-party data is not copyright or otherwise protected.

Perhaps the biggest risk is in coding the mashup – if third-party or open-source sub-routines or plug-ins are used in the development, it is conceivable that the organization might leave itself open to having the data used in ways it had not expected.

This risk is real – but no more real than any new IT development. If the developers are not careful about the origins of the code they use, just as they need to be careful about the origins of hardware, they could leave the organization open to having data stolen or viruses to be spread. Most organizations have long-since learned how to safeguard against the spread of viruses in the workplace, so this is more a case of using common sense rather than avoiding the potential of mashups.

chapter 14

Virtual Worlds

Definition and Description

Virtual Worlds (VWs) are 3D online graphic environments where users create a virtual graphic representation of themselves (known as an "avatar") and are able to move around the VW interacting with other people's avatars and, according to the world, can chat, talk, build (virtual) things, fly, buy and sell virtual goods and services, dance, and, of course, have virtual sex ("of course" because pornography has been fundamental to technological innovation for a long time[1]).

VWs are more correctly known as multi-user virtual environments (MUVEs) and are distinct from *massively multi-player online role-playing games* (MMORPGs), such as World of Warcraft, since a game has a purpose. That might be to kill Orcs or build and maintain a civilization or drive faster than the other players. In a VW, however, there is no one purpose – they are environments where the users can do whatever they want.

Before exploring the value of VWs, it is worth discussing MMORPGs a little too. Not all games are the same and the interactive nature of MMORPGs means that achieving certain positions within the game often requires skills that go over and beyond how to operate a joystick. Back in 2004, Yahoo! employed someone, in part, based on the fact that they had become one of the top guild masters in World of Warcraft[2] where top players have to show leadership skills with other players over whom they have no other connection or hold (such as paying them a salary) to achieve their aims. The Chief Learning Officer from a top law firm told me they had learnt more about leadership by becoming a guild master in World of Warcraft than they had through years of executive education and post-graduate qualifications.

Business Applications

A 2008 article in the *Harvard Business Review* suggests two learnings that corporates might take away from MMORPGs. Firstly, how to incentivize through non-monetary means to motivate individuals to achieve the group aims; and secondly, information should be *hypertransparent* to assess the capabilities and performance of team members in real-time and, therefore, reassign tasks accordingly.[3] The use of MMORPGs for *accidental learning*, however, tends to occur, as it suggests, by accident amongst individuals and is still rare amongst organizations investing in learning and development.

However, more than games, the open nature and lack of purpose of VWs means that there is huge scope for organizations to embrace the technologies but this lack of focus also makes it harder for many to see the potential value. According to VW, MMORPG, and social gaming consultants Kzero,[4] there are over eighty different VWs at the time of writing with over one and a half billion registered user accounts, 70 per cent held by under-fifteen-year-olds (ranging from 29 per cent of all seven to thirteen-year-olds in Asia to 79 per cent in Australasia). Only 3 per cent of users are over twenty-five years of age, or in other terms, most business people, managers, teachers, professionals, and consultants have never experienced a VW.

This will be discussed further in Chapter 35 on the future of technology, but it is worth considering briefly that the tools, abilities, and methods of communication and interaction employed by generation

Z (or however it might be known when there is finally consensus on the nomenclature) are not currently catered for in organizations. Those young people and children will be going through higher education and joining the workforce in the next decade and in twenty years' time they will be managers and leaders. Will organizations wait for the incoming generation to change the way they do business, or will they change now, knowing how important it will be to attract the best talent? The savvy reader will try to ensure their organization at least understands what the virtual environments are and have a strategy for starting to explore possible uses. One's customers, as well as one's employees, will also expect to find goods and services in a variety of ways. In the same way Gen Y is happy to do everything online, the new technologies such as VWs will open up huge possibilities for commerce, education, social enterprise, and entertainment that, surprisingly, many organizations and people are still unaware of.

IBM's Second Life, arguably the best known VW, has over forty-one million registered accounts with an average age of thirty-six, but many are dormant or abandoned and it would not usually have more than around fifty thousand concurrent users (down from a high of eighty or ninety thousand a few years ago) and around a million unique visitors logging in each month.[5] By comparison, Habbo has an average age of fifteen, over 295 million registered accounts, and over five million unique visitors per month staying an average of forty-one minutes each.[6]

Mindark, the creators of Entropia Universe, by further contrast, signed a deal in 2007 with the Chinese government-supported online company Cyber Recreation Development Corp. to create a VW that would allow up to seven million concurrent users.[7] It seems the ambition of that deal was, perhaps, somewhat premature and subject to the *inflated expectations* of VWs at that time.

Hundreds of brands have already created an official presence in one or more VWs, from virtual stores displaying virtual wares, to campus lecture halls and office meeting rooms. IBM opened their Second Life campus in 2006 but one year later found that disgruntled workers in their Italian offices decided to take their protest to Second Life. In September 2007 around 2000 workers, union representatives, and supporters held a twelve-hour long protest in the IBM virtual offices[8] forcing the Big Blue to drop their plans to cut the workers' bonuses. IBM engage in several different virtual environments, including Forterra System's OLIVE, Second Life, OpenSim, Torque, and Unity3D for virtual meetings, distance learning, employee induction, data-center modeling, remote mentoring, and inclusive leadership training;[9] whilst they use bespoke VWs for their virtual university,[10] with useful advice for others that want to experiment with the format.[11] The cuts in travel by many organizations over recent years has seen a growth in trade fairs, exhibitions, and conferences being held in VWs (as with Cisco's Strategic Leadership Offsite[12]).

With the global market for virtual goods exceeding $15 billion[13] in 2013 there are clearly opportunities for all kinds of organizations to engage with that growing community of all ages and meet the demand for digital products,[14] or simply advertise to them through billboards, product placements,[15] and sponsored virtual events. They can also be valuable spaces for market research – where firms are able to reach international audiences for virtual focus groups and interviews[16] – as well as for obtaining customer feedback on product prototypes and designs[17] and for recruitment.[18]

Virtual worlds, as suggested above with MMORPGs, can also be excellent environments for education of all types. In 2009, Julie Shannan is believed to have been the first graduate of a qualification program conducted entirely in a VW,[19] and many universities and business schools have experimented with holding classes and lectures in VWs. Some brief examples of how VWs have been used by organizations include:

- The University of London training paramedic students who are able to interact with each other, with patients, and with their tutors.[20]
- The UK's National Health Service exploring options for delivering healthcare in the future through hospital designs.[21]
- Imperial College, London training people in the management of patients.[22]
- University of California, Davis creating a "Hallucinations Building" to replicate the experience of schizophrenia so that healthcare workers,

family members, and others can better understand how the illness affects the sufferers.[23]
- Visualizing abstract and complex objects, such as viewing DNA.[24]
- The creation of Maslow's Hierarchy of Needs to help students explore and better understand (and remember) the nine levels.[25]
- Architecture[26] and construction.[27]
- Teaching languages[28] and negotiation skills.[29]
- Teaching law enforcement, child advocacy, and social services personnel how to identify and gather evidence.[30]

Reflecting the high usage by what US educators refer to as K-12, primary and secondary school educators have been experimenting with VWs for many years now and much has been written on the possibilities and the obstacles.

In terms of knowledge sharing, any skill or process would be better shown and practiced, in 3D rather than through textual instructions. As described already, this could be anything from boiler maintenance to bomb disposal, from surgical procedures to psychotherapy, and from customer services to conflict resolution.

Risks of Implementation

Virtual worlds are not, however, without their problems, which we can summarize here as technical issues, appearance and dress codes, acceptable behavior, and communications norms.

Technical Obstacles

First and foremost are the technical issues that users and organizations will encounter. Software usually needs to be downloaded to computers to access the VWs – but many corporate IT systems will block not only the installation of unapproved software (that doesn't feature on a small list of enterprise tools) but even downloading it. The high resolution and fast-moving graphics require a high-quality graphics card, processor, and RAM – which might well prohibit both the corporate user and the individual from accessing the worlds. Finally, it is not obvious how one maneuvers in VWs. Most rely on the standard keyboard and mouse (or trackpad), which means that the range of movements one can do (walking, running, flying, sitting, dancing, shaking hands, nodding the head to agree or disagree, raising one's hand, holding a virtual object, etc.) are not intuitive. The growing use of mobile and tablet devices means that future MUVEs will need to think carefully about the user-interface.

Things are, however, changing. Facebook famously purchased the virtual reality headset manufacturer Oculus Rift[31] (as mentioned before) and technologies are being developed that allow users to interact with VWs through gestures and without needing to use keyboards or joysticks. These new technologies will open MUVEs to a far larger audience – if the barriers to entry are low and people do not need training on using or engaging with a MUVE then clearly this will open them up to the non-geeks. Just as Nintendo's Wii created new markets that Microsoft's Xbox or Sony's PlayStation consoles could not reach with complicated and user-unfriendly handsets.

Appearance and Dress Codes

When I started exploring VWs I met some people in Second Life who I would later meet in person and I noticed how rarely their avatar looked like them. The hair color might have been similar, but the avatar, as perhaps one should expect, had a fantasy figure or physique. Men showed an athletic, muscular build and were permanently twenty-six years old. Female avatars tended to have accentuated hour-glass figures, long flowing hair, and would often strut around in stilettos and risqué clothing. I was conscious that the same could be said of my avatar, who was a healthy male in his mid-twenties whose only similarity to me was the hair, skin, and eye color – which, of course, I chose on setting up the account.

Rather than have someone see my twenty-six-year-old avatar first and then be visibly shocked when seeing the saggy middle-aged man that reality has made me, I decided to make my avatar as ugly as possible. The feature-settings on Second Life allowed me to put everything up to "11." I allowed my avatar to have a saggy behind, several spare tires around his waist, and male breasts. I set all the facial features to the extreme in eye symmetry (or rather, asymmetry), nose size and alignment, chin and jaw shape, and I ensured the avatar had a skullet (bald on top of the head but with long hair down the back). The result of the changes, and with the same standard clothes the avatar was "born" with from the Second Life inventory, was a figure that would not look out of place as a Hells Angels bouncer from an illicit desert drinking den in the mid-1970s. Not, one might argue, the most appropriate image with which to represent my organization and engage in dialogues with others interested in exploring the business and education potential of VWs. So, to counter this, I thought that with shorter hair (at the back) and a suit, my avatar would be sufficiently business-like to be a suitable representation of myself. However, rather than buying a virtual suit (and trying to claim for it through expenses at my organization, which I am not sure I would have been able to do) I looked for and found an option within my standard Second Life inventory that said "black men's suit." On clicking the option, however, not only did my avatar suddenly have a smart black suit, but he himself had turned black (I later noticed the option said "black man in suit"). It was the same avatar with asymmetric eyes, crooked nose, saggy behind, and so on, but it now had black skin rather than white and African features.

Rather than changing back I decided to keep the avatar like this (perhaps readers should know that I am a white, middle-aged man). Interestingly I noticed people (or rather, other avatars) suddenly treating me differently – as if they were making the same assumption that I had made that the avatar is an accurate representation of the person – and that, therefore, I must be a black man. Unfortunately, the change in behavior from these virtual strangers was not entirely positive. The advantages of this, of course, are that role-play suddenly becomes more real and it allows users to experience the world from another point of view. The disadvantage, of course, is that it showed me how superficial many people can be, even to the cartoon-like image they see on the screen. In 2008 a study showed people were less likely to help black avatars compared to white ones.[32] Many people have embraced VWs precisely because it allows them to be something they are not in the real world. Disabled people can move without hindrance. Those who, due to their appearance, lack confidence in the real world can interact and be sociable without their confidence letting them down. There are those who like to cross-dress or who feel they have been born in the wrong gender. Interestingly, however, a study in 2007 showed that 14 per cent of female avatars were in fact male, with only 4 per cent of male avatars being women in real life.[33] Going back to the stereotypical and accentuated hour-glass figure many female avatars have, it has been demonstrated that female avatars show far more skin than do their male counterparts.[34] There are those who choose not to appear human at all but have avatars that look like gorillas, penguins, aliens, or "trans-humans". Since 2011, Second Life has offered this option in the standard avatar inventory.[35]

The questions, therefore, for any business context (or educational one) are: What boundaries should be set, if any, on how people appear and behave? Is it appropriate for a teacher (even of adults) to appear dressed in revealing outfits or as a non-human avatar? Should they be expected to have an avatar of the same gender or ethnicity to their real-life one? For experienced users of VWs, those who have not taken time to personalize their avatars are seen as new and inexperienced and, therefore, less worthy of their attention.

Acceptable Behavior

Related to the issue of what species and gender an avatar should be and how it should be dressed is the issue of behavior. One would assume that the same rules apply for social interaction in a VW as apply in real life, but that is often not the case. Stripped of the stabilizing influence of peers seeing the real person, many people behave differently online. On a simple level this can be seen in how they may chat in an online forum, using abusive language or dismissing fellow users in a way they would not dream of doing in a physical meeting. The physical, if you will, behavior of the avatars is also open to abuse. What do you do if someone comes in to your virtual offices and refuses to leave (as with the Italian IBM workers)? What do you do if an avatar obstructs you or "touches" your avatar? Researchers have been exploring the idea of the self and the different behaviors between the online and offline persona since VWs first appeared and it is clearly not a subject that can be adequately dealt with here. Suffice to say all users of VWs for business purposes will need to think of these issues. That doesn't mean, however, that organizations should not engage with VWs. There are risks and there are benefits. Readers are urged to put the risks into perspective and explore the potential benefits more.

Communication Norms

Finally, as with teleconferences and multi-way video-conferences, communication can sometimes become awkward. Should you communicate through text, or by using headsets and speaking over the VW? If the latter, how should someone ask to speak next in a meeting? Raising their virtual hand, or textually asking to speak? Again, these are easy issues to solve, but they need to be considered before embarking on any interactions in VWs. Just as many organizations have handbooks on what kind of behavior is expected of staff, and just as many organizations publish guidelines to help staff understand what kind of behavior is expected of them in social media, organizations need to think about creating guidelines to help staff understand better what they can and what they should not do in VWs, particularly whilst there as representatives of the firm.

chapter 15

Gamification

Definition and Description

Gamification is when products, services, processes, or events include elements and features of game design to make them more engaging. This might range from collecting points or being awarded badges, to completing levels of achievement and competing with others on leader boards. For location-based social network tools such as Swarm (see Chapter 12) this means earning points for each check-in and badges for new types of location or checking in more often than your friends.

The principles are easy enough for any organization or even department or team to employ and they are no different in principle to the top-sellers lists traditionally used to motivate sales teams. Gamification has simply taken the tools used for generations (motivating boy-scouts and girl-guides by rewarding achievements with badges; publicizing the employee of the month), put a fancy word on it, and placed frameworks around how it can be used consistently and successfully within organizations.

Business Applications

There are numerous examples of marketing campaigns, customer engagement, and educational programs that embrace gamification to encourage users to connect with brands, complete training modules, and make repeat visits to websites and stores.

In the context of enterprise uses of gamification, there are already a range of organizations working on integrating gamification within their different processes, such as SAP, IBM, and Deloitte.[1] A gamification app can be integrated, for example, with customer relationship management (CRM) software such as Salesforce, so that managers can set targets and a visual display shows how each member of the team is performing.[2] Airlines have long used gamification, rewarding frequent flyers not just with points but also with "tiers" giving yet further benefits and encouraging loyalty to the brand.

If a knowledge management system used a wiki, contributors could earn points or ratings for the quality and quantity of entries, showing the organization who the best contributors are. On-boarding and training programs within organizations could use badge-collection and level achievement to reward progress through the learning resources. Gamification has the dual effects of making users want to use a system and also making their usage more visible to others (such as peers and superiors) thereby encouraging others to engage and helping the user raise their profile in the hierarchy within the organization.

Risks of Implementation

Gamification is about motivation and much has been studied and written on the subject, from motivating children through positive reinforcement (rather than focusing more on punishing poor behavior) to the role pay-increase plays in achieving higher productivity (e.g. compared to increasing the status of the employee) or encouraging people to donate blood. Clearly the wrong motivator will not work and time and money would, therefore, be wasted in trying to reach an outcome that the gamification will not achieve in sufficiently high numbers. Some customers or staff might resent feeling sucked into a game they didn't want to play – when all they wanted to do was buy a product or work hard.

By the same token, gamification might disincentivize people from engaging – sales staff, for example, who meet targets but never manage to get to the top of the leaderboard might start to resent the system and the people who play the game. Or it might incentivize employees in that particular area to such an extent that they neglect other parts of their jobs.[3]

Organizations also need to be wary of making the rewards in their gamification system so valuable that having a customer or employee achieve the rewards damages profitability.

And so?

It is not enough to "build it and they will come." A manager, leader, or organization can have great intentions of embracing the above tools, even investing money in developing and implementing them, but that is no guarantee of successful implementation. Part 2 will discuss how an organization can make the innovation take hold.

Part *2*

Why it Matters

chapter 16

Spreading the Word

Gabriel Tarde first talked of the diffusion of inventions or, as he called it, "the law of imitation" in the late nineteenth century[1] and asked why it is that some innovations would be widely adopted whilst others, seemingly equally valid and innovative, would not. This is self-evident from even a cursory glance at the latest technologies. Facebook has managed to succeed to a scale that Friendster, Friends Reunited, Plaxo, Bebo, MySpace, and the enormous resources of Microsoft's Live Spaces could only dream of. Instagram, one of dozens of apps allowing users to apply retro-filters to photos and share them on social media became the dominant player in the field, despite other apps having better filters or more personalization options. Apple's Newton PDA in the early 1990s and Microsoft's Tablet computers a few years later didn't get the market penetration either of them expected, despite the technology press praising both sets of products.

Some of this is to do with the timing of the product, as will be discussed in Chapter 35 on the future of technology, but there is usually a raft of reasons why some things succeed where others fail. The question of how to spread an innovation through a community, be it a department, the wider organization, a social class, country, or even globally has been much studied. Those interested in this area are advised to read Everett Rogers' book *Diffusion of Innovations*,[2] that traces systematic research into diffusion from the 1940s onwards. Research into the diffusion of hybrid seed corn in 1943 sparked the field of study, with diffusion defined as "(1) [when] an *innovation* (2) is *communicated* through certain *channels* (3) over *time* (4) among the members of a *social system*."[3]

It is worth spending a little time on this to see that the spread of social technologies has fundamentally followed this pattern. The question then becomes how it is communicated, over what period of time, by whom, and to which members of which social system.

Innovation

An innovation does not have to be an object or product, but can be an idea or practice, so long as it is perceived as new by the individual or organization concerned. With technological innovations there are two components, hardware and software. These may or may not be combined. For example, a smartphone is the hardware and usually comes with an operating system installed, such as Apple's iOS, Google's Android, or Microsoft's Phone operating systems; but the apps created by third-party developers are what bring the devices alive. In this case, there are three levels of innovation: (i) the device; (ii) the operating system; and (iii) the apps (of which there are hundreds of thousands to choose from). Anyone intending to purchase a smartphone, therefore, may consider three separate technologies in addition to which network operator they wish to sign up to. Some will be guided by the number of apps available in the app-store for that operating system. For some the operating system takes priority and within that subset they will choose a compatible device. Others will go by the device and happily accept whatever OS it comes with. Clearly there is a big difference between different users – geeks may be guided primarily by the OS, whereas the majority of the public may be attracted by screen size, for example. Some will accept the device that comes with a particular contract with a network operator as cost is the primary factor in their decision making.

Furthermore, the innovation must have some benefit for the potential adopter. A key question is whether the innovation will solve a perceived problem. Any uncertainty about the potential advantages or disadvantages of an innovation will mean that the potential adopter will seek information to manage that decision.

An important issue, particularly with social technologies, is that of *technology clusters*, where various innovations are grouped together in the minds of potential adopters. The result is that the experience of one of the technologies will influence the adopter's opinion and perception of the other technologies in that cluster. Using Android on a cheap handset may cloud one's opinion of the Android OS, rather than the handset or handset manufacturer. Someone who uses an Apple computer is more likely to choose the Apple brand for their smartphone, regardless of advantages other brands might offer them.

This is an important issue as social technologies are often not technologies in themselves, but terms used to describe a range of tools and technologies that allow users to create content and interact with one another both synchronously and asynchronously. As Facebook is currently the leading social network and a prominent example of social media, there is the danger that anyone who dislikes Facebook (or simply refuses to use it) might generalize all social media and social technologies in the same way. Equally, a new technology that seamlessly integrates with Facebook is, thanks to Facebook's ubiquity, more likely to succeed over a technically superior tool with a more complicated "sharing" mechanism (this is one of the key factors behind Instagram's success). It also means that someone who is already using Facebook, for example, is more likely to also use Pinterest – they have already overcome the hurdle of understanding the potential use of social technologies and are more open to experimenting with new ones.

Another way of thinking about technology clusters is to compare what Moore[4] called the two extremes of a spectrum of innovation – *continuous innovations* and *discontinuous innovations*. *Continuous innovations* are those that require incremental change and are, therefore, technology clusters. The important feature for implementing social technologies is that once a person or social group adopt one technology within the cluster, they are more likely to also adopt others as there will be less effort involved in accepting the change. *Discontinuous innovations*, meanwhile, are those that require specific investment and retraining (or behavior change) by the user. Clearly adoption is harder when it is with discontinuous innovations – it requires more of the adoptee – but that does not mean it cannot happen incredibly fast.

The world-wide web, for example, was a discontinuous innovation inasmuch as even users who already had suitable personal computers needed to purchase a modem to access the internet and contract a dial-up connection (or later on, a broadband connection) from an internet service provider. Many people also needed to purchase the personal computer – which would have been a considerable investment for some, particularly when the potential benefits were unclear (there were few websites available, little opportunity to do online shopping or banking, and electronic communications required the user's social network to also have invested in the new technologies). Adoption of the web, therefore, was slower in the 1990s and speeded up in the 2000s, but given the impact it has had on our lives, on business, on society in general in just twenty years or so, it is difficult to suggest that adoption was slow.

An important element of developing new products is understanding the customer – the intended audience. The new product, or innovation, needs to meet a need. If the existing products perfectly satisfy the customers' needs, then the product will not gain traction.

Those who are not using social networks in their personal lives often tell me that it is because they have no need for them – if they want to talk to someone they just pick up the phone, text them, or meet them for a coffee. If needs be they could always email – a technology that has proved its worth through ubiquity. It wasn't that long ago that friends and family told me they didn't need a mobile phone – because if they really needed to talk to someone they could use a public phone and why would they need to call someone that urgently? Social technologies, as described in Part 1, improve communications, processes, knowledge sharing, and cohesiveness amongst a social group. Of course no one *needed* social technologies – they could have continued to communicate in the workplace using email, or prior to that, phone and internal memos on paper. The fact that some people in some organizations adopted email, and later social technologies, gave them a competitive advantage through faster communications and greater synergies across departments, through the supply chain and greater customer loyalty. The need, therefore, for the other organizations was to simply keep up with the industry and try to remove the advantage their competitors had.

As well as meeting a need, the innovation has to fit the intended adopter's lifestyle, values, past experiences, and requirements. A poor experience with one technology (such as an early version of Android on a cheap handset) might put the potential adopter off trying a similar but improved technology. A person who tried blogging a decade previously might still be reticent to try it again – regardless of the purpose behind the blog. I had a poor experience with a range of Apple computers in the 1990s, which put me off trying other Apple products despite the marketing and the insistence by Apple devotees that Steve Jobs wasn't working at Apple when I bought those machines and it is all different now (or so they said before his passing).

There is clearly a process that individuals need to undertake to adopt new technologies. Once the individual is able to try the new technology (which in software terms means there must be a free trial period or a freemium option; and for hardware requires manufacturers and stores to allow the public to handle the new products and try them out – hence the success of the Apple Stores) they need to alter their habits to incorporate the technology into their lifestyle. Habits change through practice and repetition whilst practice and repetition might in turn be influenced by others (such as the manager, the organization, the government of the country – by setting rules, regulations or laws). An individual might find after a brief experiment that the innovation is easy to incorporate into their current lifestyle and work-practices, so the benefits of using the technology, therefore, quickly outweigh the costs of changing habits.

The actual process involved in using the new technology is also crucial – if it is too complicated to start using, it will never get past the geeks and hit the mainstream. A brand that was synonymous with ease-of-use since the start, Apple, produced guidelines in 1987 aimed at ensuring all developers built applications with the same core features (menus, icons, terminology, etc.) so that users would find new programs familiar and easy to use.[5] Good website design demands that sites follow certain expectations that users will have as to how navigation works, how to get to the home page, and so on.

Astonishingly, it is something that many designers and developers still ignore, with the result that the biggest complaint of new technologies, ranging from smart TVs to smartphone apps and from digital cameras to e-commerce websites, is not knowing how to perform a particular function, which to the developer was obvious. If the innovation needs an instruction manual, it has failed. This is why there is a growing branch of software development focusing on the user experience (UX) and the user-interface (UI).

On a personal level, I chose not to engage with video games such as with the Xbox 360 or the PlayStation. The controller was not intuitive and I was not prepared to invest the necessary time to learn how to use it. As mentioned in Chapter 14, this is one of the reasons why virtual worlds are not yet ready for mass consumption – the user interface needs to be obvious such that people will be able to find their way around it without reading any instructions.

With the advent of touch-screen devices, voice control, handwriting recognition, and wearable connectivity, digital innovations are becoming more and more integrated with normal activities and, as a result, more intuitive. Having said that, the perception of complexity is indelibly linked, unsurprisingly, with the adopter's cultural background, generation, and experience of similar technologies. If you have never seen a TV, for example, you are unlikely to quickly understand the concept of a VHS video recorder.

One of the biggest problems facing the computer security industry is how to make the user experience of online banking, or social networking or e-commerce, as simple as possible while also making it harder for hackers to break. Passwords, to be more robust against hacking, should include upper and lower-case letters, numbers and punctuation, and be as long as possible. Unfortunately, most people then forget their passwords and settle for the most common that are currently used: Password, 123456, and 12345678[6]).

The rise of the internet and peer-to-peer sharing has given the errone-ous impression to many, particularly younger users, that everything digital either is free or should be free. The Freemium business model mentioned already means that many products and services have a low obstacle to new users trialing them, but free isn't enough – if a service is difficult to sign up to, such as asking for excessive personal information, then this will override the free access for new users.

For example, one can sign up to Facebook relatively easily, but it is only once one has connected to friends and contacts and begun to interact with them that the value of Facebook can be seen – but this is a sig-nificant investment in time and effort. If one blogs diligently but no comments are posted on the blog and there do not appear to be any readers, the blogger is eventually going to give up and divert their ener-gies to something where they feel there is some kind of benefit. It is difficult to see the short-term benefits of building a knowledge sharing network within the organization – it might take months or years before the body of knowledge is used by others and built upon. Job-seekers who complete their LinkedIn profile cannot rely on that alone to find them work. And they cannot be sure when they successfully find work that the LinkedIn profile played a part in their new employment.

The innovation also benefits from being seen to be used and enjoyed by others. With hardware, such as smartphones, people can see the device being utilized in the street. With software or online services, however, this is more difficult. The water-cooler moments in offices, schools, and social gatherings may make some users feel left out because they are unable to comment offline on an online conversation or internet meme.

Conversely, online tools in the not-too-distant past did not allow sharing. Sharing options now feature across the world-wide web, allowing users to

Like something to their Facebook friends, +1 it to Google+ or Tweet it to Twitter, for example. However, new social networks struggle not only to be known but also to attract new users away from their incumbent networks. Using *member-get-member* promotions to encourage existing customers to sign-up their friends and family to a service is, arguably, the only way some services can gain traction.

As shall be discussed below, something that influences take-up of social technologies in the workplace is the knowledge that it will raise their profile within the organization or subject community – it is not enough to see others using the social tools to be interested in using them one-self, one also needs to know that one will be seen to be using them. Otherwise, what's the point? It is like shouting into the void.

Furthermore, related to this, is the need for others to be using social media for them to work. One person can use a smartphone and gain value from it whilst being the only one within their community with such a device – but the very nature of social technologies requires a community to be using the network or channel for the messages to be disseminated. This explains, in part, the exponential nature of social technologies – they only truly add value when there are millions of others using them, who all suddenly get that added value.

In summary, for a social technology to succeed:

- It needs to meet some need not currently met.
- Potential users need to be able to try it, easily.
- Users need to see the benefits of others using it as well as seeing the benefits themselves.

Communication

The communication channel, that is, the medium through which the communication of the new technology takes place, will usually directly affect the take up of the innovation. Mass media, or *old media* as we defined it earlier, such as radio, TV, and so on, is good for reaching large audiences and raising awareness. Interpersonal channels, however, or face-to-face exchanges between two or more people are often more effective in getting people to accept new ideas, particularly if they have some area of common ground, such as their socioeconomic status, education, locality, or job – such as working for the same organization. In recent years, electronic communications such as viral internet messages have bridged the gap between the former two, by allowing messages to reach mass audiences quickly but also incorporating an element of interpersonal communication since the messages will usually be transmitted from one person to a personal friend or colleague, who then forwards it to their friends, and colleagues and so on.

These last two channels are essential for diffusion as most people rely on feedback from trusted peers before adopting an innovation (they are *homophilous*). Most attempts at diffusion, however, involve *heterophilous* people, that is, those who are not similar, such as when a technical expert or change agent attempts to introduce a new technology to a group of non-technical people.

A simple parallel would be the recommendations on eBay as described in Chapter 3 on crowdfunding, where large numbers of ratings by heterophilous people are needed before they are trusted as much as a recommendation from a homophilous person, or "one of us."

It is worth considering the formal communication process when attempting to implement innovations across an organization. In such cases, the communication is very much aimed at educating the workforce, and as such, education theory can be helpful. For example, neuroscience suggests there are three elements to consider when teaching:[7]

1. The *recticular activating system* transmits information better if it is something new or different. This explains why we are more interested in new gadgets, functionalities, features, and content. It also clearly feeds through to the "observability" described earlier – we notice the new and the different precisely because it is new and different. Designers of new products and services need to differentiate sufficiently that their potential customers, users, and adopters will

be enticed by the novelty; but not differentiate so much that there is no perceived compatibility with the existing lifestyle of the target groups. This also helps explain why products and services should be regularly updated – not just to eliminate bugs in the system but also to rekindle the interest the user had in the technology.

2. The *amygdala's affective filter* lets data through better when there is a stress-free environment – which explains why the technologies need to be easy to use. Feelings of stress or frustration in the user in trying to understand how everything works are not conducive to long-term adoption of the social technology.

3. If the learning is fun, more *dopamine* is released, and the learning is more likely to stick. Much of social technologies, given that they are used so widely for non-business purposes, could be considered "fun." It is reasonable to assume, therefore, that for social technologies to work in the workplace, they also have to maintain an element of fun. If it is a bore or a burden it is unlikely to stick – which is the main focus behind *gamification*.

Time

Success is relative and deciding whether or not a new technology has been successfully implemented or not is not obvious. Some innovations are before their time. Some achieve a high-level of diffusion relatively quickly. As shall be discussed further in Chapter 19 the decision to adopt a new technology, from first being aware of its existence, through trialing it and then adopting it long-term, will vary widely according to the technology and the individual or social class. It took thirty-eight years for radio to reach fifty million users, thirteen years for TV, just four years for the Internet[8] and a matter of months for the mobile game Flappy Bird[9]. Mobile phones first appeared in 1979 but weren't ubiquitous until the turn of the century.

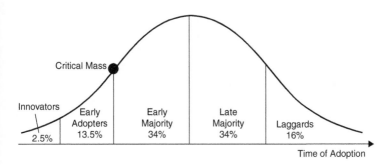

FIGURE 16.1 Rogers' bell curve

All innovations and new technologies go through a growth curve known as Rogers' Bell Curve[10] (see Figure 16.1) which plots the rate of adoption over time. The curve shows a long, slow period where only the *Innovators* are aware of the new technology, with marginally more growth as the *Early Adopters* discover it. It is only when the technology hits *Critical Mass* at around 15–18 per cent of the market that it enjoys a sharp increase in penetration as it starts to be adopted by the *Early Majority* and then, following the peak of the curve (the average time of adoption), the *Late Majority*. Finally, the *Laggards* are the last ones to jump on the bandwagon.

It is useful to compare the diffusion process with the product life cycle[11] shown in Figure 16.2. Products, or new technologies, will only become truly embedded in the system if they reach the majority of potential users within that system. By the same token, the product will only begin to stabilize and make good returns in the "maturity" period, that is, when it is serving the majority of that community.

The time taken for the life cycle could be a matter of months, particularly with new technologies where new, improved models are produced so quickly that no one model enjoys the maturity period for very long. Conversely, some products and services, such as MBA degrees, are arguably within the maturity period over a century after launch and are likely to remain so for some time to come.

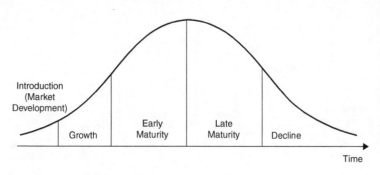

Introduction
(Market
Development)

Growth

Early
Maturity

Late
Maturity

Decline

Time

FIGURE 16.2 Product life cycle

Social System

The social system, as described above, is the community who are all working towards solving the same problem or achieving the same goal. When the community is an organization or company, it is clear that one organization is not necessarily going to behave the same way as another. When the organizations are in contact with each other, they may be siblings of a parent group, customers and suppliers, competitors or complementors, and both their relationship with each other and their individual experiences with an innovation will affect the adoption of that innovation.

That is, one business might produce an app for customers to access their services on smartphones. Their competitors are, therefore, going to be influenced – positively or negatively – by that action and will either follow them by developing their own apps or will choose to differentiate themselves from the first-movers by highlighting other elements of their service, such as (for example) more personalized and less automated customer relationships. Equally, the first-movers might have been influenced from within, by individuals or groups who feel the need for such an app or, for example, from an agency with which the organization works on other products and that has championed the concept of an app for the organization.

There is of course the danger that internal stakeholders who champion the development of a new technology may inadvertently push the organization away from that direction if they previously championed another unsuccessfully adopted or implemented innovation, regardless of the merits of the new proposal and equally regardless of the reasons behind the failure of the previous attempt to innovate. The lesson for all, then, is not to judge new technologies based on the experience of previous ones or the previous champions – but to try and assess each innovation on its own merits.

That decision to embrace the social technologies might come from an individual, a group, or the leadership. An individual might, for example, unilaterally decide to set up a Facebook account for the organization to meet a specific need they have (such as testing new product ideas, engaging the customer base for marketing purposes, or as a recruitment tool by the HR department). An individual might decide to start a wiki to put down the best practice in his or her own area so that others can learn from and build on that knowledge. Many of the successful implementations of social technologies that we will look at later on have been thanks to an individual deciding to champion the innovation and set it up.

A collective decision, in the case of an organization, would most likely be a management committee or a consensus of the members of a department to embrace the technology. Conversely, there will not be many examples of social technologies being successfully implemented thanks to democratic decisions discussed here. Rather that they have seen an individual take the lead and have decided to get on board.

The decision could come from the leadership or figure(s) of authority. This can be a double-edged sword in that some organizations adopt new technologies better when the decision to do so and strategy for implementation come from the bottom-up – that is, from the workers themselves.

As shall be shown in the following chapters, many of the successful implementations of social technologies in the workplace have been thanks to individuals and departments deciding to by-pass internal systems and embrace social networks or other social technologies through the back-door, without any formal decision by the organization to do so.

Furthermore, one of the questions that shall be explored in later chapters is how to answer the question "What's in it for me?" – helping individuals see what benefits there are to them if they help others by sharing their knowledge. There are two ways the organizational hierarchy can help this. One is to make it company policy (and part of people's jobs), so that employees have no choice in the matter – by explicitly mandating use of social technologies within the organization. Alternatively, implicitly endorsing it by having the leadership use the social technologies. Individuals are more likely to share best-practice or other useful knowledge with the organization as a whole if they know that the CEO will see their entry. The CEO could, for example, "Like" the entry, thereby explicitly endorsing the employees who embrace the new tools.

Finally, there is often a chain of decisions that need to be taken in order to enable individuals and groups to embrace social technologies. For example, it might be that the marketing department is unable to physically connect to social networks such as Facebook or LinkedIn due to the IT policies of the organization blocking social media sites. Until those policies are changed (or a "work-around" is found) the decision to implement the technologies is academic.

Decisions to adopt innovations, therefore, can come from a variety of sources and there is no hard-and-fast rule that one system is better than another. Decisions by individuals can work well when there is a culture of experimentation and endorsement from peers of those taking the plunge. By the same token, an organization that is traditionally resistant to change is unlikely to experience widespread adoption of social technologies just because one person or even one department chose to embrace them.

In summary, for social technologies to take hold in an organization, they should ideally be communicated by people close to the adoptee at the right time in the product life cycle and according to Rogers' bell curve (too early and the messages will fall on deaf ears). The decisions to embrace the technologies should come from the right source for that social system.

chapter 17

Deaf to the Word

Some messages are delivered at the right time by the right people but still fall on deaf ears. There are reasons why some innovations have a high adoption rate in a community compared to other technologies; and there are reasons why some adoption rates might appear different.

There are three main obstacles to messages getting through and being acted upon: (i) pro-innovation bias; (ii) individual-blame bias; and (iii) recall problems.

Pro-Innovation Bias

I have spent most of my life insisting on embracing and promoting new technologies. Whilst not being an early adopter (I am an "early knower" – my wallet doesn't allow me to adopt the latest technologies as frequently as I'd like), I've often seen the potential benefits to the individual and the organization of embracing a particular technology. Those technologies, however, have not always been embraced by the individuals and organizations I was talking to or working for. I admit to having what Rogers and Shoemaker in 1971 defined as *Pro-Innovation Bias*[1] – that is, the assumption that an innovation *should* be adopted by the members of a community when, for a variety of reasons, the innovation may not suit the habits and practices of that group. In the past I would suggest that the group in question change their habits and practices. They can do this, of course, but that is a whole other challenge.

For example, many enterprises have benefitted from implementing social technologies, but that does not mean they are suitable for all. What is far more likely is that the organization structure and culture will determine whether or not any significant benefits can be obtained from social technologies. The bias also means those affected tend to ignore reinventions of the innovation.

Nonetheless, a pro-innovation bias by those aiming to introduce the new technology does not mean organizations will not be able to adopt – merely that care must be taken in managing the change, *incentivizing* participation, and ensuring processes are adapted to the new system.

In terms of researching how to successfully implement social technologies in the workplace, I, being pro-innovation in this instance, have looked for ways in which organizations have successfully embraced the technology, the factors leading to that successful adoption, and ways the successful adoption might be mimicked by other organizations. It would be quite easy for another author who is not a fan of social technologies to demonstrate how many organizations have tried to adopt social technologies and yet have failed to diffuse them throughout the "social system," and my extrapolation, making the case that the technologies are doomed for widespread adoption. It is seeing the failed attempts at first- and second-hand that lead me to try and find a framework to help those who are "pro-innovation."

If the potential adopters are not pro-innovation, the task of implementation will clearly be far, far harder. They already have a range of processes in their organization to do everything they need to do – that is why they are able to get paid at the end of the week or month. "If it ain't broke, don't fix it" is the cry of many – but these would also have been the words of those against the internal-combustion engine in the late nineteenth century when horses and carriages were tried and tested technologies that met all known needs. Likewise, many could not see the point of the growth of word-processing software in the 1980s and

1990s that did away with typewriters; and the use of touch-screens to replace cursors being moved around displays by arrow-keys or mice.

Therefore, I urge any reader who has read this far, suggesting a pro-innovation bias, to avoid being dissuaded by naysayers simply because there have been others who have failed in the attempt. If you don't try, you will never succeed. And there are plenty of success stories to make the case that everyone should explore the technologies in question.

Individual-Blame Bias

If individuals do not communicate adequately with colleagues through-out an organization, who is to blame? The individual or the organiza-tion? *Individual-blame bias* focuses on the individual rather than the system; and diffusing the innovation through the social group rather than, for example, changing the group structure and culture itself.

An organization's failure to embrace new technology is not nec-essarily down to the technology; or due to the early adopter trying to encourage greater usage. Whilst successful adoption can sometimes be ascribed to the efforts of one individual to get colleagues to use the new technology, as described before, failure is often the result of users being unable to connect to the various platforms, or a known or suspected dislike of social technologies by the leadership of the organization. If we don't like a particular member of the team or organiza-tion, how likely are we to listen to their advice on new technologies (or anything, for that matter)?

Recall Problems

When researching the diffusion of an innovation, researchers map the take-up of the innovation over time, to differentiate between the early adopters, late adopters, and so on. Not everyone, however, remembers (when asked) how they first tried and then adopted a new technology. The longer the period since adoption, the less likely the adopter is to remember why they first tried the technology, who suggested it or helped them, the original intention for trying it, and how engaged peers within that social system (or colleagues at work) were in adopting the same technology.

This also explains, for example, confusion and misinformation (though not deliberate) when finding out why adoption failed. It might have been due, for example, to the organization culture not being ready; to technical problems connecting to the social technology of choice; the formal obstacles within the organization (e.g. from one's line manager, the HR Department, or company policy); or a lack of perceived benefits (but which may have been due, in turn, to insufficient take-up of the innovation by peers, thereby negating any potential network effects).

If an early adopter attempts to embrace an innovation that requires network effects, as most social technologies do, for how long will they persist with the innovation before abandoning it? Groups of early adopters, meanwhile, are likely to provide each other with the necessary network effects, which explains why the innovators of Silicon Valley adopt new technologies faster than those in many other parts of the world. With the world-wide web everyone has access to the new technologies more or less simultaneously, but if you don't have anyone to share with, the "share" button is redundant.

It is easy to dismiss innovations of all kinds, and social technologies are an easy target for criticism precisely because of their popularity amongst consumers – the reasoning being that if it is used by the general public it clearly has no place in business. Those who are keen to embrace social technologies, therefore, should be under no illusion that everyone will agree with the proposal. For deep-set reasons, many will try to find fault with the technologies or, if the decision has already been made to implement them, they will work against the strategy and, potentially, poison the open minds of others. This negative influence clearly needs to be addressed, as we shall see later on.

chapter 18

Some are More Equal than Others

Whilst all countries have access to the world-wide web (censorships and firewalls notwithstanding), not all citizens of those countries have access. The method of accessing the internet, furthermore, is not uniform. Hence, the ability of individuals and organizations within some countries to adopt a new technology is dependent in part on their geographic location and contributes towards a widening in the socio-economic gap between *adopters* and *laggards*. This gap (the "digital divide" – explored further in this chapter) can be seen within developed nations with, for example, the best prices for utilities (such as gas and electricity), insurance, and air travel being available to online purchasers; but also between nations with the more connected and developed societies moving exponentially ahead of developing nations.

These differences are not a reason to not try and implement social technologies within an organization (in any nation) but, if anything, they should encourage those in all countries and at all levels of society to attempt adoption to avoid falling further behind. Laggards do not benefit from not adopting innovations (except in the belief that they prefer traditional methods of whatever it is…) but often need help to ensure adoption is successfully achieved.

The Digital Divide

Internet connection is of course no longer restricted to desktop and laptop computers. Mobile devices, from tablets such as the iPad and Google Nexus range, through smartphones, down to WAP enabled mobile phones, allow various levels of access to the internet and its services. The growth of mobile devices and their ability to connect to the internet has allowed many developing countries to leapfrog more developed ones in levels of access as they no longer need to rely exclusively on physical landline and broadband cables being extended to remote corners of the country and individuals, families, and small organizations are more likely to be able to afford a mobile device than a "proper" computer.

The United Nations (UN) agency the International Telecommunications Union (ITU) measures adoption of information communication and technology (ICT) across the globe.[1] Figures show, for example, that mobile penetration in developing nations was 90 per cent in 2011, up from 78 per cent in 2011, from 23 per cent in 2005, and 8 per cent in 2001; compared to 122 per cent, 114 per cent, 82 per cent, and 48 per cent respectively for developed nations (there are now more active mobiles than there are people – with some people having multiple devices).[2] The report also shows that the top ten countries on its ICT Development Index (IDI) are from Europe, with the exception of the Republic of Korea and Japan. Mobile broadband is also growing fast in the developing world, at 21 per cent in 2014 compared to 8 per cent in 2011, whilst 84 per cent of people in developed countries have mobile broadband subscriptions – or, in other words, have an active smartphone. This compares to only 27 per cent of people in the developed world having a fixed broadband connection and 6 per cent in the developing nations – growth has almost stagnated as the convenience of mobile broadband overrides any advantage a fixed line might bring. There is still a large divide between costs, with mobile broadband costing ten times as much in the developing world (as a percentage of gross national income per capita) as in developed countries, and up to thirty-five times more expensive in Africa compared to Europe. As might be expected, the bottom ten countries according to the IDI are developing nations, with all but one (Papua New Guinea) in Africa.

The ITU takes the Republic of Korea, ranked number one on the IDI (recently overtaking Sweden), as a benchmark to judge how quickly other countries, according to whether they are *developed* or *developing*, reach the same levels of broadband penetration (mobile and fixed), usage, and number of connected households. The most recent report from the ITU at the time of writing shows there are around seven billion mobile subscriptions (compared to the current world population of 7.1 billion people) and it estimates that 40 per cent of the world's population, 2.9 billion people or 750 million households, are online (1.9 billion in developing nations, 980 million in developed countries).

As one might expect when there is already high penetration of broadband in developed nations compared to developing ones, the rate of growth of penetration in the developed nations is slowing whilst that in developing nations is increasing – both converging on a growth rate of around 5 per cent per annum.

Three Stages to a Digital Society

The ITU report measures adoption of ICT on three criteria: *Readiness* (the infrastructure and physical access) and *capability* (the skills required to make use of the technology), which both then drive the *use* (the amount the technology is used) that leads to the *impact* of the technology in that society, that is, the outcomes and the way in which digital technology is changing the society.

Developed nations are improving "ICT use," having already established access and developed the skills needed through formal education, media, and natural adoption in society. Developing nations, however, are still focusing on (and making the most gains in) improving the infrastructure.

Three Stages to a Digital Organization?

The findings from the ITU report suggest a few insights into how organizations might best adopt social technologies:

1. If there is a correlation between organizational use of social technologies and national use, it is reasonable to assume that, for example, an organization located in Niger (languishing in bottom position of the ITU's IDI) will find it harder to implement social technologies than the Republic of Korea, in first position.

2. It is reasonable to assume that the digital divide as shown by the IDI also corresponds to organizations. If that is the case, it is logical to also presume that the organizations that adopted the internet and online communications early on are further advanced in adopting innovations such as social technologies. Hence, conversely, the barriers to creating the infrastructure and boosting skills in laggard organizations are likely to prevent them from being able to leap-frog over the early adopters of earlier technologies – as has happened with fixed broadband penetration being superseded by mobile broadband.

3. It is also reasonable to assume that organizations follow the three stages of evolution (where *readiness* and *capabilities* lead to *use*) as defined by the ITU; which should help organizations focus their energies on ensuring that readiness and capabilities are in place to maximize ICT impact.

The IDI as defined by the ITU consists of a range of sub-indices, as already described, that measure infrastructure and access (such as the level of broadband penetration, how many people have mobile phones or access to home computers, etc.); capabilities (how literate and computer literate people are and, therefore, whether or not they can access the internet and the services it offers, as well as how many people have had a secondary or tertiary education); and usage (how many people actually use the internet).

Therefore, it can be presumed that an organization in a country with high numbers of users and fast connections can be assumed to find it

easier to implement social technologies; because the
employees will often already have experience of the
tools in question (and certainly of similar ones)
through their personal use of the internet. By
the same token, an organization based in
a country with a poor infrastructure,
a low level of secondary education,
and little personal experience of the
internet is likely to face more barriers
to getting its employees to embrace social
technologies. That is not to say it cannot be
done, but the organization in question would need
to exert more effort in training its staff and installing the necessary
broadband infrastructure.

chapter 19

Deciding to Do Something

The seed corn study in 1943 developed the idea of a five-stage inno-vation – decision process that all individuals must go through before adopting an innovation – a process that has not fundamentally changed and which will be explored in more detail in this chapter:

- *Knowledge* – that is, awareness of the existence of the innovation in question.
- *Persuasion* – when the person or organization concerned decides whether or not the innovation is useful.
- *Decision* – when they actively adopt or reject the innovation, that is, they make a conscious decision to try the innovation or not.
- *Implementation* – when they put the innovation to use, when they trial it.
- *Confirmation* – where the adopter seeks approval from others that the decision made was the correct one.

Confirmation is important as disapproval may cause the decision to be reversed – either abandoned completely or exchanged for an alternative innovation.

Knowledge

> *If I had asked people what they wanted, they would*
> *have said faster horses.*
>
> Henry Ford

Another way of saying this is that Ford's customers had a need (faster autonomous transport) but didn't know how to articulate that. It is not the job of the customer to come up with the solution either, that is the job of the innovator. The marketer must then make the customer understand that the innovation meets those needs.

Social technologies are a range of tools that allow interaction, content creation and consumption, and collaboration by large numbers of people. For example, it is difficult to say that there was a *need* for more self-publishing, but the increase in self-publishing would have been impossible before the invention of the various social technologies.

At the level of an organization, the employees will often complain of the organization being "siloed," with different departments not speaking to one another about what they are working on, with the potential, as has happened often, for different departments to be simultaneously developing the same new tool or product in different ways. Those employees will not usually express a *need* to collaborate more but they will complain of politics within the organization and of "others" making their jobs more difficult by not sharing their knowledge. It is always easy to blame others or the lack of tools that would allow easy knowledge sharing, for example. However, many organizations do not allow individuals to use new technology without it being sanctioned by a particular department – such as that responsible for ICT. In general one will find that the organizations that have adopted social technologies early on are the same ones that have an open attitude to employee use of information technology (IT) – although those that inhibit experimentation (due to the information systems and technology – IS&T – policy or fears of cyber-attacks, viruses, or other malware) will not always be behind with social technologies.

A fear of security breaches to company IS&T systems causes many IS&T departments to err on the side of caution and lock down computer permissions for all staff so that they cannot install software themselves (thereby being unable to take advantage of open-source software or apps) or access certain areas of the internet (such as Facebook). Yet, as mentioned in Chapter 1, McAfee has failed to find any examples of disasters occurring through the organizational use of social technologies (or Enterprise 2.0). In many cases, individuals have managed to implement social technologies within their departments by finding a "back-door" through which they have been able to circumnavigate IS&T policies – for example, by installing a standalone computer, completely unconnected to the corporate network, with its own broadband access.

The fear, however, still dominates the policymaking of many IS&T departments and they often set policy rather than follow it.

The "knowledge" part of the innovation decision process is, itself, made up of three types: (i) Awareness knowledge; (ii) how-to knowledge; and (iii) principles knowledge.

Awareness Knowledge

Whether or not the individual knows that the social technologies exist. For our purposes, everyone knows about Facebook, although they will often not know of the possible benefits to their organization; and many more will not know about LinkedIn, blogs, wikis, and virtual worlds. How one learns of an innovation, as described already, is also important in setting one's expectations of its use and capabilities. Whether the information comes from the organization's leadership, a less-respected colleague, a TV ad, a discussion with a friend, or one's children will all affect how we perceive that innovation.

How-to Knowledge

Whether the person is able to use the social technologies correctly. This is clearly where training and education of an organization's workforce comes in and how the IS&T readiness of a country will affect the amount of training and education required. This includes not just *how* one gets on a system, posts entries, rates colleagues, and searches for information; but also the etiquette of how one should express things, what information should be posted, what level of peer feedback is acceptable, and what is not.

Principles Knowledge

Whether or not the person knows why the innovation works. In the case of social technologies this would include knowledge of how networks are created, the changing rules related to user-generated content, and an understanding of the viral nature of information flow through the internet. Arguably this level of knowledge is not necessary for users to engage effectively within an organization – they need to know the *what?* and the *how?* but not so much the *why?* This is information that only change agents, champions, and technical-support staff might need.

Common sense (and research[1]) shows that those who have status and position in a social network (the old fashioned kind, such as an organization or community) and who have a good level of education and access to media are far more likely to be early knowers. If people are connected to others, talk to them and keep abreast of the news, of course they are more likely to know about innovations! However, the *bleeding obvious* is important in identifying, as we shall see later on, those within an organization who can help others engage with the new technologies.

Furthermore, these characteristics are similar to those found in early adopters when compared with later adopters – with the important difference that the knowers do not necessarily go on to adopt the innovation (e.g. deciding that it is irrelevant to their needs).

According to Moore, all technological innovations start out as *fads* – lots of potential that generates enthusiasm within the "in crowd" (which would be the *early adopters* or *mavens* – discussed further in this chapter) but little market value.[2] Following this point is the *chasm* where the rest of the world observes and decides whether or not to adopt the innovation. The issue, Moore says, is to create the mainstream market – achieve *market maturity* according to the *product life cycle* by reaching the *majority* according to the *diffusion process*.

Moore provides a revised technology adoption life cycle (see Figure 19.1) that clearly defines the chasms between the groups and illustrates how movement from one group to another is not always fluid. In short, getting on the bandwagon with early adopters within the organization is never going to be enough. The impetus and drive to adopt the new technologies *can* fall into the chasm – and this might occur at various times as the different groups adopt, leaving another gap before the next group joins in. The take-away from this is that many attempts to implement social technologies in organizations have failed because they fell into the chasm – there wasn't enough drive to push adoption from a test group or core circle of champions to the next stage. That is not impossible, of course, but needs to be built into the overall strategy of how to implement the technologies.

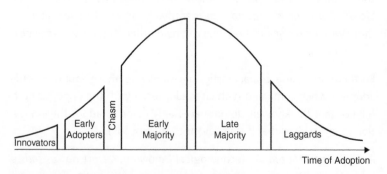

FIGURE 19.1 Moore's revised technology adoption life cycle, showing the "chasms" between adoption groups

Persuasion

Clay Shirky says:

> *real revolutions don't involve an orderly transition from point A to point B. Rather, they go from A through a long period of chaos and only then reach B. In that chaotic period, the old systems get broken long before the new ones become stable.*[3]

That is not to say, however, that organizations must undergo a long period of chaos before they are able to properly implement social technologies. Stability is required for an organization to be sure of the expected outcomes of a new technology, but the current path from old media to social media could be described as being in chaos. Things change relatively quickly and organizations need to be aware of the changes outside as well as inside the organization. In marketing terms, organizations have to consider using all three types of media (old, new, and social) – and the production (or operational) possibilities, as well as the potential for collaboration available through social technologies that are not immediately apparent to most.

As has been mentioned before, the channel of communication through which the potential adopter was first made aware of the innovation is, potentially, going to have a huge influence on their perceptions of that innovation. In some organizations, if a person from the IS&T department suggests a knowledge management system based on social technologies, many within the organization will assume it is an IS&T issue, a technical issue, and as such nothing to do with them. Some might consider the proponent of the new technologies to be "empire building" or getting involved in matters that don't concern them. By the same token, having a young member of staff explain the purpose of the tools to an older generation may put the senior staff member on the defensive, making them feel out of their depth or as if they are being railroaded into adopting something they don't wish to. They may even perceive that they are being forced out of the organization – since the organization will have no further use for that person once their knowledge and experience has been safely distilled into a knowledge management system for everyone else to take advantage of.

Decision

The decision to adopt an innovation can lead to continued use or the adopter may decide to abandon the experiment. Equally, a decision to reject the innovation can lead to re-evaluating the decision later on (and becoming a *late adopter*) or continuing to reject the innovation.

Many decisions will be to trial the innovation for a fixed term and in limited circumstances. This is one of the ten tips Gary Hamel recommends for encouraging innovation so that the business does not expose itself initially to unknown risk.[4] Trials can also, of course, be undertaken by peers of the organization (competitors, collaborators, etc.). Seeing a competitor gain a competitive advantage by having adopted a particular new technology will increase the likelihood of adoption.

Decisions to adopt, however, as already indicated, can lead to later rejection (*discontinuance*), either *active* – when a decision to adopt might have even included a trial – but then followed by rejection – or *passive* or *non-adoption* – where the decision to adopt was not taken in conjunction with a change process to consider how the business should properly integrate the innovation. In the case of social technologies, this might be where an organization creates a corporate blog but then fails to maintain it, because it doesn't fit with the established PR strategy, the organization is suddenly wary of the potential for confidential information to be inadvertently broadcast, or ownership for the blog is given to the wrong department (such as IS&T, rather than marketing or communications).

To prevent this happening, a feedback mechanism is needed that constantly monitors, measures, and reviews the process of implementation to ensure that the innovation "sticks."

The Tail Wagging the Dog

According to Ward and Peppard,[5] a distinction should be made between the strategies from the IS department and the IT department – where IT is concerned with the technology issues (*how* to do something) but IS is concerned with requirements of applications, business needs, and identifying *what* needs to be done.

The important lesson to take from this distinction is that IS&T must educate the business to help influence strategy according to what is *now* possible, but the decisions on what should happen, when, and why must come from the business strategy. Whether or not an organization is to engage with its customers through a smartphone app or whether or not employees should be encouraged to share best practice through a knowledge management system is, and this should be clearly obvious, a decision for the business to make and not any level of the technical division. IS&T departments should be there to support and deliver the decisions and strategy as dictated by the business. This does assume that all three strategies are aligned, but the question quickly arises as to whether or not the IS&T strategy *is* aligned with that of the business.

Furthermore, an important question is whether or not social technologies enjoy the same relationship as other strategic information systems. Organizations are like people – there are similarities and generalizations can be drawn, but they are all different from one another. Some organizations believe they need to develop infrastructures and services in-house, either to create competitive advantage, avoid having to change existing processes, or keep the technologies proprietary. Some, however, will ensure the IS&T department only supports the business strategy through the organization's use of external tools aimed at the end-user.

Others, meanwhile, will only support the internal tools and provide no help to the organization's use of external tools and social technologies. They try to mitigate the risk of something going wrong by simply blocking or strongly discouraging the use of the platform in question, rather than finding other methods – such as training and education, finding other solutions to protect their corporate networks, or perhaps using a network of "super-users" who can provide support but are not formally in any technical function.

Key Success Factors in Strategic Information Systems

Ward and Peppard also list seven success factors for the implementation of strategic information systems, which again should be self-evident, but are worth detailing here:

1. External, not internal, focus – even in the case of knowledge management, which is fundamentally internally focused, the end result should be better service for the customer, a quicker development time-frame for new products, and consistent policies and practices across the organization.
2. Adding value, not cost reduction – implementing an internal micro-blogging platform should be to improve communication amongst staff in different areas of the business, for example, and not a way to cut email traffic, thereby reducing email server-costs and support staff.
3. Sharing the benefits – the benefits of an organization using social technologies have to be available to the whole organization. This should certainly be the case for knowledge management systems but also means that insight gained into a particular customer segment through social media engagement, ideally, gives benefits to other departments and users and not just those directly involved with that customer interaction.
4. Understanding customers – social technologies in themselves will not help an organization understand its customers better. Companies

striving for customer intimacy have managed to do so long before social technologies came along. Nonetheless, the very nature of social technologies comprising mass publishing by the crowd should make it easier for organizations to understand when there is unhappiness with products and services. Dell's experience of blogging, as described in Chapter 4, and its implementation of a social media monitoring department is a fine example of exactly how that can be achieved.

5. Business driven innovation, not technology driven – as before, organizations should decide to embrace social technologies based on sound business reasons, rather than because a new craze is sweeping through the industry press or the IS&T department want to show off their creative skills.

6. Incremental developments – can the system be improved over time or is it a once-off implementation? In the case of a knowledge management system, this might be initial sharing of texts, followed by images and other files, followed by peer reviews and ratings of best contributions, followed by tagging for easy access, and so on.

7. Using the information gained – there is no benefit to having all employees dump the entire contents of their brains on the most sophisticated knowledge management system that allows for intuitive search, peer recommendations, and integrated knowledge maps connecting all areas of the business, if no one uses the resource to learn and gain benefit from someone else's knowledge.

IS&T Generic Strategies

Parsons[6] produced a framework in 1983, adapted by Ward and Peppard, which shows the characteristics and implications of the generic strategies organizations use to guide IS&T from the point of view of management, the organization, IS&T, and line managers and users, differentiating between those elements that are "centrally planned" and those which are a "scarce resource."

However, the fact that social technologies fundamentally rely on the end-users for them to prove effective means that the framework must find a new space between centrally planned and scarce resource. The different roles and responsibilities within an organization will need to be aware of the implications of pursuing a social technology strategy:

- *Management rationale* – potential internal and external benefits need to be identified.
- *Organizational requirements* – restrictions on using social technologies need to be "unlocked" from the center. HR policies need to understand the potential benefits.
- *IS&T role* – provide support to access the new tools. Unlock restrictions on accessing new tools. Implement new criteria to see what constitutes a threat to the internal IS&T systems.
- *Line managers' and users' roles* – identify possible uses and ways for the department or individuals to better communicate and collaborate with each other, across the organization and with the customers.

Implementation (Putting the Innovation to Use)

This stage involves behavioral change, where the adopter or adopting organization must purchase or otherwise obtain the innovation, install it, learn how to use it, integrate it with other systems, and implement support mechanisms in the event of a malfunction or other problem. For some social technologies use in organizations this is as simple as an individual in a particular department creating a Facebook page for the organization, opening a Twitter account, or writing a blog. For a complex knowledge management system that integrates wikis and blogs to an internal social network, clearly a little more investment in time and money is required and, therefore, one can expect (though not necessarily condone) more reticence on the part of the organization to adopt the technologies.

The difference in these examples also highlights the obvious fact that the person who will use the technology (who will populate the wiki or blog, or connect to others through the social network) is often not the same person who created the original strategy. This disconnect clearly affects how well the technology will be adopted – a personal decision to engage with new tools will usually be followed through more enthusiastically than when that engagement has been mandated from above.

During implementation, furthermore, there is the possibility that the innovation will be *reinvented* – that is, that new and unexpected uses will be found for the technology. A simple example is how the internet itself was originally invented to facilitate communication between academics in select universities. That was before the reinvention by Sir Tim Berners-Lee in 1990 that allowed the world-wide web to be a channel for consuming multi-media entertainment, a shopping portal, a platform for keeping in touch with friends, an enabler for political change, and a publication vehicle for billions of people – to name just some of its current uses.

This means an organization may implement a new technology, but find it gains far more value from a previously unconsidered use than from the intended one. The problem is that the unexpected benefits will not have been considered in the decision-making process of whether or not to adopt social technologies. Equally, if organizations do not implement new technology, they are blocking potential secondary benefits and reinventions and possibly stifling internal innovation.

Reinvention, according to Rogers, occurs at the implementation stage for many innovations and for many adopters – which is a reason why heavy-handed lock-downs of company IT systems might well do more harm than good by restricting innovation and lowering the rate of adoption. Furthermore, a higher degree of reinvention leads to a faster rate of adoption of an innovation and adoption sticks for longer – which suggests that users should be free to explore the new tools and not be restricted in how they use them.

Many organizations, however, restrict the amount by which employees may personalize their computers and the way in which they connect with various websites, including social media sites such as Facebook or Twitter. If this is the case, and reinvention is unable to take place, it is far more likely to restrict or block the widespread adoption of an innovation.

Finally, as Ray-Coquard et al. suggest, if the end-users of an innovation are involved in the creation of guidelines for its usage, they are more likely to adopt it.[7] It is not enough, once again, for an edict to come down from on high that the organization must become "social." The users must be involved in the decision-making process and, as described above, be allowed to explore it – because this might lead to reinvention, which will in turn lead to greater and more sustainable adoption.

Confirmation

Confirmation is where the adopter seeks approval from others that the decision they made was the correct one. This might be through choosing the same network, blogging platform, or tagging system that others are using. It may be by being an early adopter and being admired for one's choice. It could be by seeing a report by a third party confirming that the decision-making process was correctly done. Failure to receive approval may result in the decision being reversed.

Discontinuance occurs when an adopter rejects an innovation after adoption. This might lead to *replacement* of the innovation with a newer version; or *disenchantment* of the innovation – where the innovation is rejected due to dissatisfaction with its performance.

Both types of discontinuance occur frequently with the adoption of social technologies. There are those that, for example, use the microblogging service Twitter exclusively, having previously devoted much time to "normal" blogging – an example of *replacement discontinuance*. Equally, an example of *disenchantment discontinuance* can be found in those that have tried "normal" blogging and abandoned it, being dissatisfied with the lack of demonstrable results or audience, or disenchanted with the amount of time required to maintain the blog – hence tens and hundreds of millions of blogs being abandoned each year.[8]

This is where people fall off the bandwagon. Many have tried and, due to problems with the IS&T systems, time, not feeling the benefits, or not managing to reach the intended stakeholders (customers, employees, etc.), have then abandoned the social technologies. They then say "we've tried that and it didn't work" rather than "we tried that, it didn't work because we hadn't thought it through properly, we need to put more thought into it next time."

20

What's Marketing Got to Do with it?

The High-Tech Marketing Model

The *high-tech marketing model* suggests that the way to develop a market for technological innovations is to progress through the curve for the diffusion process from left to right, beginning with the *innovators*, passing through *early adopters*, *early majority*, *late majority*, and ending with the *laggards*.[1] In this way, organizations are able to use each group that adopts as a reference for the next group, with the previous group acting as opinion leaders and building credibility.

The model does specify, however, that there is a *window of opportunity* for an innovation to take hold. If that opportunity is missed, Moore says, any advantages of being in a technology leadership position are lost and competitors are likely to catch up or overtake. However, with social technologies this is less of an issue – the advantages to the organization are not only to give it competitive advantage, but also to improve internal collaboration and communications, new ways of marketing to different audiences and whilst there may be little competitive advantage of embracing social technologies at a given time, in time there may well be a competitive *disadvantage* if the organization does not embrace it. Whilst having a good website in the 1990s and early 2000s might have provided a competitive advantage to an organization, allowing the new breed of internet surfers to access products, services, and information online, an organization that does not have a website now is at a competitive disadvantage, effectively invisible to the many millions of customers and potential customers that use the internet as part of their decision-making process.

The Effect of Opinion Leaders

As explained in Chapter 4, Webster and Wind described the decision-making unit in 1972 with the iBuild framework (*initiator, buyer, user, influencer, lodgekeeper, decision maker*) and for our purposes the important role here is *influencer* – or opinion leaders.

Opinion leaders can make a significant difference to the rate of adoption of an innovation and as we shall see later on, it is essential for an organization to have an opinion leader, or champion, for the innovation to diffuse efficiently. Without the champion, the innovation never gets past the section of early adopters. Furthermore, we shall see how the networks themselves (in which the opinion leader drives the change) are essential to successfully diffusing the innovation. Finally, not just anyone can be a champion, but the position (such as a middle manager, one of the executive team, a technical assistant) is not limited to a specific place on the hierarchy – it depends on the culture of the network.

The Effect of Networks

The networks themselves are also important – peer influence can make a great difference in the diffusion of innovations. The communication through networks has also been studied at length; such that any network will have $\frac{(N(N-1))}{2}$ different possible connections, where N is the number of individuals in the network. Clearly not everyone within a network is directly connected to everyone else, people group in clusters with occasional connections to members of other clusters. The clusters tend to be homophilous in nature with members sharing many social characteristics. Rosen,[2] however, explains how individuals gain far more from heterophilous links than those close to them and that the growth of the internet has made it far easier for individuals to create weak links with those socially and physically distant to them.

Therefore, what seems to be likely – though not proven – is that individuals who have created a large social network online through websites such as Facebookand LinkedIn, where they have many weak ties to their online "friends," are more likely to adopt innovations faster than those who maintain small, homophilous networks.

In the case of social technologies, this means that those who already engage in the social online space are more inclined to adopt new innovations and new elements of social technologies and other online technologies faster than those who do not. This is likely to be one factor exacerbating the *digital divide*.

The Pareto Rule for the Social Age

The Pareto Rule, that 20 per cent of a population provide 80 per cent of the results, has been extended for the internet to show that most user-generated content is created by a small minority of the total users. As described already in Chapter 4, Bernoff and Li's "Social Technographics Ladder" for Forrester broke the population down into seven groups, from the creators to those who completely disengage and five levels using social technologies inbetween.[3]

The research by Forrester shows that for the UK 15 per cent of people are *creators*, with 38 per cent *joiners*, 50 per cent *spectators*, and 37 per cent *inactives*[4] in 2009 (some people might be creators on one type of media but joiners on another, hence the overlap). Comparatively, this research shows, in the US 24 per cent are *creators*, 51 per cent *joiners*, 73 per cent *spectators*, and only 18 per cent *inactives*. This data is not up-to-date of course, for that the interested reader is advised to go directly to Forrester, but it is useful for our purposes here to show the cultural differences between the countries and to assume from this that the UK as a whole might be considered to be "early majority" where the US is "early adopter."

The increase in online usage (not least membership of Facebook) means that figures for 2015 would undoubtedly show a smaller percentage of *inactives* in the UK – but this highlights the issue any organization is likely to face when implementing social technologies. If a company is broadly representative of the population of the country in which it operates, it is likely to share similar characteristics for online participation. This means that an organization in the UK will have some people (37 per cent according to the 2009 figures) who will not participate with the new user-generated content. Even if this figure had reduced greatly, it highlights the issue that there are some people who will be more difficult to get onboard.

It also means that a small group will be responsible for most of the content generation. The question the organization needs to ask itself is whether that is sufficient to gain value from the new tools, or would they need greater participation to ensure true value? Are the tools set up to allow conversationalists to post without expending a lot of energy in creating long posts?

There is, of course, no right answer to this question – it will be for each and every organization to decide for itself.

chapter 21

Critical Mass

Critical Mass is a term often used but rarely defined: when enough members of a society or community have adopted an *interactive innovation* so that the further rate of adoption becomes self-sustaining. It is clearly closely related to network effects – there is little point joining a social network when there are no other members of one's community there; but when enough people are there that others feel they are missing the interaction that happens on the network, they will be more inclined to join. *Interactive innovations*, according to Markus,[1] are those where "widespread usage creates universal access, a public good that individuals cannot be prevented from enjoying even if they have not contributed to it." Later adopters are influenced by the early adopters of interactive innovations, while early adopters also benefit from the later adopters' usage. Markus terms this *reciprocal interdependence*; for example, an early adopter of the telephone probably didn't have much fun until more people adopted the innovation and they had, therefore, more people to call.

As can be seen from Roger's diffusion process (see Figure 19.1, Chapter 19), the speed of adoption accelerates greatly after reaching critical mass. The requirement of *critical mass* is essential for the effective diffusion (and adoption) of social technologies. One of the fundamental concepts of social technologies is that the content is user-generated. This requires two things to work properly: (i) users who want to generate content; and (ii) users who want to consume the content generated by others.

That content might be blog posts, Twitter feeds, or wiki pages. It might simply be status updates on social networking platforms and the mere "connection" between users that enables other users to see one's contacts (as with LinkedIn).

The concept of the *critical mass* was explored in Malcolm Gladwell's *The Tipping Point*,[2] where he describes four criteria necessary for an idea to pass the *tipping point* or *critical mass* and become widespread: *Mavens*, *connectors*, *stickiness*, and *context*.

The term *mavens* comes from a Yiddish word meaning people with *knowledge* or who *understand*. According to Gladwell, mavens are an essential first step in spreading an idea. Rogers would refer to them as *early knowers*. It is the mavens who know about new ideas or innovations and spread the knowledge to their friends and colleagues. Mavens do not need to be well known "gurus" in the technology field (or whichever area the innovation is in). They could be, in fact, relatively anonymous people. They may be outside the organization, they might be family members or friends and completely unconnected from the organization in question – but they are known to *connectors*. They are the sparks that see the potential in an innovation and communicate it to someone, the connector, who can do something about it.

Connectors are the people who, if mavens tell them about a new idea or innovation, will spread the information to a wide circle of people. Where the mavens are early knowers, the connectors are the means of communication. The connectors do not discover innovations or new ideas, nor are they early adopters. But they are an essential step in spreading the news.

The role of the *champion* is most certainly a connector, but might also be a maven. The original idea doesn't need to be theirs, but they are the ones who every organization needs to drive through the change across the company – they know people at every level.

Stickiness is essential for any innovation to gain traction and pass critical mass. An innovation must have a *sticky* quality that will make users want to return to it time and again. For social technologies, each tool will have its own level of stickiness and its own sticky quality. For a reader to return to a particular blog frequently it must have regular, relevant, and compelling content. In order to check their account regularly a Facebook user needs to see news feeds of their friends, to find out what they are up to, and see whether any of them have posted personal messages. The fear of missing out on the latest gossip ensures approximately half of all Facebook users check their profiles several times a day.[3]

Context – or the *power of context* according to Gladwell – is the environment in which the idea or innovation would take place. When thinking about social technologies in the workplace, if an organization's IS&T (information systems and technology) policy prohibits access to social media sites (such as blogger.com, Facebook, or Twitter) then the best *mavens*, *connectors*, and *stickiness* in the world won't embed the innovation throughout the organization.

Organizations that hope to embrace social technologies, as with any new technology, will need some combination of the above four elements. The maven, as explained, might be a CIO, but it could be someone alien to the IS&T department who happens to be highly knowledgeable about technology. Or they may be outside the organization – but in that case they must be close to the connector as they have to be able to reach everyone in the organization, or at least reach the sub-connectors in each department. This *might* be simply an internal communications system, but this champion is more likely to be a change agent – someone who has the knowledge (from the maven) and the persistence to ensure the new technology is adopted across the organization. The connector is more likely to be a CIO or someone in a similarly central role who can get the message through at all levels.

The technology in question needs to be sticky. Whilst most social tools have proven their stickiness with the general public, there needs to be a compelling reason for the technology to be used within the organization. Facebook is sticky on the individual level, but for an organization to embrace it they need to see that it is an important branding opportunity, or a way of engaging with specific audiences, or a tool to aid recruitment, and so on. There needs to be an *incentive* to use it.

In addition, the environment within the organization – the *context* – must be conducive to using the new technology. This might be a relaxing of IT policies; it may be recognition by HR departments that engaging with social technologies are in the company's interest; it could be the requirement for the organization to think about what it wants to achieve through using social technologies, so that users engage with a purpose.

The context also describes the way in which the technology is viewed within the organization. Clay Shirky said, in *Here Comes Everybody*:

> *Communications tools don't get socially interesting until they get technologically boring. The invention of a tool doesn't create change: it has to have been around long enough that most of society is using it. It's when a technology becomes normal, then ubiquitous, and finally so pervasive as to be invisible, that the really profound changes happen, and for young people today, our social tools have passed normal and are heading to ubiquitous, and invisible is coming.*[4]

Finally, there is a constraint on the size of community that can have a *genuinely social relationship* with each other. Dunbar[5] claims that the size of the human neo-cortex ensures that no more than 150 people can truly know each other in any social network and is the reason that the social network Path limits a user to 150 connections, contrasting with the fashion on Facebook of people acquiring as many friends (or connections) as possible. Many of us, of course, have far more connections even in a professional context. My LinkedIn connections list is over 2000 at the time of writing, but having attended dozens of conferences and taught thousands of postgraduate students, all of whom I have met and "know," I recognize of course that these are connections. I cannot truly *know* them – even if I wanted to.

The point here is that large organizations should understand that introducing social technologies will not suddenly create a networked organization – nor will it make everyone friends with each other nor suddenly share all their knowledge nor trust the opinions of others.

However, bearing in mind that organizations are already created in clusters of dozens of people, known as offices, departments, or practice groups, for example, they should find that knowledge is shared within those clusters. And occasionally people within the clusters will have connections from other offices, departments, or divisions with whom they will share information from their cluster. Some organizations deliberately limit the clusters to approximately 150. W.L. Gore & Associates, of Gore-Tex fame, create new offices when one exceeds 150 in size.[6] In contrast, IBM's online collaborative "Jam" events have involved 150,000 people from 104 countries and sixty-seven companies[7] (although it should be mentioned that Jams are specific events rather than ongoing collaborative environments).

Innovations in Organizations

Studies of organizational innovativeness have not managed to find a magic formula for implementing change and yet they have shown that some organizations are more innovative and embrace change quicker than others. Many studies have focused on the leadership roles rather than the end-users, with the result that the studies tended not to provide true representations of organizational behavior. Some studies have suggested that larger organizations are more innovative,[1] but this was long before the free and low-cost tools that social technologies provide came along. It is now far easier for small organizations to embrace social technologies with low risks, given that little investment is required to start using them and they often, by their nature, allow the smaller organization to tap into a far wider talent pool through crowdsourcing than ever before.

However, size *is* important – it is a good predictor of organizational innovativeness as it is easy to quantify and larger organizations tend to have spare or previously unidentified resources, such as employee expertise, that facilitate the implementation of innovations.

size is important

Having said that, many of the innovations that have changed the internet have come through start-up companies, one or a handful of people with a new idea that they bring to market. However, research suggests that large organizations are more likely to adopt those innovations (and, therefore, themselves to be more innovative). It is small and medium-sized enterprises (SMEs) that often struggle with adopting new practices and tend to be more subject to internal power struggles and politics that might prevent an idea from one area of the organization taking hold in another.

The Innovation Process in Organizations

Organizations go through two fundamental stages in the innovation process: (i) *initiation* (that is, up to the point of taking the decision to innovate); and (ii) *implementation* (post-decision).

Initiation

The initiation process is sub-divided into two stages:

- *Agenda setting* – the issues faced by the organization that lead to a belief that innovation is required. The agenda-setting stage might come at a time of a strategic review within the organization or perhaps after an employee survey that has highlighted that synergies are not being created across the organization, knowledge is being lost when people leave, best practice is not being shared, or efforts are being repeated to achieve the same goal due to a lack of collaboration and sharing.
- *Matching* – an attempt to find an innovation that "fits" the organization's agenda. This could be a wiki for sharing best practice, a blog for project management, an internal social network to work as a people-finder, or a folksonomy system to aid sorting, categorization, and improving findability.

The failure of many organizations to embed innovations such as social technologies is clearly due to the second stage of implementation.

Implementation

The implementation process is also sub-divided, this time into three stages:

- *Redefining* and *restructuring* – where the innovation is reinvented to "fit" the organization or the organization undertakes restructuring to adapt to the innovation. Redifining might be the use of a blog that was originally intended as an online journal with a single author gaining multiple authors and being used for project management, for example. Restructuring could be anything from decentralizing IS&T functions so that departments are able to manage their own blogs, wikis, or Facebook access (for example) to creating a matrix organization where similar roles across the business are now connected, driven by the improved communication through social media.
- *Clarifying* – when the innovation and its role in the organization are better defined.
- *Routinizing* – the innovation becomes embedded in the organization, loses its "new" status, and becomes a part of the *status quo* – or "invisible" as Clay Shirky suggested above. It is routinizing which, arguably, is the biggest obstacle to implementing social technologies in the workplace. Organizations need to focus clearly on how they can embed the changes and ensure employees and other stakeholders use the new tools as a matter of course.

Organization Structure and Innovativeness

The level of innovativeness of an organization, according to Rogers, depends on the following characteristics, although some of these do not seem to be relevant to social technologies.

The leadership's attitude to change is clearly important. However, many organizations have managed to buck this trend by implementing social technologies "informally" within departments, bypassing central IS&T and formal approval from the organization's leadership.

Large organizations, as before, are more likely to be innovative but not if the organization is centralized. When employees have more knowledge or more expertise then the organization is more likely to be innovative, but not if they have a formal and rigid bureaucracy.

If the organization is *networked* (by Goffee and Jones's measure, as explained further) and if it has spare resources within the organization then it is more likely to be innovative (to put it another way, if people have time to experiment then they are more likely to collaborate, and this will engender more innovativeness).

There is a self-perpetuating truth here that innovative companies will be more innovative. That is, those that have a less rigid structure, empower their employees more, have highly-educated workers who enjoy each others' company, and where there is enough spare capacity for people to think and, therefore, to innovate are more likely to adopt new innovations.

Old-fashioned, centralized, hierarchical organizations are less likely to cede power to staff in any way. There are, of course, exceptions to this rule. The UK's Ministry of Defence, for example, has adopted social technologies as a recruitment tool, allowing potential recruits to see what life is like for serving personnel with guidance for employees on how to use social media.[2]

Finally, the more "open" an organization is to those outside the organization, the more likely it is to be innovative. Highly secret and paranoid organizations (fearing industrial spies at every email) will not embrace social technologies quickly, although companies like Apple, notorious for being very closed and secretive, have clearly been among the most innovative companies too.

Zaltman et al. have shown that certain characteristics that were useful for an organization to initiate the process of adopting an innovation (such as low centralization, high complexity, and low formalization) were precisely the characteristics that were likely to impede *implementation* of the innovation.[3] This is because a centralized strategic process would be better at driving change through an organization and ensuring the innovation was embedded (for example, through implementation via HR practices and incorporation into performance appraisals and measurement criteria). However, such a centralized decision-making unit might impede the innovation first being tried.

The counter argument to these studies is that there are some characteristics which might suggest that an organization will be quicker, or slower, to embrace social technologies, but these are not rules. There are many organizations with all the "negative" characteristics that have embraced social technologies, just as there are many with the right ingredients to be innovative but who fail to implement and keep the innovations.

It is not just down to the organization – it is also down to other factors too.

chapter 23

All Change Please

Technological Change in Organizations

There are five traditional strategies for implementing technology changes according to Eason,[1] which range from the more difficult (from the user-adaptation point of view) revolutionary change to the easier, evolutionary: (i) the big bang; (ii) parallel running; (iii) phased introduction; (iv) trials and dissemination; and (v) incremental evolution.

All of these strategies are still relevant for social technologies – an organization can choose which (or a combination of which) ones it wants to use – deciding, for example, that all internal communications are suddenly going to be exclusively broadcast through Twitter (a *big bang* strategy) or allowing employees to use whatever tools they wish to see what values and reinventions might occur (an *incremental* strategy).

Organizations that have successfully implemented social technologies, however, have not tended towards one particular strategy. That is, no implementation strategy has proven to be more reliable for social technologies.

One strategy that often does not work is to make an innovation available in the organization and assume that it will be embraced by the employees, otherwise known as "if you build it, they will *not* come." If it is

if you build it, they will not come

self-intuitive and easy to access, it is likely there will be initial uptake at least as employees jump on the bandwagon to see what the fuss is about. But even intuitive technology needs promotion and a communications strategy is needed across an organization to explain what the changes are about and prevent falling off the bandwagon as it trundles along.

We shall explore later on whether formal strategies work better than organic implementations where word-of-mouth provides the necessary distribution of knowledge.

A Culture for Change

Nationality Counts

Gladwell refers to various studies that highlight the cultural differences across countries that have led to plane crashes. He cites a Fischer and Orasanu[2] study that showed how first officers would use hints to try and tell their captain about a potential problem (without forcing the captain to lose face), where captains would use commands. As hints were often ambiguous the semantics of the message were often lost. Female pilots were found to prefer using indirect and more conversational speech, whereas their male counterparts would tend to be more direct.

There were also important differences of culture. For example, in collectivistic cultures where there is group influence, such as in Korea, China, or Indonesia, ambiguity in speech is used far more than in individualistic cultures, such as the UK or USA. Furthermore, cultures that are dominated by a belief in hierarchy and where "normal" workers must be respectful to senior management (such as in Korea or Japan) may find that the collaborative nature of social tools is seen as a threat to the status quo and the opportunity, therefore, for workers and customers to freely communicate through social technologies is missed.

Hofstede[3] lists four dimensions – power distance, uncertainty avoidance, individualism and masculinity – that affect the way societies, as well as the people and organizations within those societies, behave, based on cultural differences.

Power distance is the inequality in a particular society, be that society an organization or a country. The Power Distance Reduction Theory[4] suggests that subordinates will try to reduce the inequality (or power distance) between themselves and their bosses, whereas the bosses will try to increase it. However, Hofstede claims that the level of power distance is determined by society, such that the levels vary across occupations, countries, and gender. This was determined from surveys that looked at the perceived style of decision-making by superiors, colleagues' fears of disagreeing with superiors, and the type of decision-making preferred in the superior. The suggestion then is that the ability for an organization to connect effectively and share knowledge across job divisions and hierarchies will be strongly determined by the country in question.

Uncertainty avoidance refers to the level to which a particular culture tolerates ambiguity. Hofstede plotted countries on a scale (the Uncertainty Avoidance Index – UAI) and states that the top five countries on the UAI (i.e. those that rely on rules, procedures, and plans) are Greece, Portugal, Guatemala, Uruguay, and Belgium. Conversely; the bottom five – those best able to tolerate ambiguity, or those that rely least on rigid procedures – are Hong Kong, Sweden, Denmark, Jamaica, and Singapore. Given that social technologies rely on flexibility and flow rather than rigid procedures, one would expect there to be a correlation between the successful implementation of social technologies and the position of the country on the UAI. Our research, however, discussed in Chapter 26 has found no such correlation.

Hofstede also discussed *individualism–collectivism*, or the scale used to determine whether a culture was individualistic (such as the USA) or collectivistic (e.g. Guatemala – at the other end of the scale). Hofstede notes that in collectivistic societies such as China the individual is driven by the need to "save face" (or not lose face) rather than being inner-directed. Such cultural traits have a strong bearing on how organizations in those societies adopt certain innovations. In the case of social technologies, one might assume that a collectivist society would be more likely to adopt technologies sooner rather than an individualistic one; although the very nature of social technologies giving the individual more freedom to explore networks and information and to express themselves suggests that social technologies do not conform to a correlation on the individualism–collectivism scale. Once again, however, the research discussed later (see Chapter 26) does not support such an assertion.

Finally, *masculinity*, as one would predict, refers to the different roles expected of, and usually provided by, the different genders in a particular society. Men are expected to be more assertive, according to Hofstede, while women more nurturing. If an organization rewards what might be considered "masculine" goals (such as winning new business), it will tend to promote men. If the organization is inclined to reward "feminine" goals (such as the nurturing required in healthcare or education), then it will tend to promote women. The most "masculine" countries by this measure are Japan, Austria, Venezuela, Italy, and Switzerland. Finland, Denmark, The Netherlands, Norway, and Sweden are at the other extreme. It could be argued that social technologies require more "feminine" influences so that people share and collaborate, rather than aim for personal achievement. Again, however, the research does not support this and there are no significant differences between the adoption of social technologies by countries at different ends of the masculinity index.

What these studies also show is that the dominant culture of an organization might correspond to the country in which it is situated, but it might be more aligned to the culture of the parent company culture – for example, a US company operating in Japan may assume the culture of the US or of Japan or a hybrid of the two.

Organizational Culture Counts

Goffe and Jones[5] believe that organizational culture can be plotted as a function of *sociability* and *solidarity* with each position on the two-by-two matrix of these two factors capable of having a *positive* effect on the organization, or a *negative* effect.

An organization that is high on solidarity but low on sociability is *mercenary*. This might be suitable for sales teams where individual targets are pursued with little regard to the success or failure of one's peers.

An organization that is high on sociability but low on solidarity is *net-worked*. Such a culture might be appropriate amongst office staff, for example, who see each other on a daily basis, may live nearby and meet socially, and who are concerned for the long-term success of the organization.

An organization that scores low on both levels is *fragmented* – there is no cohesive culture, which might be appropriate for certain organizations, for example, that combine sales staff (who are more mercenary) with content-creation teams (who may, by the very nature of their work, need to collaborate with colleagues and are, therefore, networked).

Finally, if an organization is high on both *solidarity* and *sociability* it is known as *communal*. This seems to, on first glance, be the ideal position for an organization to be in, but what is most important is that the culture is a *positive* one. A *positive fragmented* culture, for example, might be a better fit for an organization than a *negative communal* one.

The effect that this might have on the ability of an organization to implement a social media strategy appears to be that organizations with networked or communal cultures will embrace social technologies best. This is not necessarily the case, however. It is far more likely that an organization that has a good fit between the performance measures and the use of the technologies will benefit. For example, a sales team with a mercenary culture is more likely to engage with social technologies if they are appraised using a balanced scorecard approach that measures their contributions to central knowledge sharing or through 360° feedback as well as the traditional sales figures. That is, so long as it is in the interests of the organization's stakeholders to use social technologies, be that through the dominant culture and desire to collaborate or through refined targets, they are more likely to implement the new technologies. However, it is fair to say that an organization high on *sociability* is likely to be more ready to share knowledge and help others within the organization.

Organizational Change

Burke and Litwin's model of organizational performance and change[6] lists what they consider to be the twelve most important organizational variables when trying to implement change and shows the interconnect-edness of all the variables and, therefore, how change cannot happen in isolation from the rest of the system or organization.

The model lists the *transformational factors* (external environment, leadership, mission, strategy, culture, and individual and organizational performance), which drive what Burke and Litwin term the *transactional factors* (structure, management practices, systems and processes, work unit climate, motivation, individual needs and values, and task and individual skills), which in turn drive the individual and organizational performance that feedback to the transformational factors.

The important lesson from Burke and Litwin is that, given how everything affects everything else, attention must be paid at all times to the change, lest it adversely affects the other areas (or, going back to Moore, the innovation falls into the chasm).

Organizations can decide where to focus – on the transformational factors (these tend to be major organizational changes) or on the transactional factors (e.g. process changes, partial restructuring, or changes to the reward system).

For most implementations of social technologies, the changes will concentrate around the transactional factors. They could involve fundamental shifts in the organization's strategy, as was the case at Goldcorp[7] and Eli Lilly[8] who changed their business models to crowdsource new business and production ideas. As such, the main focus of the change should be on:

* *Management practices* – the specific behaviors of managers when doing their jobs; do they collaborate with staff, insist on specific systems, or do they allow a level of innovation, for example?
* *Systems* – policies and procedures; which include reward systems, resource allocation, budgeting, knowledge management. If performance appraisals and bonuses focus on individual tasks, they are less likely to share and collaborate.

- *Structure* – the division of employees into business units, lines of reporting and so on; which of course is related to the clusters and affects the network effect of the organization.
- *Work unit climate* – the relationships between peers, superiors, and subordinates; whether the environment is a sociable one, by Goffee and Jones's standards, or one of solidarity.
- *Task requirements* and *individual skills* – whether or not employees have the skills to do what is asked of them and if training might be required.
- *Individual needs and values* – the psychological factors that drive the individual; which of course relates to motivation structures and how the organization can encourage or inhibit certain workplace behaviors.
- *Motivation* – what makes the employees want to achieve targets; which is a combination of their individual needs, ability to do the job, the climate, and most of the other factors above.

What is not apparent from Burke and Litwin's model is which of these factors are relevant for successfully implementing social technologies and whether or not there are factors that will inhibit adoption.

chapter 24

Management Choices

Given the participative nature of social technologies, management also needs to decide its position with regard to implementing the change. McLoughlin and Clark[1] plot management choices when implementing new technology on a two-by-two matrix measuring the approach by the workforce (from participative to non-participative) against management organization (from top-down to bottom-up). Logic suggests that a successful implementation of social technologies – which requires, by definition, high levels of user-generated content – will be where management have allowed the impetus for change to come from the bottom-up rather than mandated down from on-high, and that the approach to the workforce will be one of participation.

This is an assumption, however, and is better tested by comparing real examples of successful implementations of social technologies, as we shall see.

Unanswered Questions

The literature provides many models and much previous research on the diffusion of innovations and implementing change within an organization. The following questions, however, remain unanswered and shall be explored in the next chapter:

- How are organizations using social technologies successfully – just for marketing and communications or also for collaboration, knowledge sharing, and crowdsourcing?
- Is there an optimal size of organization that can successfully embrace social technologies, or do multinational companies with tens of thousands of employees simply divide into clusters on internal social networks?
- How long on average did organizations take to embrace social technologies?
- Where do the success stories lie on the diffusion of innovations "s-curve" and do they, therefore, tend to be innovators, early adopters, or early majority?
- Have successful implementations involved technology clusters, or are there success stories that have concentrated on only one social technology?
- How was the new technology communicated through the organization and is it essential for an organization to have an opinion leader, or champion, for the innovation to diffuse efficiently?
- If it is essential, then does it matter *who* the champion is – that is, whether they are internal to the organization or not; and at what level – a middle manager, one of the executive team, a technical assistant?
- To what extent are the networks themselves (in which the opinion leader drives the change) essential for successfully diffusing the innovation?
- Did the drive to embrace social technologies come from the leadership, or the bottom-up, and what was the decision-making process – was there a participative or non-participative approach to the workforce?
- To what extent does user participation in the adoption of an innovation benefit the long-term implementation of it?
- Who owned the change – the information systems and technology (IS&T) department, individual departments, or another specialist?
- If the organization rejected the technology, why?
- Is there a correlation between organizational use of social technologies and national use, according to the information communication

and technology (ICT) Development Index (IDI)? Does the digital divide as shown by the IDI also correspond to organizations – that is, are the organizations that adopted the internet and online communications early on further advanced in adopting social technologies, or are the barriers to creating the infrastructure and boosting skills so low that organizations are able to leap-frog over the early adopters of earlier technologies?

• To what extent do organizations follow the three stages of evolution as defined by the International Telecommunications Union (ITU); and how can they best focus resources to maximize "ICT impact"?

• What is the role of IS&T departments in embracing social technologies? To what extent does an organization need to develop infrastructure and services, or does it only need to support the business strategy as it uses existing tools aimed at the end-user?

• Has there been any reinvention of the technology and if so, how has this affected the appraisal of the new technology – as the results cannot have been predicted? Are the people who use social technologies in the workplace also heavy users at home? Did organizations that have successfully implemented social technologies tend towards one particular implementation strategy and is there a particular implementation strategy that has proven to be more reliable for social technologies – an innovation which by definition requires input from the users? To what extent does that strategy need to be formal – as opposed to organic where word-of-mouth provides the necessary distribution of knowledge?

• What are the specific factors, according to Burke and Litwin's model, that organizations that have successfully embraced social technologies have? Are there any factors that will block attempts to embrace the new technology or are there any factors that are present in all successful implementations of social technologies?

Knowing the answers to these questions will help understand what drivers are necessary for embracing social technologies and what obstacles need to be avoided.

25

Separating Fact from Fiction

Getting some Numbers

This book is based not just on common sense but also on research. The literature discussed in the previous chapters left many questions unanswered. To try and answer these questions, a survey was created and divided into the following five sections.

Use of Social Technologies or Similar Collaborative Tools

This section asked what social technologies organizations are using or have tried and abandoned, how they are used, what the primary use is, and if they have not "stuck," then why the implementation failed.

Strategies and Champions – How Organizations Embrace Social Technologies

The aim of this section was to find out what systems the organizations had used to implement social technologies, for example, to see if re-invention had taken place, or if there had been an explicit strategy to embrace social technologies and, if so, where it had come from. We also asked whether or not the change had a specific champion within the organization, what its role was, and how the change was communicated. The questions were posed with a view to establishing if there was an overwhelming preference for implementing social technologies in a particular way:

- Is having a champion essential?
- Does a particular communication method work better than another?
- How important is employee input into creating the strategy?

Attitudes to New Technology

This section was aimed at uncovering attitudes towards new technology. Whilst it seems self-evident, it is worth exploring if those who successfully use social technologies are also early adopters of other new technologies, and if there are any *technology clusters*. This also covers any explicit or implicit incentives to use social technologies within organizations.

Furthermore, a series of questions specifically enquired about the individual's or organization's attitudes by asking them to agree or disagree with seventeen statements including:

- My organization is innovative.
- My organization encourages collaboration and knowledge sharing.
- My organization or business unit provides the physical access necessary to use social technologies.

The aim here was to see how technology-orientated the individuals and the organizations were, how innovative they perceive themselves to be, and what obstacles they see as preventing full implementation of social technologies.

Organizational Culture and Corporate Character

As discussed in Chapter 16, it is worth considering if there is, as might seem intuitive, a correlation between those organizations that successfully implement social technologies and their corporate culture. The Goffee and Jones "Corporate Character" questionnaire was included in the survey as an indicator of the culture, although it should be stressed that for a complete measure, according to the Goffee and Jones framework, both qualitative and quantitative data would be needed.

Personal and Organizational Information

The final section asks individuals some personal demographic information, such as their age, gender, and job role. It also asks some questions about the organization itself, such as size, turnover, the country of location, and, referring to Hofstede and Gladwell's theories in Chapter 16, the location of a parent company, if applicable.

Unexpected Learnings from the Survey

The survey was disseminated to several thousand business people in different international locations through different media (e.g. email, social media such as LinkedIn and Twitter) and there were two important lessons learnt from this process.

The term "social media" – the term used more often in the survey – was viewed as a fad and not worthy of attention. This assumption is based on the fact that the first invitations used the term social media – for example: "Please help us with this research into using and avoiding social media." The second sets of invitations, however, used the term "new technology" instead of social media and received far better response rates. Among the people who received the invitation to take part in the survey via LinkedIn or Twitter and who were, therefore, personally comfortable with using social media, it is surprising how many maintain the idea that social media isn't a serious business topic.

It was only after the fact that it became clear that the tools being used and the way they were being proposed and adopted by organizations stretched further than the term social media implied and would, in fact, be covered by the term "social technologies."

It should be stressed that of course a significant problem with such a survey is that participants self-select and, therefore, are not necessarily representative of the whole population. Nonetheless, there were sufficient respondents who had successfully implemented social technologies and those who had not for the results to make sense and for conclusions to be drawn.

Qualitative Research: Interviews

The survey gave the numbers. Interviews were then conducted to gain insight. The interviewees ranged from clerical and administrative roles through to managing directors and C-level executives in a variety of roles and organizations, public sector and private, large and small, UK and non-UK based, and at different managerial levels. The only common factor in all interviewees was that they had direct personal experience of using or implementing social technologies in their organizations.

chapter 26

Findings from the Research

The organization sizes ranged from those with fewer than fifty employees to those with over 10,000; and with revenues ranging from under £1 million per annum to over £1.5 billion. That is, contrary to McKinsey research,[1] there is no correlation at all between the size of an organization and its likelihood of implementing social technologies.

Furthermore, there seems to be no correlation at all between the location of the organization and its uptake of the technologies, although McKinsey's research showed that companies in the USA were more likely to successfully implement the new technologies. Nor is there any correlation between the industry sector and the likelihood that an organization will embrace social technologies.

This does seem odd. Intuitively, again, one would think that technology companies are more likely to embrace social technologies than, for example, accounting firms or educational organizations. Also, whilst it might be true that the sector helps ensure an inherent "readiness" for embracing new technologies, the research shows that there are examples of successful implementation of social technologies in one form or another in all types of organization.

Having said that, the McKinsey research suggests that high-tech and telecoms organizations have been more successful at adopting the new technologies than manufacturing companies; and smaller firms (with revenues below $1 billion) have also had fewer barriers to success. There are, of course, examples from all sectors of how it has not worked, and there might be a far more important correlation with the organizational culture.

The McKinsey research, furthermore, highlighted three factors that made a significant impact on successful implementation of the technologies:

- Lack of internal barriers to adopting social technologies.
- A culture favoring open collaboration.
- Early adoption of the new technologies.

We shall look more at the internal barriers to adoption and the organizational culture. As for early adoption, it helps no one to know that they have missed the boat. That is, an innovative organization that adopts early technologies such as Web 2.0 is more likely to successfully implement them, surely in part due to the innovative culture of the organization that allows early adoption and experimentation to take place. However, those who have not been early adopters can still successfully implement social technologies and that is very much the purpose of this book, to show the pitfalls to avoid and the best practice when attempting to adopt. The bandwagon has left the coach-stop, but it's never too late to jump on. Better to be a Johnny-come-lately than a luddite, technophobe, or stick-in-the-mud.

Organization Culture

The theory on organization culture was that organizations that were, according to Goffee and Jones, *networked* would be better at sharing knowledge and collaborating on social technologies than *mercenary* ones. It appears to be a self-evident truth that a group of people who work together for the good of the organization are more likely to embrace tools that help them help each other; whilst a group of people who are obsessed with individual targets and objectives will only use the new tools if they can find a personal direct benefit.

If you want to participate in social technologies, you need to become a social organization
> Head of Digital Engagement, central Government Agency

The research shows that there is, indeed, a positive correlation between sociability and solidarity – the higher individuals ranked on sociability the higher they were likely to rank on solidarity. That is, the more "sociable" an organization, the more likely they are to also be aligned to achieving the aims of the organization.

the more "sociable" an organization, the more likely they are to also be aligned to achieving the aims of the organization

Furthermore, the results show that most organizations that had embraced social technologies were, according to Goffee and Jones, *communal*. Whilst there were communal organizations that had not embraced social technologies, it should be clear that "communality" is not a causal link for their implementation. Although differences in organizational culture might make the difference between successful and unsuccessful use of social technologies, there is, as yet, no proof of such a difference existing.

To put it another way, an organization that does not have a communal culture should still be able to successfully implement social technologies and, certainly, the idea that people within an organization do not get on should also be no obstacle to implementing social technologies. It just might be a bit more of a struggle to get them collaborating and sharing.

McKinsey's research[2] showed that almost three-quarters of organizations using internal social technologies used them to get internal information quicker, two-thirds reduced communications costs, and over half reduced travel costs. All of these benefits of internal usage are not specifically related to helping one's colleagues, but improving efficiencies and cutting costs – aims of all organizations, surely.

Having said that, once again the caveat is that the data only included people who opted-in to complete the survey and there was only one response per organization. Therefore, those who responded might have felt they had a communal culture when many within the organization may not. All interviewees suggested that their organizations were somewhere on the spectrum between the middle and the networked end, with everyone working towards the improvement of the organization. There was, however, one significant exception. In one very large technology organization, the interviewee explained how Enterprise 2.0 was not very much used in his own division of sales, where everyone had their own targets, and was more popular in the HR, learning and development, and research divisions.

One of the main obstacles, furthermore, to adopting Enterprise 2.0, mentioned by several of the interviewees, is proving to end-users that there is a direct benefit to them, answering their question of "What's in it for me?" If they are unable to see a personal benefit, they are not incentivized to use the Enterprise 2.0 tools.

Attitudes to Technology

There is an important correlation in attitudes towards new technologies and engagement with Enterprise 2.0. This seems obvious also – if an organization is more innovative, then it is more likely to try social technologies, which means that it is more innovative.

The flip-side to this equation is that if an organization is not, generally, very innovative (e.g. using old-fashioned IT systems internally) then it is less likely to successfully engage with social technologies. This finding is, as described above, borne out also through the McKinsey research, and suggests that one of the best ways an organization can guarantee successful adoption is to be an early adopter. But having identified one's organization as slow to adopt innovation, one can then start to think about the mechanisms that need to be implemented to encourage adoption.

The Use of Social Technologies in the Organization

The research shows that there is no one "correct" way to use social technologies in an organization. Some organizations are using wikis, status updates, and blogs for internal knowledge sharing whilst others are using platforms such as Facebook and Twitter to reach the general public.

All the social tools are used by several organizations and there is no tool that is the preserve of individuals – rather they are used by teams or the entire organization. McKinsey's research, once again, bears this out, with "traditional" social tools being the most popular – such as social networks, video sharing, blogs, and collaborative document editing. Curiously, a relatively simple tool to implement, tagging, is only used by a fifth of organizations surveyed by McKinsey, less than 10 percent use mashups, and none use peer-to-peer. It is possible, however, that mashups are being used but not recognized as such because they are part of an overall ERP system. Peer-to-peer tools are often used in an organization but usually referred to as a central drive or document repository, such that individuals can access documents by others but don't refer to it as peer-to-peer.

What is also clear, however, is that the implementation of social technologies, or Enterprise 2.0, is uneven across all the organizations involved in the research. Even those who had a successful knowledge sharing solution in place complained of it not being used across the organization and having better uptake in some departments than others.

Mavens + Champions = Mampions?

Around half the organizations surveyed who used social technologies claimed to have had someone who championed the new technologies. The champions occupied a range of positions from senior executive and director levels through to administrative roles, with management and department heads taking an important lead in championing the technologies. But the primary criterion for any organization is that the champion be an enthusiastic proponent of the technologies.

Many of the interviewees insisted on the necessity of a champion, explaining that: "Having an enthusiastic and internal champion who can identify the benefits" is important and that "You need a maven who is an expert in a subject area."

> *It helps to have the presence of a senior executive or a credible and authentic highly-regarded expert in a particular area who can become a patron and encourage or validate usage. A lot of the motivation comes from the kudos of being seen by a senior executive.*

> Experience Architect, Global Broadcaster

The champion does not have to be from the leadership either, but if they are, this will help with incentivizing uptake. Equally, the official appointment of a champion can send signals to the organization that social technologies are approved of by the leadership.

The champion might be at the departmental level, or might be at the organizational level. There can, of course, be more than one champion. An "official" role might be created, such as head of digital engagement, with a remit to ensure effective take-up of social technologies by employees across the organization. However, they may need the additional seal of approval by the CEO to demonstrate to the organization that the appointment is part of an overall strategy and is viewed as important by the leadership. Equally, the official role might require a network of champions in teams and departments. Again, these roles could be official or unofficial. The organization could create "super-user" roles so that within each department there is one person tasked with not just being the local go-to expert on how to use the technologies, but also with encouraging uptake and usage, as well as ensuring the technologies are factored into strategies and processes within the department.

An informal, self-appointed champion can also be effective, but will require more persuasive influencing skills to encourage uptake by peers if not officially endorsed. In some cases, the champion was someone who decided to unofficially start using social technologies to better perform their own role, and through demonstrating the success of the new technologies has helped others realize the potential and that the risks had hitherto been exaggerated.

Adoption Process

Just over half of the people surveyed did not have a clear strategy before starting to use social technologies but simply started experimenting. Of those that did have a strategy, over two-thirds say that staff were involved in creating that strategy and three-quarters believe that staff involvement in creating the strategy helped with adoption.

What the interviews repeated time and again, however, was the importance of having a *reason* to engage with social technologies. An organization has to think through what it hopes to achieve, which audience it hopes to engage with and how it intends to maintain that engagement in the long term.

The timeline of adoption, as explained above, could not be usefully drawn, but the survey did show that the drive to implement social technologies came from a variety of sources including champions, the leadership, the marketing department, and in over a third of cases, from individuals across the organization (who could be considered champions within their departments).

The survey also showed that there was no consistent approach to communicating the new technologies across the organization and no attempt to use the same communications strategies that would be used when advertising or communicating with external audiences or customers.

With the implementation of new technology within an organization, one would assume that the communication of the new technology would itself use technology. However, almost half of all cases learnt of the new technology through word-of-mouth – about the same as through email and the intranet.

What is also significant is that no one form of communication dominates. This suggests that various methods need to be used to try and reach as much of the audience – that is, the potential users of the new tools – as possible. It also appears that no organizations, neither from the survey data nor the interviews, used the kind of marketing tactics for internal communication of the new technology that they would when advertising to customers.

The AIDA framework for advertising and marketing, used since first defined in the nineteenth century by E. St. Elmo Lewis, describes how an effective communication process should create:

- *Awareness* – make people aware of the existence of the product or service.
- *Interest* – capture their interest and demonstrate the benefits of the product or service.
- *Desire* – make them want the product or service.
- *Action* – make them want to buy the product or contract the service.

At best it appears that most organizations stop with "awareness," assuming that a formal corporate communication, email, or newsletter to disseminate a message is going to fire the imaginations of its employees and spark widespread adoption.

To put this another way, there is no prescriptive process that will help organizations communicate an intended adoption of social technologies. Some have used word-of-mouth, others email, others existing internal communications tools. It is not enough to say in an all-staff email "We are going to begin using X to communicate" – although this will work for some. Equally, it is not adequate to rely on individuals to disseminate the information personally through their departments.

What is more likely to work best is a combination of all these methods of communication so that as many people as possible receive the news through their preferred medium. Communication, however, is not enough to get individuals or an organization as a whole to embrace an innovation.

Behavior Change Theory

Social marketing theory, meanwhile, uses marketing theory and techniques to effect behavior change and focuses on the criteria necessary to get individuals to adopt a new practice, such as wearing seat-belts, recycling more, or giving up smoking.

Prochaska and DiClemente's Stages of Change Model (also known as the Transtheoretical Model)[3], lists six steps, which are relevant for implementing social technologies as follows:

1. *Precontemplation* – the individual is not thinking about social technologies at all.
2. *Contemplation* – the individual acknowledges there might be a benefit in using social technologies, for example, recognizing that greater interaction within an organization or better customer engagement is required, and starts to think seriously about it.
3. *Preparation* – these are the final adjustments before taking action, such as telling others of an intention to get online or asking for advice and reading books on how best to implement social technologies.
4. *Action* – such as creating accounts on Facebook and connecting to friends, family, colleagues, and like-minded organizations; or beginning to create and post content.
5. *Maintenance* – perhaps one of the hardest things for many who have tried to embrace social technologies is the sudden realization that they need to post content on a regular basis, read content posted by others (in the organizational sense, this involves responding to customers, becoming a good netizen and sharing content posted by others, and generally becoming an active and proactive member of that particular network or technology).
6. *Termination* – which, in our example of implementing social technologies, might be when the user has embedded the new technology into their work-life and daily routine. They check their social media accounts (internal or external to the organization) regularly, respond to queries, post content, and have fully included it within their marketing strategy or knowledge sharing processes – or whichever function they have put the technologies to use for.

Linkenbach and Perkins's Social Norms Theory[4] suggests that people adopt a new behavior when they believe "everyone else is doing it." There is much to this when discussing social technologies – one cannot obtain the *network effects* discussed before if one does not have a sufficiently large network of acquaintances with whom one can interact through the new technologies. Numerous organizations and individuals join Facebook because they believe everyone else is there and, therefore, they are missing out on some information, gossip, or interaction.

There is, of course, a distinction between perceived and actual behaviors, with the perception of everyone being on social technologies being enough of a driver to encourage others to join. As described before, there is still a Pareto rule in effect with the creation of content on social technologies and the majority of people "lurking" and observing rather than actually posting content. There is also much debate on how many people are actually on the different platforms, with "registered users" being a far different metric from "active users."

Fishbein and Ajzen's Theory of Reasoned Action suggests that the best predictor of a person's behavior is their intention to act,[5] which depends on whether they think they will get the desired benefits and what others, whose opinions they value, think about it. As already discussed, what one defines as benefits could be crucial – an individual might greatly benefit the organization by sharing information but not achieve any personal benefit either by increasing their personal knowledge or their status within the organization. Therefore, there needs to be a clear connection between the individual benefits and the organizational benefits. This could be through publicly acclaiming those who give to the organization (knowledge, time, expertise, etc.) or embedding the process and practice within an individual's job description or performance appraisal, such that their benefit is in knowing that they are doing part of the job they are employed to do.

Mars famously awarded a 10 per cent daily bonus for punctuality,[6] so it should not be beyond the realms of any organization to tie adoption of a technology to a financial reward. But, once again, there are other non-financial ways to endorse and promote adoption.

Social learning theory[7] and social cognitive theory suggest that much of people's learning comes from observing others and being rewarded for the new behavior, rather than simply using trial and error to discover new behaviors. In the context of encouraging people within an organization to adopt social technologies, this links up nicely with social norms theory in that the belief that others are using the new technologies and, ideally, the physical proof that others are using them – by seeing them using them in the same organization, team, or social setting – is likely to work together to encourage others to adopt.

Nudge theory[8] suggests people can receive strong encouragement to adopt the technologies by making them the default channels of communication, for example, such that people would have to consciously opt-out (something not everyone is able to do within an organization anyway). For example, if a leader tells their team they only want to see updates on a specific project on a team-blog or microblog and that emails are banned, people will, by default, adopt quickly.

Duhigg suggests we can change behaviors through creating opportunities to develop new habits,[9] which would mean, for example, having employees check their internal microblogging platform for organizational updates first thing every morning. For an individual, it might be the habit of posting updates on a corporate blog every Friday afternoon, or responding to status updates and queries on a social network at a particular time each day. The creation and adoption of norms with email etiquette happened relatively quickly and organically. Whilst many of us find the burden of dozens (or more) of unread emails every morning when we get to the office stressful enough, and the idea of having to answer other communication channels, such as microblogs, an unnecessary extra burden, the issue tends to be one of exchanging one channel of communication (such as email) for another (such as a microblog).

Furthermore, for managing emails or microblogs, the issue is not one of technology but one of time management, and readers who identify that as an issue are advised to read more about prioritizing work, or setting aside specific times of the day for answering emails rather than obsessively checking and answering every few minutes.

Kotler and Lee highlighted common themes from all these models for behavior change that, whilst not guaranteeing success, will contribute towards it.[10] Users will clearly need a positive intention to change to the new behavior, the necessary skills to achieve that behavior, and the belief that it fits their self-image. The self-image comes down to an individual and communal belief recognizing that social technologies are productivity tools and are to be welcomed in the workplace, not shunned, and an understanding that the advantages outweigh any disadvantages. There also, very clearly, need to be no environmental constraints – no blocks or obstacles to embracing the new technologies. We shall look more at the issue of obstacles in Chapter 27.

Investment Costs

The budgets invested in Enterprise 2.0 vary widely across all sectors. The vast majority claim in the survey to have spent next to nothing on implementing social technologies, with many not knowing (suggesting the resource cost is not being measured) and with a handful suggesting an investment of £1,000 to £50,000. There are a few responses though showing costs of £80,000, £100,000, and £200,000 per year and one response suggesting £1 million to £2 million over five years (or £200,000 to £400,000 per year).

That the costs vary widely is to be expected – depending on whether the organization has purchased an Enterprise 2.0 solution (such as Lotus Connections from IBM or Microsoft Sharepoint) that offers internal blogs, wikis, microblogging, discussions, and so on, or whether free publicly available tools (such as Facebook and Twitter) are used. Many of these tools allow personalization and branding (such as the Wordpress blogging platform) at a low cost.

What the survey responses also show, however, is how little is being measured. To establish an effective Enterprise 2.0 solution, with collaboration and engagement from internal staff, whether or not the audience is an internal or an external one, takes time. Most organizations still do not have a dedicated manager of their social media presence (and knowledge management systems, by definition, require multiple content creators across the organization). It is, therefore, difficult to judge how many "manhours" are spent managing the social technologies across an organization and arguably so much time might be wasted in measuring those hours that the benefits of social technologies may be lost.

Clearly, therefore, Enterprise 2.0 is not free. Time, after all, is money, as one survey respondent noted.

Return on Investment

As described before, those who seek to prove return on investment (ROI) with social technologies are likely to be sorely disappointed.

The social media managers that do exist (and it is worth noting that the roles are almost always "social media managers" rather than "social technology managers" – emphasizing the bias towards the use of media to engage customers but ignoring the many other options) are often not asked to prove engagement or show a ROI. But, as with all online metrics, you get what you measure. If the principle metric by which success of a website is measured is visitor numbers to the site, the web team will spend most efforts on driving traffic to the website, regardless of the quality of the traffic. If the visitors are not signing up for newsletters, downloading PDFs of articles, or purchasing on the site then is this the traffic you want? If the metric is how many visitors complete a purchase online, this would not show the specific benefits of different marketing strategies to drive traffic to the site. It would not show, for example, new versus existing customers.

A combination of different metrics need to be used and, of course, the most important thing is to ensure that the metric can give, as Avinash

Kaushik calls it, an "actionable insight."[11] If the metric doesn't help you adjust and improve what you do, then it has no real value. The same could be said for social technologies. Social technologies are used, as described before, for many purposes.

The point made by many is that one should no longer measure (or even attempt to measure) ROI but that one should measure rather more intangible returns[12] such as:

- *Return on engagement* – the return of time invested engaging an audience, customers, or community in online conversations.
- *Return on participation* – where participation and content creation on social technology platforms is measured.
- *Return on involvement* – where interaction or points of contact with the customer in the social technologies space is measured.
- *Return on attention* – how well the audience's attention is captured.
- *Return on trust* – where an organization builds trust with its customers, which then leads to loyalty and referrals.

These measures, however, do highlight the problem of how one defines "engagement" in a conversation. Is it, for example, the number of people who have read a post; the people who have commented on it; or the people who have shared it on other social technologies? Another issue is whether positive comments and responses are rated in the same way as negative ones. If a disgruntled customer complains on social media, this is engagement, but the organization might not consider it a sign of success.

I believe it is a sign of success, however, as it is better to know what customers take issue with than just assume that everything is fine. Without feedback, we cannot grow. Without knowing there is a problem, we cannot address it and seek a solution.

Many new tools measuring social technology engagement have algorithms to show the right balance of positive and negative engagement (based on sets of keywords and phrases), although the software is not yet able to identify irony. In short, whatever metric is used to try and measure engagement, it will be inherently flawed.

Nevertheless, the fundamental principle underlying these new measures is that social technologies are an investment, but more (usually) of an investment in time rather than capital outlay. Organizations need to listen to the conversations taking place and participate in them when appropriate. They need to behave in a manner that is contrary to the traditional way of issuing corporate communications where all copy is approved in advance. The requirement of social technologies to have an instant response, for that response to be seen as "authentic," "honest," and "non-corporate," and for those responses to take place on a variety of platforms (blogs, wikis, social networking, microblogging, etc.) and individual brands worldwide, means that employees of the organization must spend sometimes considerable amounts of time listening to the conversations taking place. Listening takes time, even with software to help identify mentions of a brand.

The return on that investment of time can take the place of traditional marketing spend in raising brand awareness, but is far more potent in generating customer loyalty, brand loyalty, and winning new business through referrals. At the most basic level this might be the system Amazon.com introduced shortly after launching in 1995 for recommending books to customers based on what other purchasers of the same books also bought ("Customers who bought this item also bought…"). On the down side it could be business lost as a result of negative feedback through social media, as was the case with Jeff Jarvis's blog posts against Dell computers in 2005. As described in Chapter 4, Jarvis's blog gained support from thousands of other dissatisfied customers and was a key driver in Dell's decision to change its customer services policies and procedures.[13] On another level, however, it could be that the very openness of the organization and its willingness to engage in conversations with customers and stakeholder communities brings it to the attention of audiences it would otherwise not reach.

The use of social technologies tools, furthermore, can have a direct effect on improved knowledge management (through enabling the easy sharing of information across the organization that may improve processes or service), communication tools (reducing email overload and ensuring all stakeholders have access to all information), customer services (e.g. getting customers to advise each other), and new product development (where customers suggest the changes and improvements to existing products). Those positive effects, however, are as difficult to measure (over what period of time and how many projects would shared information apply?) as the time invested in the first place by the employees.

Many organizations do measure those effects. One of the interviewees, the Managing Director of a global telecommunications organization that provides Enterprise 2.0 platforms to multinational corporations, explained how they need to prove the ROI in their written proposals to prospective clients and have to underwrite those claims.

Furthermore, various books – such as McAfee's *Enterprise 2.0*[14] or Qualman's *Socialnomics*[15] – list case studies of organizations that have made huge gains from embracing Enterprise 2.0. Whilst the benefits of sharing either within an organization or externally with customers has been repeatedly proven (and over several years, with McKinsey publishing a report[16] that showed that high-tech companies, organizations with revenues of over \$1 billion, and B2B operations are more likely to report measurable benefits), social technologies are still considered new. I have taught and worked with hundreds of people, from Gen-Y postgraduate business students through to senior managers and leaders and every level in-between that still view social technologies as a waste of time and feel that any sharing of information is to be avoided at all costs. These people, particularly in the case of the senior levels I have spoken to, tend to view information as power (even though they do not articulate it so clearly) and that to share information with others, even within the same department and possibly subordinate to them, would create untold risks to the organization. Perhaps their main fear is that the risk is to them, not the organization, and that rather than inspiring their teams through the information, they prefer to manage by dictat and removing the opportunities for the teams to understand the reasons behind certain decisions or to participate in creating ideas to solve the issues at hand.

As discussed already, when asked how much organizations had invested in social technologies, whilst some responses ranged from small-change to £400,000 per year, most responded that there had either been no monies invested or that they were unable to quantify them.

Kaplan and Norton[17] explain how intangible benefits cannot be measured in the same way as tangible ones, and McAfee believes that IT investments should be considered in the same way as research and development (R&D) rather than as a new machine tool. In short, there is plenty of research on how businesses have benefitted from using Enterprise 2.0, but those returns should not always be measured in monetary terms – the figures are likely to be flawed and misleading.

In summary, the fact that social technologies have real business benefits for the organization has been proven on many occasions. The doubt only comes on putting a figure to that benefit, which will allow it to be measured as a normal investment within organizations. This surely explains why so many organizations do not invest in the technologies and allow the employees to use free tools on the internet that require no monetary outlay. Some organizations are able to specifically quantify the time spent by limiting the management of the social technology engagement to one person – but this does not take account of benefits from internal collaboration and knowledge.

27

Obstacles and Excuses

Social Technologies

An important focus of this research has been to try and identify blocks to adopting the innovation – to find out why some organizations succeed where others fail. The free-text responses to why the respondents' organizations had made no attempt to implement social technologies have been grouped in to five principle themes, one of which indicates the late adoption of the organization (they are in the process of initiating an Enterprise 2.0 strategy). The other four are: (i) not for us, thanks; (ii) it's not worth it; (iii) too risky; and (iv) here be luddites.

Not for us, thanks! (or "it is not relevant to our organization/sector")

An example of this type of response was: "We are a firm of commercial lawyers and cannot see its relevance to the work we do." That they cannot see its relevance does not mean, of course, that it is not relevant – as shown by the two interviewees from the legal sector, one from a global firm the other from a regional practice, that have embraced social technologies for knowledge sharing. But clearly there are many organizations that fail to see the potential benefits of new technology, preferring to do things the way they've always done them. Other responses in this theme included:

- We are a micro-company and have not perceived the benefit of using social technologies.
- The property industry is usually ten years behind cutting edge thinking and I work for a small business that is more concerned with other business issues.
- I think my organization will implement limited social technologies. It asks for a totally different approach to the market and employees that will take some time.
- We are a specialist operation with no general use.
- No benefit to the organization.
- No reason to use this media.
- Not suitable to the business – business to business. Selling a service that is not suitable to the social arena.
- It currently sees no need to use them.
- We are a B2B supplier of specialized consultancy services to a large but specific business sector and do not believe that the use of social technologies as a means of contacting, communicating with, or otherwise interacting with our target client groups would be effective.
- Because it doesn't fit with our audiences/key stakeholders.
- ROI and customer and employee demographics.
- Not relevant to our core business.
- Not technically advantageous to the company.
- We are a university department most of whose work is based within the department. We are not really trying to reach out to clients.
- I think at the moment it is a mixture of whether it is relevant to our business and time to be able to setup and manage efficiently. There is probably also a certain amount of technology phobia involved.
- No specific business requirement to implement them.
- The target groups are not the right ones.
- Not considered relevant within a blue chip organization.
- Unsure of their value added in a B2B market such as ours.

Clearly the main obstacle is believing that social technologies only have value when dealing externally with consumers and the general public, completely ignoring (or unaware of) the potential internal or business to business (B2B) benefits.

Given the range of sectors covered in the survey and the interviews, there can be little doubt that there are plenty of success stories to show that all organizations and sectors can use social technologies.

It's not worth it (or "the organization does not see the business benefits")

> *Social technologies is not a technical issue, it's a people and engage-ment issue. Once people understand the benefits they'll start using it.*
> Director of Operations, Global Executive Search Firm

This obstacle is similar to the first obstacle and is all about incentiv-izing usage – as mentioned before – and proving the business case for Enterprise 2.0. Once more this appears to be due more to lack of understanding of the tools available than the lack of benefits. This is why a champion (and one with access to the leadership – a mampion if you will) is so important, to show all the potential benefits to all stakeholders.

Other responses under this umbrella included:

• My organization is missing an amazing opportunity.
• The media does not show our brand in the correct manner – not viewed as "professional" or business related.
• Lack of research into any benefit. We are just starting to consider looking into it.
• My organization lacks awareness of the real value it can bring; it is also a bit afraid to charter into this unknown territory; afraid to lose control; no formal organization to move this.
• I do not know. Perhaps they are viewed as distracting to the workforce.
• Not sure. Probably no business case has been established.
• The organization is small, less than fifty employees. In implement-ing social technologies it would require a resource to focus on this

element. In our organization, with scarce resources there are other higher priorities for the business's survival.
- A lack of understanding of the benefit to be derived from the use. The new marketing director will help in this regard.
- Lack of knowledge on how to use effectively.
- Cannot see the value for our business versus the time it would take to manage.
- No perceived value.
- Not well understood or no identified benefit.
- Not enough time in the day to do everything.

It is worth thinking about these arguments against adoption. Many of them would be used against any new technology. How many organizations failed to have a corporate website in the 1990s because they only saw the potential benefits of the internet in B2C transactions? How many people within organizations, at all levels, fail to remember that organizations are made up of people? When marketing B2B, one is not dealing with an organization, but with people. As discussed in Chapter 3, it is true that the decision-making unit might be more complicated within a business and each of the sections within the iBUILD framework (initiators, buyers, users, influencers, lodge-keepers, deciders) for an organization might contain several individuals – but they are all still people. They still commute to work, use email and phones, stop for lunch, have productive and unproductive meetings, experience enjoyable days and frustrating projects. And the ability for those individuals to share their experiences and knowledge and to learn from their peers (within and outside the organization) should be the same, regardless of whether they are selling widgets for an industrial widget-controlling system or they are providing personalized packets of domestic widget substitute.

Too risky (or "Security concerns, fear, and lack of control")

There are those for whom all external influence is a threat, for whom there is risk at every turn, and for whom the only way to avoid having an accident is to never leave the house. This is an exaggeration, but not a huge one. There are, shockingly, still many organizations where employees have no access to the internet – they are unable to even download a file transferred through a system such as wetransfer.com or yousendit.com (many others are available). It would be interesting to know the rationale behind this, if it is fear of viruses and hacking, or fear of employees wasting their time reading celebrity gossip on the web. Responses on the subject of security included the following:

- Our senior management does not want to use social technologies as they think they will be only used by trouble makers.
- This is something we don't master for the moment and there is a long tradition of prudence.
- They do not match company's need – security.
- Security restrictions and cost.
- Social technologies are banned due to security issues arising from opening up company networks to the online world.
- Because of bank security implications.
- Still viewed with suspicion and as a way of finding a new job rather than helping the organization.
- We find social technologies as a business tool for our purpose to be unsuitable due to a number of privacy laws. We are aware that a lot of our staff are on social networks on a personal basis though.
- We are connected by server to our German parent company who use a webwasher [a filter] so the use of social media sites is not available to everyone.
- It would be opening a can of worms – having to mediate what gets published and where.
- We are a company that operates primarily in the defense market. We have determined through observation of various events that implementing social technologies has potentially dangerous consequences to the business and its staff. We have, therefore, banned the use of staff company email addresses for this purpose.
- We are a wholly B2B businesses, with a small number of international customers, several of which are government departments with security related business.
- There are security issues as well as management of the time individuals spend on them.

- The quality/stability of our shared network.
- The webmaster/IT department sees no valid reason or value in using Twitter at the moment or Facebook/LinkedIn and blocks access for all.
- Social technologies by definition are an open source of information, so the risk of misuse is too high.
- I believe that the tools have not been used because of perceived negative uses that there may be.
- Our organization is not geared for the twenty-first century and not set up in a way whereby such social technology tools would be best utilized (such as a convoluted and lengthy sign off process).
- Data security issues.
- In order to use it has to be approved and evaluated by the corporate IT and legal departments.

These concerns cover the fear that confidential information will be released to the general public over social technologies. Companies are physically blocking access to public sites like Facebook and Twitter for fear of organization computers being exposed to viruses and malicious attacks. Information first leaked by Edward Snowden in 2013[1] showed how the security agencies of the US and the UK have been illegally spying on domestic, personal, and private communications including email and phone records on a global scale for years. Meanwhile, viruses have been on computers for a long time, transferred originally via diskettes, then through wired connections, USB memory sticks, email, and fake websites. The existence of viruses should not stop someone using email as a productivity tool, nor using their computer to produce documents through word processing software. All that is required is for users, individually or through their organizations, to be made aware of the existence of viruses so that they can use best practice to avoid downloading them accidentally, and to ensure suitable anti-virus software is installed.

The alternative, of course, is that we will be doomed to writing everything by hand (and not on pads from which indentations of the script can be recovered), only conducting conversations face-to-face (and far from prying ears) and ensuring our employees are only ever allowed to socialize with other employees within the same organization (in case they might discuss company business with someone outside the firm). These options are clearly ridiculous, so once one accepts the fact that modern life involves electronic communications with others, one must accept the fact that this comes with the risk of espionage and sabotage (which, let us remember, existed long before email). Blocking access to technology will help reduce the accidental data loss or corruption of data by third-parties implementing malicious software but it will not eliminate it. Better than blocking social technologies, organizations would do well to educate the workforce on how they should engage with them. As with many things in life, education is the best protection.

Many interviewees cited physical obstacles to social technologies, even though the survey showed no correlation between the IT department blocking physical access to social technologies and the uptake of them. A number of organizations, for example, have resorted to installing stand-alone computers that are not connected to the organization's internal network but that can connect directly to the internet and have drawn up rules on what data can and cannot be put onto that machine. In summary, IT departments blocking access to social technologies is unhelpful and in many cases is a significant obstacle to embracing them, but resourceful employees will find ways to work around it if necessary. IT blocks are a factor in preventing organizations from embracing social technologies, but they are not insurmountable.

> *A big challenge in the public sector is deciding who is empowered to say things in public.*
> Head of Digital Engagement, Central Government Agency

These reasons also cover the concern within some organizations that social technologies cannot be controlled – one cannot control the messages if they are being disseminated by hundreds or thousands of employees on public sites. This is a particular concern within the public sector, but is also a concern for sectors subject to government regulation, such as the pharmaceutical industry or the big four accounting firms, where no preference for a particular organization can be shown if there is also a professional relationship. This means that a link to a Facebook page could be construed as endorsement, although once again the main issue here seems to be trusting the employees to do the right thing. Training and information might need to be offered to make it clear what is and what is not allowed, but that is all. Written guidelines are also useful. Most people like having a job and are not willfully going to jeopardize it by getting their organization into trouble with the authorities. All they usually need to avoid this is better information as to what they should not do and why.

Training and information might need to be offered to make it clear what is and what is not allowed

As mentioned before, McAfee[2] goes to great lengths to explain how he has sought evidence of Enterprise 2.0 disasters from conference attendees and CIOs for several years with none actually having occurred. Furthermore, all the fears of using external social technologies ignore the potential benefits of using them within a closed group, such as internally to the organization.

The fear, in short, is unfounded, and trust is listed by several organizations as the one ingredient without which social technologies will not work.

Here be luddites (or "the organization does not embrace innovation or new technologies")

This response is closely related to the "attitudes" part of the survey where a direct correlation was found between those organizations who had a positive attitude towards innovation and the uptake of new technology. If an organization is old fashioned in its attitude, this will be a severe impediment in implementing social technologies.

Responses related to the luddite tendency include the following:

- There's a lack of focus and or knowledge; we have difficulties in seeing trends.
- We're a very traditional company that doesn't appreciate what IT can offer.

- The business is very conservative and historically has been somewhat paranoid about IT (security) and personal (mis)use of social technologies etc. There has been a recent review of the use of social media for marketing communications but the budget holder was unconvinced of its value in an industrial setting. We have only just got to grips with e-mail for marketing communications purposes!
- We lack knowledge and expertise.
- The marketing and PR departments have not evaluated their benefits properly and are too much stuck in "old fashioned" ways of communicating.
- The organization needs more information about crowd sourcing – we haven't had time to incorporate the rest.
- We haven't really got beyond email to be honest. Interestingly, many members of staff appear to have Facebook accounts but it is not used as an organizational tool.
- Besides use of intranet the topic is ambiguously discussed in the press/media and 'older' management is rather unwilling to work on these issues because of personal aversions.
- The company has a central IT team who are mostly concerned with maintenance of the systems, the work population is mostly over thirty and predominantly manual workers, the IT systems are pretty old.
- We do not yet have a Web 2.0 technological platform in the organization.
- There is no overall understanding of social media, especially the latest technology.

Technology Discontinuance

In addition to not embracing social technologies, the survey asked why organizations had experimented and later abandoned the technology – *discontinuance* as it is known in *diffusion* theory.

The reasons given in the survey for abandoning certain social technologies have also been grouped according to the following themes: (i) that's not the way we do things; (ii) it takes too much time; (iii) hitting a (fire) wall; and (iv) what does that bit do?

That's not the way we do things (or "Incompatible with the current organization practices")

The comments shown here highlight the importance of having a strategy – of having thought out what the organization hopes to achieve from using social technologies:

- It's not a way of working for us.
- We trialed Facebook in [a particular office] but local staff were so put off by the negative comments they were getting they didn't want to engage with the users.
- It's not effective for us at the time.
- It wasn't useful at all. It didn't fit in our strategy, based on personal contact.
- It didn't work (probably because it was very poorly thought out).

Ignoring feedback, as some organizations do, will not tend to improve user experiences.

> *It's happening anyway – you either evolve with it or you aren't involved.*
>
> Community Manager, National TV Broadcaster

It takes too much time (or "We are not prioritizing it over other time-consuming activities")

Some organizations abandon social technologies due to the time commitment that is required to maintain them, as shown with comments such as:

- Twitter is too time consuming.
- We may soon abandon blogging because it's just not being read and we cannot post consistently.
- There's a lack of time – and it did not seem to meet business needs.
- We are considering abandoning blogs as they are time consuming and do not seem to deliver enough value for the time required.
- Only my department used it, and this became a burden.

This is a concern expressed by many active users also. When deciding how to embrace social, or indeed any new, technologies, the organization needs to consider how much time individuals might need to properly share documents internally or engage with customers on Facebook. If no allocation is made for these tasks, for example, by including them in performance appraisals, they will not receive the time and attention they need to succeed. And of course time is money, so the time needed by one person to update a blog (half an hour to one hour per week?) might be good value when considering the potential reach, but it also means that person has one hour less to do other tasks. This is not a problem of the social technologies, nor is it a problem specifically of time management, but of prioritization. If the social technologies are given due priority within the organization and within the departments that are implementing them, then the time will be appropriately used for them. This means the strategy has to be in place. On implementing social technologies, the organization needs to consider what the purpose is, if it replaces other activities and what priority the organization will give it.

Hitting a (fire)wall (or "Play abandoned for security concerns")

Despite the IT obstacles (as described earlier) preventing some organizations from embracing social technologies, they were also cited as an important reason for abandoning social technologies. Some of the comments on this issue included the following:

- Security – we are unable to make the Wiki secure enough for our purposes.
- Our blog was not accessible onsite due to a "websense" filter which would not be released by IT dept.
- Out of security reasons these functionalities are blocked on the company network.
- Reasons: 1. data security issue; 2. avoid using the internet for private purposes.

I have run numerous sessions on embracing digital tools to a wide variety of public and private sector organizations, many of whom have admitted – when asked if they had "Liked" their organizations' Facebook page – that they are unable to access it from within the organization. This is surely a ridiculous state of affairs – where the public messages from an organization provided on Facebook are not shared to people within the organization whose jobs, in some cases, are to engage with customers and other external stakeholders. Like a paranoid military regime, high levels of security might keep an organization's IT infrastructure clean of malicious influences, but it also stifles business, inhibits expression, and eventually fails.

What does that bit do? (or "Lack of knowledge or training")

Any strategy to engage with social technologies must include an element of training for employees. One of the interviewees, however, explained how his global telecommunications firm (which provides IT services for other organizations) set up training for whole departments in different organizations and then used cross-organizational communities of practice for the end-users to share what worked and what improvements could be made. More and more training firms and consultancies offer to teach employees how to engage with the tools and embrace the change. But the internal champion, as described already, is more likely to get long-term buy-in once the training course ends or the consultants go home.

The following comments show how important the role of the champion is:

- I tried Second Life but found it too complicated and it wasn't very user-friendly and felt seriously strange.
- We abandoned virtual worlds as unpredictable.
- Wikis were too difficult to build and get participation for.

There are three types of training that should be considered by organizations when trying to implement the new technology:

1. Installation and set-up

    - Not all new technologies need a "techie" to install them. One of the key attributes of social technologies, for example, is how individuals with only a limited background in programming can set up blogs, wikis, or Facebook pages for individual or organizational use. However, there are many nuances and specific configurations on different platforms that a beginner might find daunting. As a result, organizations should consider the use of champions to help set up the different online tools. If the platforms being used allow for personalization and branding, the marketing department might want to get involved by sharing brand guidelines and a range of company logos and imagery in different sizes and resolutions for employees to use.

- Instructions on how to set up different technologies could be created and shared throughout the organization. As has been mentioned now on many occasions, IT departments shouldn't need to get involved other than to unblock access to the platforms in question.

2. User friendliness

- Once new technologies have been set up (e.g. this might include installing the "client" on an individual's computer, which would allow them to participate in a virtual world) the user might still find themselves flummoxed as to how to proceed. I found Second Life very confusing to engage with and never seemed to find the time to sit and practice with the controls to make my avatar do anything more than walk clumsily and fly. After an initial interest several decades ago I have since avoided video games thanks to their ability to sap my time and leave me drained and frustrated (having stared at a screen for a number of hours without blinking only to fail at a particular level on a game and not quite achieving the score I had hoped for). A reason for not engaging in the generations of consoles that came out in the 1990s and beyond was the complete confusion I faced when trying to work out which button on the handsets did what function in a particular game. I know, I'm old. The creation of the Wii consoles by Nintendo in 2006 understood the potential audience who felt alienated by the complexity of the experience with existing consoles. However, the point remains that some tools are more user-friendly than others. Some, even those which are used by many millions, such as Facebook, are not intuitive and users might need guidance on how, for example, to adjust privacy settings or share information within certain groups.

- This lack of "usability" is important for designers and creators of online experiences. A typical danger of having a developer create a website with no input from someone trained in the user experience is that the developer might create a hierarchy and functionality that makes perfect sense to them but no one else. An organization, therefore, would do well to consider what level of training might be needed to help users start using the new technologies. Whilst any user of a word processor should understand the icons in most blogging platforms that embolden, italicize, or underline a text, they might not find the process of loading an image or linking to another page equally intuitive.

3. Usage guidelines

- All organizations would do well to have clear guidelines on using social media specifically and social technologies in general. Ideally, to obtain better buy-in from the employees, they could be crowdsourced from within the organization. Regardless of how they are created, they should cover the following at least: (i) what employees should and should not say; (ii) what voice they use (and how they can be authentic); (iii) whether or not to sign or otherwise identify themselves (e.g. using initials on a Tweet); (iv) how imagery and audio/visual media should be used; how to avoid copyright issues; (v) what defamation is, its possible consequences, and how to avoid it; and (vi) how to ensure employees are up-to-date with official messages from the organization, to avoid inadvertently contradicting them or, if they do contradict, to turn this into a positive of how the organization trusts its employees.

If an organization's marketing materials talk about the benefits and intended uses of a particular product, an employee could give considerable added value explaining to potential customers any exceptions to this. For example, a manufacturer of Smart TVs might explain the attributes and features of the TV and how its two SCART connectors allow it to connect to a DVD player and a set-top box. An employee might help a sub-segment of the intended audience by explaining how to connect three SCART connectors so that those with multiple devices are able to have all their machines plugged into the TV simultaneously.

How employees should engage with others is also fundamental to these guidelines. How often they should publish; what language they should use; what they should not say; how familiar they should be and how they should maintain their privacy online; what involvement would be considered excessive by an organization; and when it would be appropriate for them to participate in an online conversation. In addition to the rules restricting how pharmaceutical organizations communicate with potential customers and how financial entities must distinguish between official advice and unofficial chat, a lot of organizations seem to ask themselves if it is appropriate for them to use social technologies. I would argue that it is – but each organization and each sector will have nuances of how they should engage. The UK's Ministry of Defence encourages service personnel to use social media but not to provide information that might be used by the enemy. Individual comments might seem innocuous but in conjunction with hundreds or thousands of other posts could paint a picture of troop movements or strategic intentions. A recent exercise with postgraduate students on this very topic came back with the same answer, after studying dozens of Twitter pages and Facebook pages for organizations such as cemeteries, funeral parlors, and children's hospices, for example, who used social media to engage with fundraisers, it is clear that no organization cannot find some value in engaging with stakeholders.

As has been said before, it all comes down to who the stakeholders are, whether they are employees, suppliers, investors, regulators, consumers, end-users, or the general public. As with all marketing and communications, all an organization needs to do is analyze their habits, behaviors, and needs and then devise a strategy that will meet the needs of those stakeholders.

How to Do it

chapter 28

A Framework for Engagement

Readers will by now understand the importance of exploring, if not actually embracing, new technologies and of avoiding the knee-jerk reaction of rejecting change. What the research also showed are the key areas that need to be considered before an organization should think about engaging with social technologies – a framework for successful implementation of social technologies in an organization. Like many frameworks, much of this will seem self-evident. In fact it is self-evident to many who have successfully implemented social technologies as these points of focus have arisen from the research of the success stories as described in Part 2.

The purpose here, therefore, is to distill the learnings from that research into a practical methodology that can help organizations avoid embarking on a project to adopt social technologies that is doomed to failure. It is also aimed at those within the organization that are frustrated by the general lack of interest in the technology – the colleagues who still think that "social" is either indicative of communism or Facebook and that neither are good for developing a business or other large organization.

Like most business models, the framework does not give you the answer, but is a way of

Like most business models, the framework does not give you the answer, but is a way of structuring the analysis

structuring the analysis. Within each element of the framework, a range of decisions will need to be made (Figure 28.1). Ignoring one of the six elements, however, will ensure that the implementation of social technologies eventually fails. The framework involves the following elements:

- Strategize.
- Incentivize.
- Trust.
- Champion.
- Engage.
- Review.

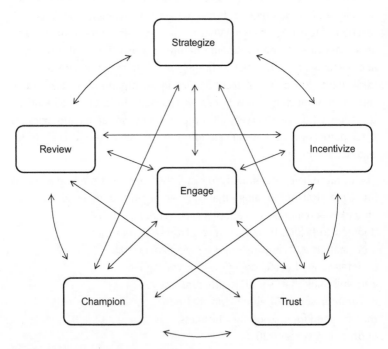

FIGURE 28.1 / **The SITCER™ framework**

The acronym, SITCER™ (others are available), is intended to help the reader remember the framework and, therefore, implement it more readily (or use it when trying to achieve internal agreement to embark on using social technologies). Exactly what one needs to do with the six elements of SITCER™ will be explained in the following pages. The elements are interconnected as they all need to be considered, and reviewed, in conjunction with one another. It is not enough to develop a strategy if it has not taken into account the champion; and, for example, the incentivization structure will need to be reviewed frequently. The reason, however, that "engage" is at the center of the framework is because it is at the heart of social technologies. Every process and strategy in the world, no matter how well intentioned, will ultimately fail with social technologies if engagement is not at the center of all discussions – how to engage, who should engage with whom, and so on.

chapter 29

Strategize

As mentioned in Chapter 23, there is a persistent fallacy within many organizations and certainly with regard to the adoption of technology in the organization that, to paraphrase the 1989 film *Field of Dreams*: "if you build it, they will come". This was true in the early days of the world-wide web when organizations would create websites assuming their offline customers would come online. This was true during the dotcom boom when numerous start-ups created businesses based on the idea that they would generate thousands or millions of web visitors to view their unique content and that, therefore, they would be able to sell multiple advertising spaces to fund the start-up. This is true in the age of social technologies when organizations create Facebook pages assuming their customers will "Like" the page, which will somehow generate direct or indirect benefits for the company. This is true of organizations that create Twitter accounts and Tweet information on behalf of the company (be it special offers, announcing new content, or responding to customer queries) but don't have a plan on how to get their customers (existing or potential) to follow their Twitter feed and actually experience the Tweets. This is true of the organizations that pay tens of thousands to create apps, which don't get downloaded by their target audience.

Market research in to what the customers want is important but not the only issue under the heading "strategize." Organizations need to think carefully about what they want to get out of social technology and how much time they want employees to spend on it. And the employees themselves should, ideally, be included in the planning process. Finding out what the intended stakeholders need is fundamental and will help with the conversation about whether the tool is intended, for example, for knowledge sharing or project collaboration; if it is aimed at reaching new audiences or as a vehicle for customer feedback; how the target audience (customers, employees, suppliers, other stakeholders) will learn about the tool; who will be responsible for the tool; who will take ownership; and, of course, under whose budget it would sit. The strategy would need to include a timetable of implementation but also of engagement, whether it would be used 24/7 to monitor customer services, for example, or if it will only be manned during office hours.

The organization, the "dog," must wag the tail of technological development. A former colleague referred to the "Ta-Dah!" form of information technology (IT) development. This was where the information systems and technology (IS&T) department would work in secret for months, or even years, on a project that had received no input from the rest of the organization, no focus groups, no collating user requirements, no analysis of the target audience, and which was eventually released much as a magician might pull a rabbit from a hat. The organization didn't want the rabbit, they wanted to see a person sawn in two, but by that time it was too late to change anything. The rabbit was let loose and often referred to but rarely seen.

This example of the sunk-cost fallacy, as described in Daniel Kahneman's *Thinking Fast and Slow*,[1] should be borne in mind at all times. If a project isn't working or if a strategy isn't bearing fruit it should be abandoned regardless of the time, effort, and money invested so far. Many organizations, however, will settle for the rabbit rather than insisting that their development team go back and work out how to saw the magician's assistant in half, let alone put them back together again.

High Level/Low Level

At the highest level the organization (and for this one could include the department that is able to implement social technology independent of the mothership) the leadership need to consider what they want to achieve. If they want to achieve a *communal* culture according to Goffee and Jones's model, they need to encourage sociability amongst the employees and ensure the HR policies and key performance indicators (KPIs) simultaneously encourage staff to work towards the benefit of the organization to achieve the stated goals.

This might mean that the organization needs to ensure the employees actually know what those stated goals are and social technologies might be used to disseminate that information in addition to being part of an over-arching strategy to improve the corporate culture.

If the intention is to have continuity in process by creating a databank of knowledge from senior, outgoing executives, once again the strategy has little to do with the technology itself. It has to do with how to engage those senior executives to share their knowledge. How can the organization be sure it is then found and used by the more junior members of the team? How can the knowledge sharing process be built into the everyday processes of the organization, so that new employees and old understand that new projects and old would benefit from trawling through the past experiences to see where improvements and efficiencies can be made?

If the organization wants to increase its communications and marketing activities to reach a specific target audience through the means of social technologies it should first ask itself "Why?" Why that target audience is relevant; why they are targeted; whether they are existing or potential customers; or whether they are simply a segment who currently receive a lot of media attention. If one wants to target teenagers it would be better to look at Pheed or Snapchat than Facebook. If the organization's intention is to reduce recruitment costs by engaging through social technologies, then LinkedIn, or Xing if recruiting in Germany, might well prove to be a better tool than Facebook.

The following, therefore, is a simple checklist of
what to consider and questions to ask during the
strategy consultation. There are no universal
answers, but every organization will need
to ask: What? Why? Whom? Who?
How? How much? When? Where?
How many?

What?

What do you want to achieve?

An organization might have several issues it hopes to
resolve by implementing social technologies, which may require different approaches. To begin the process, the organization will need to ask
itself the following questions:

- Do you want to engender knowledge sharing and create a knowledge
  management system?
- Do you want to improve customer intimacy by having customer
  services answering queries on a range of platforms?
- Do you want to encourage a community amongst the customer base
  and have your brand ambassadors help other customers with tips and
  tools?
- Do you want to open up your product development process to the
  crowd?
- Do you want to identify new channels to place ads on?
- Do you want to encourage customers to create content about your
  products?
- Do you want to create a "member-gets-member" system for customer
  acquisition?
- Do you want to collaborate with your supply chain through social
  technologies?
- Do you want to be seen to be an innovative organization?

The answer to the question "What do you want to achieve?" could be
self-evident. It might be a simple decision of using social networks for

recruiting graduates out of university. It might be aimed at engaging with new potential markets. However, to arrive at the answer, readers might want to conduct a strategic analysis as they would for any major decision for the organization. Look outside the organization at the state of the market, the industry, the economy, and the world. Look at the competition and find the space that the organization can compete in efficiently and effectively. Look within the organization, find its core competencies, the shared values, the corporate culture and see what social technologies best fit. It is better to use a technology that suits the existing work practices or organization's strengths than to try to adopt one, however trendy it might be, that would involve a funda- mental change in employee behaviors and, therefore, face greater resistance.

It is better to use a technology that suits the existing work practices or organization's strengths than to adopt one

Why?

The "why?" is important as it will help you refine the "what?":

- Why create a knowledge management system, for example?
  Is the knowledge held by the outgoing senior executives still relevant?
  Is it explicit knowledge that can be located elsewhere (e.g. through a bought-in database)?
  Is it likely to be used by junior members of the organization (notwith- standing the issues of incentivization, which shall be discussed later on)?
- Why engage with customers?
  Is there something about the current systems for customer services that isn't working?
  Are customers currently kvetching on social media and is the organi- zation's hand being forced into engaging in the social space?
- Why crowdsource product development?
  Is it to save money?
  To engage with the user-base?

To access a greater number of opinions, options, and potential solutions than through only focusing internally?

Whom?

Whom do you want to target? Again – it is worth supplementing this question with a "why?" just to be sure the audience is relevant. If you want to use Facebook for recruitment:

- Is it easily accessible in the target country?
- Is there a better network or social technology that could be used?
- What is it about traditional recruitment practices in the organization that is lacking?
- Is the system broken (if not, why fix it)?

Who?

Who is going to actually manage the process within the organization? We shall get on to "champions" later but it is worth defining who has ownership of the social technology:

- Is it every department?
- Is it HR?
- Is it Marketing?
- Is it IS&T (if you, the reader, have read all the previous pages, I am hoping that you will already know that the only reason for IS&T to "own" the technology is if they are the ones targeting the audience – for example, to share knowledge amongst in-house developers on the best way to resolve certain issues). Who is the actual person, not just the "department" who will be responsible for managing the social technology?
- Do they have sufficient seniority, or freedom, to post messages on behalf of the organization?
- If not, why not?
- In addition to the issues of trust (see Chapter 31) do they have access to the information to be able to engage through the social technology?

- If they are within the customer services department, are they empowered to resolve customer issues there and then? There is little point creating the impression of a customer services department that will respond instantaneously through social technologies if the customer is told that the person manning the platform (such as Twitter or the Facebook page) will have to get back to that customer at a later date. The most likely outcome of that would be for the customer to then use the twitter or Facebook pages to complain about the organization.

How?

What are the channels that will be used?

- What social technologies will be employed to achieve the "what?" by the "who?" for the "whom?"
- Will it be one channel or several?
- Will this be part of the employee's formal job description and, if so, how many hours per day or week should they spend on it?
- If there are several people dealing with the channels, how will each know if the other is dealing with a query?

How will the customers or other stakeholders know with whom they are talking?

- Will a system be bought in, or developed in-house?
- Will an "enterprise" access be purchased for the technology or should staff use the free "public" version?
- If audio-visual materials are to be produced, what are the desired production values?
- Should videos (e.g. to be posted on YouTube) be of a quality that would not look out of place on mainstream TV, or should they be done as quickly and as cheaply as possible?
- If the former, do the requisite skills already exist or would new staff need to be recruited to film and edit the footage?
- If the latter, what training would be required with the existing staff?

- How are you going to build up a following, if necessary, on the platform of choice?
- How many followers will signify that the message is reaching a significant sample of the population?

How much?

What budget will this endeavor have? Whilst many social technologies are free to use, they take time.

- How much time would be expected from the individuals tasked with owning the technologies, and what would happen to their existing duties?
  Would more staff need to be recruited simply to cover these extra actions?
- If an enterprise edition of the social software is purchased, how much would that cost and what internal IS&T support would it require to get it working?
- If social technologies are intended to be used for advertising, what is the budget, over what period of time, targeted to what audience?
- Would this budget be shaved from existing budgets and, if so, what activities would have to be reduced to make up the shortfall?

When?

Will the social technology be manned 24/7 or only during office hours, or over extended office hours that, for example, cover two time-zones?

- Would employees need to do shifts to ensure responses can be near-instantaneous?
- If responses would only be expected once per day, as they might with emails, for example, would that be made clear to the customers or other stakeholders so as to manage their expectations?
- Would it be justified (depending on the industry and the purpose of the use of the social technology) to have a delay of twenty-four hours in hearing back about an issue?
- When will the new strategy be implemented?

* How long is it expected to last?
* Is it ongoing or a fixed campaign?
* When would the review period take place?

Where?

Where will you communicate the new strategy and its place within the organization?

* How will employees learn about it?
* How will the end-users learn about it?
* Will you need a marketing or communications campaign simply to talk about the new use of social technologies for marketing and communications?
* Where will the social technology "sit" within the overall communications channels or, for example, within the internal platforms and intranets already in place?

How many?

How will the success or failure of the social technology be measured?

* What does success look like?
* Is it in the number of followers or the number of Tweets/posts/pokes/likes/+1s or Pins?
* Is it in the engagement with the target audience and how do you define that engagement?
* Do you only count those who respond to the organization or also those who read the messages or see the posts?
* Do you only count those who download the app or those who engage via the website on a mobile device?
* Why is engagement a measure of success?
* Can you honestly put a value on each post, response or interaction?
* What is the minimum return that will be tolerated for the strategy to continue?
* To every metric, as Avinash Kaushik says, you should ask the question "So what?"[2] If a metric does not give you enough information that

will allow you to improve things or make a decision on whether or not to continue, then don't bother with that measure! So whilst proving ROI is important for many organizations, much of the measure of return that one could choose to produce to show ROI is irrelevant for the long-term health of the company. For example, having *x* thousand or million "Likes" on Facebook will look good in a report but is it actually making a difference to the bottom-line?

- Is customer satisfaction up since the creation of the organization's Facebook page?
- Are sales up?
- Are referrals up?

Equally, when considering knowledge management, showing how many documents are being created is nice but doesn't actually help if employees are not using the system to search for knowledge, process, and insight. Showing how many searches take place is no good if the right documents are not found. Demonstrating that employees are searching and reading a certain number of documents might be good, but if it doesn't create efficiencies elsewhere in the organization (e.g. through improved processes, better judgments, or greater employee satisfaction – which, in turn, reduces employee turnover) then it might be reasonable to ask what benefit the investment in the social technology has had.

However, to be able to properly measure those efficiencies might create such a lot of extra work that there is a good chance it is cheaper to simply implement the technologies and then measure, much further down the line, if sales are up, employee turnover has decreased, or mentions of the brand in the press have increased. This will be covered in Chapter 34.

Summary

In short, no one should even consider thinking about the merest possibility of discussing the potential implementation of even the tiniest form of social technology without first thinking about what it would

be used for and why. Have a strategy. Have a plan. Make sure
it fits. If the strategy is a stretch for the organization, it
might make sense to have more realistic ambitions.
Better to walk before you run and better to crawl
before you walk. But it is better still to avoid
standing idly by while everyone else in the
industry is moving.

avoid standing idly by while everyone else in the industry is moving

chapter 30

Incentivize

Whether through creating personal goals and objectives, encouraging knowledge sharing, or showing that the leadership are listening and approving, the main focus of this part of the framework is to answer the question "What's in it for me?" By the same token from "strategize" that one cannot simply use social technologies and expect customers or others to flock to them, one needs to incentivize employees to engage with the tools too. In the case of knowledge sharing within an organization, there are plenty of reasons why an individual might not want to share their expertise. Many might (perhaps rightly and certainly justifiably) assume that it is what makes them employable. If they were to share their knowledge with the rest of the organization they would become dispensable and do themselves out of a job. That knowledge or expertise could be how to connect printer "X" to a locked-down work laptop using Windows 7, it could be tips on negotiating with supplier "Y", it could be the best strategies to employ when creating a contract for clients with requirements "Z," or it could be knowing who to talk to to get X, Y, and Z dealt with efficiently.

"answer the question "What's in it for me?""

Incentivized Lurking or "What's in it for me?"

One man's incentive is another man's turn-off.

Digital Communications Professional,
Central Government Agency

The term "incentive" suggests a reward for using the tools, where "motivation" is, in some cases, more appropriate. The question is, therefore, how an organization should motivate employees to use social technologies.

One global pharmaceutical company, for example, built engagement with public social media sites into the performance appraisal of individuals within the sales and marketing departments. Employees were tasked as one of their objectives for that year with "listening" to the conversations taking place in public fora on their specialist (disease) area – what another interviewee referred to as "incentivized lurking" when they heard about it. The intention is to set objectives for the next year based on actually engaging with the public groups. This method was chosen for two key reasons:

- It ensured the public's conversations on those diseases and, often, on the company's products, would not be ignored internally.
- It gave individuals time to understand the tone of conversations taking part, where corporate "PR" language would be particularly unwelcome.

Survey respondents and interviewees suggested putting essential corporate information on the Enterprise 2.0 platforms, such as CEO updates, accessing expenses forms, or conducting training.

Others mentioned that the culture motivates, through the specific promotion of knowledge sharing and showing. As one interviewee put it, it is no longer the case that "knowledge is power" but one must now "give knowledge away to show that one has it and is willing to share."

An easy, and cheap, method of incentivizing staff to participate is having the leadership take an active role. If, for example, everyone knows that the CEO posts and responds on an enterprise microblogging site, occasionally "Liking" the posts and posting updates, then staff understand that to be seen and recognized by the hierarchy, one would do well to use the tools of communication that they have endorsed. If there are organization blogs, the leadership could occasionally comment on the blogs. Other organizations have specific objectives for engaging with social technologies; although the rewards are not always financial.

> *Money is the last thing you should be thinking of.*
> Ex-Director of Knowledge, Global Broadcasting Firm

The Managing Director of a global telecommunications firm that implements Enterprise 2.0 solutions in other organizations says there is an age issue – where the younger ones do not need much incentivizing, but the older ones often do. But that incentivization does not need to include financial rewards, it could be simply praising good work or giving out staff awards, treats, or weekends away.

> *Highlight the good – don't punish the failure.*
> Managing Director, Global Telecommunications Firm

The other incentive that appeared often in both interviews and survey responses was showing people what is in it for them. This is clearly an issue more for an organization driven by individual targets rather than organizational advancement, but suggests that – when thinking about the Goffee and Jones's framework – perhaps there is no difference in how different cultures embrace social technologies, so long as the incentives are there for the target-driven *mercenary* employees to get personal benefits whilst the organization also benefits.

How to Make Them Care

The incentive for staff could be setting individual objectives on sharing knowledge internally or engaging with audiences externally. It could be relating those objectives to financial bonuses or other rewards schemes. It could be creating a culture of sharing within the organization that ensures individuals think first about their teams, departments, and the organization, and only second about their own personal benefits. It might be showing that the leadership of the organization are listening to the conversations taking place, that they approve of social technologies, and that they engage with them too.

There is no one method to incentivize engagement with social technology – but incentives must be aligned to the culture of the organization and the aims of the social technology strategy.

incentives must be aligned to the culture of the organization and the aims of the social technology strategy

Incentivization is fundamental to the SITCER™ model as it is to everything – how to motivate people and to help them see what personal gain they will get. This can involve culture change, or simple training about the benefits. It might involve a new regime of performance appraisal and bonuses, or simply demonstrating from the top that knowledge sharing is not only approved of but actively encouraged and a route to higher visibility within the organization. Through that the "love and belonging" level of Maslow's Hierarchy of Needs[1] (by contributing and becoming a more central part of the organization) are met; or even the "self-esteem" level (by being praised and recognized for the contributions made and feeling that one has helped others).

What about Outsiders?

Finding ways to incentivize people to adopt social technologies should not just be limited to internal users of the tools. The target audience will also need to understand why they should bother to follow an organization's tweets, engage with them in a virtual world, read their Facebook posts, watch their videos, or help peers through crowdsourced customer services.

If the product or service has "fans" as well as customers, it shouldn't be difficult to get the fans (or early adopters) to engage with the organization through whichever platform is best suited. Through the fans, through the creation of content, and the visibility of the network it is more likely, then, that others will follow suit and sign up.

Life is Just a Game

As discussed in Chapter 15, employing elements of gamification could help encourage engagement by both internal and external users. Simple leaderboards showing those who have participated the most might be sufficient within certain platforms or for limited uses, such as showing which employees have shared the most documents that others have found useful. Regular contributors might earn "badges" for types of contribution, which could appear on their profiles.

Customers can be encouraged through the use of a points system where, for example, they earn points for each "engagement" with the brand and then earn discounts or gain access to exclusive content after collecting a certain number of points. Rather than tangible benefits, those points might lead to users having special features on their profiles or access to exclusive content.

In the case of an internal knowledge management system, problems could be posted with a view to encouraging multiple users to respond to the challenge with potential solutions – the solutions then being voted on by other users to find the one that seems most relevant or innovative.

Making the platform fun to use is also a way of encouraging usage. There is a mistaken belief that B2B marketing must be "formal" or that organizations in certain sectors are only focused on results. The tendency is to forget that all organizations are made up of people – and all people like to have fun (although how "fun" is defined might be quite different from person to person). A good manager will know that a happy work-place is more productive, and fun does not have to be anomalous to serious business. Creating a system where the users need to undertake a series of challenges or complete various levels can make the process feel more like a game.

Whatever Works

Each person and each situation will be different. Some people will respond well to public acknowledgement. Some will like badges and points. Some will need it to be part of their job description and built into their performance appraisal. Some will need cold hard money. Whatever works, works. But what is clear is that a successful strategy that has not considered how to incentivize users will be an exception, not a rule. It will most likely have developed a series of mechanisms to motivate the employees already, such that engaging with social technologies is simply considered another feature of the working day that employees should get to grips with. Staff will be happy in the knowledge that they enjoy their work, their colleagues, their workplace, and the direction the organization is going in.

chapter 31

Trust

Trust and honesty were key terms used time and again by the interviewees. There is an implicit assumption within social networks and social media that when connecting to someone else, they are going to respect that connection and not "spam" you. There is an implicit assumption that when downloading apps from unknown companies, they will work properly and not use your data without your knowledge (let's not discuss the small print loopholes that officially mean users give permission but in reality are never read).

Modern society operates on trust. In many countries, such as the UK, a verbal contract is still binding and writing it down simply gives the parties easier recourse to action if the other reneges on the agreement.

There is (much abused) trust with our politicians. We vote for them and expect them to actually do what they promised. We expect people in positions of trust (those who take care of our money, our health, our education, our safety) to uphold those expectations, which is why we are more shocked and disappointed when bankers, doctors, teachers, or the police are seen to have abused that trust. To request a UK passport, identification is confirmed through countersignatories who must be "a person of good standing in their community"[1] and from a recognized profession – a list that has expanded beyond doctor, lawyer, or accountant to include teachers, travel agents, journalists, and funeral directors. The suggestion being that "mere" office and shop workers and manual laborers are not to be relied upon to confirm someone's identity, even though research shows the "ordinary man or woman in the street" is more likely to tell the truth than civil servants, government ministers, and politicians and are actually on a par with the clergy and the police.[2]

The point is, of course, that we rely on trust. We expect trust. When we give our word we expect people to trust us. When people give us their word, we expect to be able to trust them. When we employ certain professionals (doctors, lawyers, accountants, etc.) we expect them to do their best for our interests and, therefore, to be able to trust them.

Likewise, when we employ people within our organizations, we expect to be able to trust them. We seem to spend more time with the people we work with than we do the people we love (at least if counting only our waking hours) and they often have the ability, should they choose to, to steal from us personally or from our organization. Yet, on the whole, this does not happen. People repay that trust with trust – they also expect not to be stolen from and for the organization to pay them the salary that has been agreed. The exceptions that reach the newspapers and the courts are just that, exceptions – newsworthy precisely because they are not usual.

Open Access

Curiously, however, many believe that you cannot allow the rank-and-file workers of an organization to have access to social technologies as they will abuse the trust by spending all their time on Facebook. To prevent this happening, information systems and technology (IS&T) departments are asked to block access to certain sites, such as Facebook or Twitter.

> *Spending time on Facebook is not a technical issue, it's a performance management issue.*
>
> CIO, Global Publishing House

Following from what this CIO said, who often had requests from departmental managers to block access to social technologies, workers have always had a wide variety of ways to waste time if that is what they actually want to do, and with smartphone access to all social media platforms, they do not need to be at their desks on the company networks to use the technologies.

As mentioned before, there have been many occasions when running sessions on social technologies with middle and senior-level managers from large, often multinational organizations, that the response to my question of whether or not they had seen their organizations' Facebook pages was that they were not able to because access to Facebook on company laptops was blocked. These were women and men between thirty-five and fifty years of age who spent much of their time out of the office meeting clients. If employees want to waste time, Facebook should be the least of the companies' worries. The people who make the decision to block access are having knee-jerk reactions and have not thought it through.

Security

Another excuse for blocking access to social technologies is that staff might inadvertently download malware to their computers, for example, by playing a game on Facebook or clicking a link on Twitter. Whilst malware is a real issue, having the appropriate anti-virus and anti-malware software regularly updated is more likely to prevent breaches of malware being downloaded to work computers.

Furthermore, despite the attempts of scaremongering in the press to make us believe that cyber-criminals are spying on us all the time through our webcams and tracking e – v – e – r – y – k – e – y – s – t – r – o – k – e we make, we are still more likely to lose data by misplacing a USB memory stick or the laptop itself.

Better than blocking access to social technologies, an organization that wants to encourage its employees to have respect for the integrity of data and the importance of safe-guarding it would do well to consider educating the workforce about best practice. That way they could also cover the issues of opening attachments from private emails (e.g. which might not go through the company's security software filters), using USB sticks to transfer data and how to avoid leaving them on trains or in the pub, and not putting confidential paperwork in the normal recycling bin. People are not daft – but they sometimes lack knowledge of what constitutes danger, or a dangerous link, on the internet.

There is nothing wrong, in principle, with employees using their own IS&T equipment (including phones and tablets) in the workplace either. The Information Commissioner's Office in the UK even gives guidelines of the potential issues that might occur[3] and how to safeguard against them – none of the guidelines discuss blocking access to certain sites.

Defamation and Copyright

Another common excuse for shying away from social technologies is that the organization can get into trouble if employees publish comments or other materials which could be construed as defamation or would be in breach of copyright.

Once again, education is surely better than blocking. Having social media guidelines in place within the organization and ensuring all employees know about them, have access to them, and, ideally, have read them would help ensure staff understand what kinds of comments would be construed as defamation; what usage of images, audio, video, or text would be a breach of copyright; what legal and moral requirements the employees are under with company data and any information about the organization's fellow employees, customers, suppliers, or other stakeholders.

Guidelines for using social technologies should include the full range of what behavior is expected from employees. For example, the employees should know whether they are blogging, Tweeting, or posting on behalf of the organization or as an individual and when they should have a disclaimer on their page explaining that the views are theirs and theirs alone, and in no way represent the organization. The organization should make it clear what subject matter they are allowed to comment on – whether they have strict guidelines and guardrails on acceptable topics or if they are allowed to discuss anything that a customer, for example, might talk about. Zappos, the online shoe retailer is just one of many examples that shows how empowering employees creates a good customer experience and an enduring, positive, corporate culture.[4]

Clear Boundaries

In summary, most people like their jobs. They might moan about certain elements of the day-to-day routine. Some might have a better or worse relationship with their boss or their co-workers. But most people like the fact that they have a job and a salary and are not going to deliberately jeopardize either of them. If they can be helped to understand the limits of what they should and should not do online, they are more likely to conform to those limits. Better to educate than simply block. Better to guide than tether. Better to allow your employees to become ambassadors for the organization as the accumulative effect of seeing how helpful employees can have untold benefits on the reputation of a brand.

And if you find that the majority of employees are likely to speak ill of the organization, perhaps you need to look hard at the corporate culture that has developed and see what can be done to improve that.

No Defense from the Defense

Wise employers will take employee complaints as feedback, say "thank you for the feedback," and work on improving it.

The defense industry, one that by definition has been extremely focused on security, has embraced social media (and even has its own conferences on the subject[5]). Their biggest threat is not from employees sharing secrets online – if employees want to leak information, there are plenty of other ways to do it. Ed Snowden's revelations in *The Guardian* and the *Washington Post* of illegal spying by the US and UK governments on private organizations and its own citizens did not occur with any involvement of social technologies.[6]

Mistrust is Naïve

A common response to suggestions that employers should trust their employees is that the speaker is being naïve and no serious organization would last long if it let its employees do what they want.

To be clear, it is not a question of letting employees doing what they want, but treating staff as adults, not children. Treat them as you would wish your superiors to treat you. Stuff happens. Mistakes occur. Malice exists. People will abuse their organizations and leak confidential information. That has always been the case and there is no evidence to suggest that social technologies have caused more problems. But, once again, most employees are responsible adults who only want to do their jobs better, more efficiently, and with improved results. Let them.

Chapter 32

Champion

There are those amongst us who are naturally inquisitive about technology (or perhaps that should be "nurturally," if you will…), who will explore the advanced options and settings of software to see what else it can do, try new features or systems, and like our technology to work for us and fit our environment. We are the people who will probably have a "pro-innovation bias" (see Chapter 17) and who, whilst not necessarily early adopters, are most likely early knowers.

This does not mean, however, that our lives are spent with technology, that we only play videogames when out of the office, that we are obsessed with science-fiction and comics, nor that we are strangers to the outdoors, sport, or social interaction.

If anything, many early adopters of social technologies were those who had interests outside the workplace and who embraced blogging, for example, as a way of reaching out to that wider, more dispersed community. These are people who learnt to share their jogging statistics with friends and peers and compete with them through social networks. These are people who will encourage their friends to start using Facebook, Whatsapp, Instagram, Pinterest, Snapchat, or whatever the newest platform is.

These might be younger members of a team, but they don't have to be (I, myself, am no spring or even summer chicken).

Mampions

As explained in Chapter 26, the champions need to be mavens – people who know everyone. The people who know about the technology and are good at explaining or helping others embrace it also need to be known within the team, department, or organization. Having the leadership show interest and lead the way helps, but the social technology will only embed if people have a local "super user" they can turn to for help. Someone who is well versed in the organization's social media guidelines, someone who knows how to resize images for web use, someone who can show how to tag and hashtag in the right way, someone who knows the protocols that the community within that specific social technology have created (e.g. the "Follow Fridays" hashtag on Twitter: #FF, where users recommend people to follow).

The champion does not have to be a dedicated "social technologies guru." Nor does he or she need to be a member of the senior management team; they could be a middle manager or even a relatively junior member of the organization. The appointment of a champion, however, sends a signal to the rest of the organization that it is taking social technologies seriously, and becomes a focus for queries and hand-holding across the organization, encouraging individuals and different teams to get on board. In fact, rather than one champion, it would be yet more beneficial to have a network of champions across the organization, ideally one per department or division, to ensure that they can help with the micro-detail of helping individuals get with the system and not just talking about it generally.

The champions do, therefore, need to be recognized by the leadership as the internal experts and be available to help users across the organization who are unsure about using the tools in question. Putting the tools in place and expecting them to be used is naïve; particularly if no formal knowledge sharing has previously taken place.

Although this may appear to be self-contradictory, it is important, furthermore, that the champions are not members of the information systems and technology (IS&T) team.

> Social technologies are not a technical issue, they are a people and engagement issue.
>
> Director of Operations, Global Executive Search Firm

By disconnecting it from where the technical experts sit, the role of the champion is being defined as one who is not a technical expert – and, hence, that engagement with social technologies requires no technical expertise. Non-champions should not have the opportunity to say "well it's easy for you – you're a computer expert" or similar.

Turn Slackers into Backers

When seeking employees who would be suitable as champions, there are two attributes to look for:

1. They have already embraced social technologies and require no further encouragement or incentives to do so.
2. They are mavens – they know people throughout the department, division, or organization and they are known.

A good place to start is by approaching your IS&T department and finding out which employees are currently using social technologies the most; assuming there is no block on access. It might be that some teams or departments have already created a social media presence for their area. It could be, of course, that the heavy-users of social technologies are utilizing them for personal connections. If that is the case, there are two options. The employee is reprimanded and told that any future use of social technologies will result in a formal warning. Alternatively, you congratulate yourself on correctly identifying someone who has already embraced social technologies and whose keenness to use them should be turned to an advantage by having them become a champion and help others to get with the program.

Incentivizing the Intensifiers

Whilst the incentivization methods discussed in Chapter 8 are aimed at the non-champions within the organization – the people for whom the reasons to engage are not immediately apparent – it is essential to think about how the champion should engage with the rest of the team, department, or organization. The following criteria should be considered when drawing up a job description for the champions:

1. Whether the position should be full or part time and how much time per day the champion should dedicate to helping others needs to be decided first. One cannot give more responsibility and expect the person concerned to fulfill all the previous (and continued) responsibilities to the same level. One could make the champion a full-time position, but at the other end of the spectrum, one hour per week will make no difference whatsoever. Certainly, during the period of change, while the social technologies are being implemented, the champion is likely to be needed full time, but this may be scaled back as the processes and technologies become normalized. The organization might need to consider how some (or possibly all) of the previous or existing responsibilities of the champion should be redistributed amongst other staff.
2. The champions must lead by example but also help and guide others. They need to create content to ensure there is a steady stream of new material, but they also have to help others – in the physical use of the technologies, in creating a schedule of how often they should post, and in helping the users find their voice and the tone to use when posting, according to the target audience (internal vs external, B2B vs B2C).
3. The key performance indicators (KPIs) will need to be adjusted to reflect these new responsibilities; perhaps measuring the number of people they spend time with, the amount of content they personally post, the amount of content by others they assist in getting

online, and the readership of that content (numbers of visitors, time spent on the pages, number of likes, bookmarks, shares, etc.). Surveys could be created periodically to measure changes in attitudes of the employees to social technologies and this measured against the time spent by the champion with those people. Those KPIs will also need to be weighted appropriately against any other responsibilities the champion might have. It would not be fair, however, to measure and appraise the champion on the success of the social technologies if the incentives for the rest of the organization have not been appropriately set up and rolled out.

4. Realistic expectations would need to be set on the numbers of people the champion is expected to help. Spread the role too thinly and it will be ineffective, spread it too thickly and it will be economically unviable.

The formality of the role and the process for engaging with the other employees should be clarified – for example, whether or not the champion should hold scheduled "surgery" times when people can book training; if the champion should systematically go around everyone in the organization to spend time getting them connected or logged in; or if the process is less formal and people are told to contact the champion if they need help. The less formal the process, the less likely it will succeed. Not everyone likes to admit to not knowing how to use new technologies and will protest that they are too busy rather than voluntarily book time for training and assistance. It is worth having formal sessions with everyone to get them comfortable with the new process at least at the start. This is clearly more time consuming but a better guarantee that those who need help most will get it.

However, in the case that all employees are required to spend time with the champion, organizations might want to think about possible sanctions if employees choose not to do so. Ideally this will be built in to the incentives mentioned before, but the senior managers who have not bought in to the idea might prove more of an obstacle in enabling the rest of their department to engage with the champion and social technologies in general. One of the incentives for engagement might also be to set targets for the number of posts per department and the number of users logging on for a specific amount of time, in order to ensure that management encourage the change.

5. If the organization is large enough to warrant having several champions, they could be a central pool or they could be distributed such that there are specific, dedicated, named champions for specific departments. If a particular department has no suitable champions, a value judgment will need to be made on whether to train up an incumbent within the department or parachute in someone from outside and who does not have the requisite social connections within the department that will best help ensure the messages get through.

6. It is possible that the champion is more comfortable with some of the social technologies and less so with others. In this case a training program for all champions would be needed to make sure they are all on the same page and able to help and support others on all and any issues related to the social technologies.

7. When several champions are recruited, some kind of hierarchy might be useful just to ensure messages, best practice, and policy get through to them all. An internal online forum would allow them to do this organically without specific leadership, so it might be the case that someone is nominated as the "communications officer" for the pool of champions, rather than having a leader and a formal hierarchy.

8. Finally, if there are several champions, each dealing with their own department, they should be incentivized to share information amongst themselves and create links for employees to do the same. For example, if someone working on the supply chain comes across a blog complaining about the customer services department, the information can be easily passed through to the appropriate person in that department to deal with it.

Champions, mampions, superusers, change agents, social technocrats – whatever we call them, the name is not as important as the role and responsibilities. What is clear is that attempting to implement social technologies without an internal champion or network of champions will be doomed to failure.

chapter 33

Engage

In the simple diagram showing the SITCER™ framework (Figure 28.1, Chapter 28) "engage" was placed in the center, because it must be the focus of any social technology. If the organization implements social technologies but the employees do not engage with them, the exercise has been a waste of time. Likewise, if the champions drive the usage of the social technologies but their colleagues' engagement drops off after the initial training, the exercise has been pointless. The problem, therefore, is how to ensure there is momentum behind using the technology and how the organization, and individuals, can be sure that they won't allow themselves to slowly drop the social technology engagement as more immediate and more pressing issues arise.

Depending on the technology, there are plenty of tools which can be set up to automatically notify the user when there is an update – but we all know how distracting and stress-inducing it can be to have notification after notification that our email inboxes are filling up.

Time Mismanagement

Time management experts usually suggest tackling the email inbox at specific times during the day rather than having it always open, using filtering systems to identify urgent emails and those that can be left until later, and making it clear to colleagues and bosses that if they need to contact you urgently, email is probably not the best tool.

However, it is fair to say that keeping track of notifications from various social technologies as well as the single email inbox can be time consuming and merely add to the anxiety of never being able to get on with "proper" work whilst keeping tabs on what is happening. This is not just a case of monitoring mentions of the organization or the brand in social media, it could be monitoring new entries in the internal knowledge management system, seeing what colleagues have done recently through the internal social network, or observing what the competition are up to over various platforms.

When I upgraded my mobile phone a few years ago, I noticed on loading my work email details into the handset's email software "Exchange" settings an optional check-box to "receive notifications when new email arrives." I unchecked it. For the first time in months, if not years, I found myself only checking work email once a day at the weekend, rather than looking at every message that came through (which could be anything from thirty to a hundred over a weekend).

Equally, for my social media accounts I have unchecked the boxes to receive notifications every time someone sneezes in the ether. What I do is find five or ten minutes per day to go through the different social platforms I am signed up to and do a quick scan of updates, responding to some, ignoring others.

I now check those settings on every new mobile I have. I am obsessed with having "zeroinbox" on my email account, that is, no unread messages, and whilst a therapist might one day help me move away from such obsessive tendencies, I have helped myself immeasurably by removing "push" notifications. I recommend it.

This isn't, it should be stressed, going against everything that has been encouraged previously in the book. Social technologies should be embraced. Any organization that understands that its customers might prefer to be contacted through other platforms (for customer services), for example, or that the brightest minds are not always within the organization (crowdsourcing) will benefit from that. By the same token, any organization that neglects to implement an effective knowledge management system will carry on reinventing the wheel time and again; rather than, to continue the analogy, having a blueprint for wheel construction, with step-by-step instructions and a list of preferred wheel suppliers in a central repository, where peers and future employees could find it.

All this is saying is that one (and the "one" here can be the individual – you – or the organization as a whole) must find the balance between engaging with social technologies and not allowing that engagement to detract from the many other projects that we all need to constantly juggle in the workplace.

Engage, not Enrage

It should, of course, go without saying that one should aim to avoid irritating, angering, and generally making enemies of our customers, employees, or stakeholders. But let's say it anyway. If a customer comes back with a load of negativity through a social network – saying that your brand is the worst, that the customer service stinks, that everyone should avoid your organization at any cost – there are several tactics that a socially-adept organization can use:

- Ignore the feedback and assume it is simply one person complaining and that no one will pay any notice (but see, as discussed in Chapter 4, how Dell learned their mistake from that tactic with Jeff Jarvis way back in 2005).
- Take legal action to try and shut the individual up (threatening defamation, for example, most individuals are unlikely to want to go through the mess of having to go to court just to say that the organization stinks, and are more likely to simply withdraw the offending content).
- Get "friendly" members of that community, brand ambassadors, to drown the social network in question with positive statements

so that the voice of dissent sounds like an oddball and an isolated incident – many organizations have chosen this route through PR agencies, often "employing" brand ambassadors by paying for posts through Amazon Turk or other websites for crowdsourced labor.

- Simply argue with the complaining ex-customer by explaining how wonderful the organization is, how big the brand is, how many satisfied customers there are, and how much they disagree with their opinion of the brand.

- Actually say "Thank you for the feedback" and mean it (a message given on many websites after submitting a feedback page but not always given honestly). Humility in the face of such feedback goes a long way. Accepting that you (the organization) is not perfect is simply recognizing the truth – perfection doesn't exist but we can all strive towards it.

- Engage the complainant in a conversation of exactly what happened and when. Rather than using this as a means of finding a scapegoat within the organization who didn't do their job properly (although that might be relevant in certain circumstances), the organization could try to understand how to avoid the issue arising again. If necessary, new processes and protocols can be created so that said complainant, whilst only an individual at this stage, doesn't become representative of a larger but more silent section of the target market.

Engage, not Marry

Just as engaging with stakeholders should not mean fighting them over the ether, neither does it mean you have to get in to a cyber-bed with them. You're all adults – they can talk to other brands if they want to – you can sometimes express an opinion with which they are not 100 per cent in agreement. That's fine. But if we treat customers and employees as potential collaborators, rather than risks that need to be managed, we might find there are unexpected benefits.

What is "Engage"?

The reason we talk about "engaging" with an audience through social media and social technologies in general is because that is what we do with conversations. We engage in conversation. Conversation is a dialogue – between two or more people. There is a subtle but significant difference between having a conversation and talking to someone. When you talk to someone there is no indication that you actually do any listening – it suggests a one-way transfer of ideas. The whole point of social technologies is, as explained at the beginning of the book, that there is a two-way interchange of ideas, concepts, and opinions. When the pharmaceutical company discussed in Chapter 30 asked its sales and marketing people to observe the conversations and interactions that take place, it was to avoid using the wrong tone – to avoid hectoring or lecturing to the group – to avoid having the people in that community feel that they were being sold to, badgered, or shouted at.

Engaging is as much about listening as it is about talking. It is about giving the community in question time and space to air their views rather than assuming that they will only be interested in yours. It is about discussing their views too, rather than "listening" and then saying "that's lovely – now listen to this…"

Engaging is as much about listening as it is about talking

Engaging Engagement

The steps to properly engage are obvious. That is, they should be obvious. We all know how to have conversations with friends. However, some engage better in conversations than others. Some choose to use every opportunity to argue or complain such that their friends, those who have to put up with the endless arguments or complaints, either get sick of that individual or play the game and argue back and complain back. Some, such as those trained in psychoanalysis or coaching, know how to listen and focus on the other person to such an extent that they never show anything of themselves. As with much in life, there is a middle ground, where we take turns to talk. We listen to the other. We comment on what the other has said. We empathize when necessary, we show sympathy if appropriate, we confirm beliefs we share and we play devil's advocate to help them see the other side.

That middle ground is what any organization should aim to achieve when engaging with social technologies. Ask our audience (be they customers, employees, suppliers, etc.) questions; listen to their answers and probe to truly understand what they mean. When our audience asks us questions, we should answer honestly. If we don't know the answer, we should say so (bull won't last long in the social sphere where it can be proved wrong quicker than you can say "Google"). We should respond quickly. This might mean setting goals for those engaging with the social technologies (not just the champions) on how quickly they should respond to messages from the community:

When our audience asks us questions, we should answer honestly

• Answer all Tweets in twenty-four hours?
• Only during office-hours?
• Have someone "on-call" 24/7 in the virtual world of choice?
• Match the timetable of social technology engagement with the timezone of your audience?

Make your engagement fun. Are you, as an organization, able to laugh at yourselves? Are you able to show that you are human? Don't mock the competition – that just looks like bullying (if you are larger) or that you feel threatened (if you're smaller). Don't mock the community for the same reason. Be sufficiently self-confident that you can laugh at yourselves. If a member of your target community (such as a customer) makes a video mocking you, don't stifle it. Don't ignore it. Promote it! Just make sure that you don't ignore unhappy customers to the extent that they feel the need to make damning portrayals of your organization – that way even the mocking ones will be done by brand ambassadors. People who love the brand and feel comfortable with it (inside or outside the organization) will feel the confidence that they can make a joke and it won't backfire on them. Encourage that atmosphere. That encouragement can only come from the top – from the leadership of the team, the department, or the organization as a whole.

Remember, most people are human. There is a place for humor in business. The most innovative organizations of the past twenty years have truly understood this. They have endeavored to make their workplaces fun places to be – not sterile, soulless, desks with beige dividers and clock-watching staff members who are as engaged with the organization as a prisoner is with their jail.

What Should We Say?

When posting your part of the conversation with your audience, you should also think about why you are doing it. Ask yourself if your post is truly interesting, if it is something you would actually take time out to read yourself. If it is a press release, send it to the press, not your social media platforms. If it is a product release, be clear why you are talking about it through social media – for your audience to comment on it, to offer early-bird discounts, to get feedback and suggestions for improvement, or as cheap advertising. If the latter, then it might be better to rethink the post; social technologies are for engaging in conversation, so don't use them to broadcast.

If members of your audience do have suggestions to improve the product, be sure to listen carefully and pass them to your research and development (R&D) team.

How Often Should We Say it?

There is much conflicting advice about how often an individual or an organization should post through social technologies. If it is internal knowledge sharing, then only post when there is knowledge to share. You might need to consider that what is obvious to you is not to others, so there could be a good argument for sharing things which are not necessarily "new." If it is an external audience, the definitive answer to how often you should post is "it depends."

If your organization is involved in a sector that has quickly-changing criteria on an hourly basis – for example, with share-dealing, currency trading, traffic flow, or transport punctuality – you will probably want to post updates at least once per hour on your platform of choice.

For a "slower" business that doesn't change on a day-to-day basis, such as in education or law, you might choose to only post occasionally. For example, when there are news stories suitable for your students, or new cases that create precedents.

I once read advice that people, and organizations, must post on Twitter a minimum of six times per day. To do this, when you have nothing to say, is ridiculous. If your community are asking questions or discussing issues on which you have an expert opinion, then do please answer the questions and share your expertise. But if the only way you can fill that target of six posts per day is by explaining the banal, then I ask you, for the sake of humanity and all that is sane, please desist. No one cares about the latte you had for breakfast unless you are trying to engage people to talk about lattes and their relative merits as part of an over-arching strategy to change people's breakfasts – and if that is the case do please explain upon what research you have based your opinion that breakfast needs to change. Likewise, people are not interested in the weather in your part of the world – unless your business fundamentally depends on the weather (transport, construction, sport, weather predictions, etc.).

Say Again?

In summary:

1. **L**isten.
2. **E**xpress opinions.
3. **A**nswer questions.

4. **D**on't preach.
5. **E**veryone needs a reply.
6. **R**elevance, not nonsense.
7. **S**eek feedback.
8. **H**umility is best.
9. **I**nteract at all levels of the organization.
10. **P**ost often, but not too much.

This mnemonic, LEADERSHIP, is not (of course) an accident. Leaders can show leadership by engaging with social technologies. Leadership always involves listening to the stakeholders (unless you're in the army and most of us are not). Leadership is about being humble when receiving feedback. Leadership is about showing others how it's done.

chapter 34

Review

In the SITCER™ framework (Chapter 28) the "review"
element comes last not because it is the least important but because it is the end of the first iteration
of the process. But you cannot implement
social technologies and then just leave
them and assume everything will carry
on working as originally intended. The
history of social technologies is a history of
iterative developments, of users feeding back
and improving the product and the overall experience, of businesses assuming that that which cannot
be measured has no value. The internet, through the
main platforms of websites, has shown how everything can be measured,
for example on the full customer journey, all the different influences that
a customer was exposed to on their way to completing a purchase both
online and offline can be tracked. As the GPS (global positioning system) in
smartphones allows the tracking of consumers physically in the real world
as they go from shop to shop and are exposed to marketing messages,
and as this is tied in to the marketing messages they have seen online and
through social technologies, the potential to better know what works and
what does not work for the smallest subset of a target audience is immense.

Metrics can be great – statistics and business intelligence; market
research, surveys, and focus groups; analytics on everything. All this can

help us as organizations to see what has worked and what has not; what has met the customers' needs and what has fallen short. Of course, any savvy company is going to know what the customer needs long before they implement anything – but how one measures success is important.

To Measure Success, You Must Define Success

Success for social technologies will always depend on whatever the original strategy was. If it was to engage the target audience, that can be tracked. One can measure how many in that segment have engaged with the brand through the different technologies – how much time they spend doing so, how often (and to whom) they have recommended the brand, and so on. This might not make any difference to the sales of the organization – or so it seems – but one will never know if sales might have fallen had social technologies not been implemented.

If the strategy is to capture knowledge within the organization and make it easier for people to find others they need to talk to, to make it easier for individuals to share tricks, tips, and tools that work for them and might work for others, to make the process of contacting suppliers or potential customers more seamless and avoiding repletion, then all of these things can be tracked.

If the aim is to use social technologies as a channel for the customer services department to engage with customers, then the number of interactions, the number of problems solved, the number of complaints received, and the number of customers who have helped others with some technical details can all be tracked.

You and Whose Army?

There are, as was mentioned before, plenty of companies now offering different types of software to measure the impact of social technologies for organizations. They are able to identify if the mention of a brand is positive or negative. They can measure the impact of that mention; for example, if the person has an army of followers on Twitter numbering in the millions, the impact of that mention is going to be much larger than for someone who has only a couple of hundred followers.

The software can help organizations remember that whilst all customers are equal, some are more equal than others. A complaint in front of millions will need a swift and subtle response to help satisfy the needs of the complainant (and here, more than ever, honesty and humility are important – the millions will manage to see through corporate bull remarkably quickly). A complaint from a "normal" person with a relatively limited number of followers should, however, also be treated with the same level of concern.

whilst all customers are equal, some are more equal than others

Build it, Leave it and Forget about it?

Just as it is no good building a platform or a presence with social technologies and assuming, or hoping, that your target audience will flock to engage with you on that platform, you equally cannot start the project, put all the incentives and champions in place, entrust the workforce and your customers to have an open conversation, and then just forget about it. Other projects come along. Other priorities arise. Personnel change and are not properly inducted into the new systems. Other areas of the business might have ignored (or simply not known about) the social technologies and start to create one for themselves in isolation, or a campaign that makes no reference at all to the social technologies.

Strategy

The strategy – whilst hopefully founded on the best analysis of the industry, the sector, the competition, the customers, and the organization itself – might suddenly be faced with an unexpected turn of events. The world economic collapse in 2008 is a good example. It could be a new conflict involving one or more of the countries with which you do business (and in whose languages you engage through social technologies). Perhaps a new product – a substitute – comes out of left field and makes the core offering of the organization redundant. It could be that the social technology landscape has changed and new tools or platforms have arrived that supersede the incumbent dominant one, which will require a review to see if the new platform should be adopted at all, partially or completely; to see through trials if it is relevant for the target audience and if so, over what timescale it should be adopted.

Therefore, as with any strategic initiative, the strategy itself will need to be reviewed periodically. In part this is to see if the situation is relatively unchanged for the strategy to still be relevant. Whilst the strategy might have originally been focused on sharing knowledge within the organization, if it has proven to be a great success then it might be expanded to include the use of social media for marketing, or crowdsourcing product development. If the implementation has not been a success, then lessons should be taken so that the issues are resolved and the same mistakes are not made during further possible implementations of the straegy.

Incentives

The incentives must be reviewed to see if they are still relevant and attractive for the target audience. For example, should financial salaries increase in line with inflation? Should other benefits be introduced? Can key performance indicators (KPIs) be set across the organization to encourage greater engagement without neglecting the core offering from the organization? Is the implementation receiving sufficient attention from the executive board and is that attention obvious? It might be that a full-scale review of what would motivate the target audience is required.

Trust

Trust will remain unchanged, one hopes, but it is always worth reflecting on this. One would need to see, for example, if there have been instances of employees abusing that trust. Have customer complaints through social technologies caused more remedial work by the customer services department? Has there been a noticeable drop in productivity with employees spending too much time on the social technologies (perhaps the incentives are too attractive and have not been appropriately balanced with the core targets for the business)? It might be the case that management need some training in how to manage poor performance, only now identified through excessive use of social technologies. It could be that trust has been repaid in spades with productivity, employee satisfaction, and customer satisfaction up and customer services complaints down. We should trust others as a rule. Not to do so makes us all paranoid and the world a dark place. But we should temper that trust with pragmatism and review it periodically to make sure it is still warranted.

Champion

The organization, as they would with all employees, should review how well the champions have been doing their jobs and helping others get on the platforms. Through appropriate KPIs, metrics, and feedback this should be perhaps the easiest of all the review processes. However, as mentioned before, we need to be careful not to blame the champions for a failure that might have occurred elsewhere in the framework, for example, through inappropriately set incentives or a flawed strategy.

Engage

Metrics can help measure the quantity of engagement through the number of posts, number of likes, number of reads, or amount of time on the site in question. Simple online analytics tools can show this data for the organization as a whole, the department, the team, and the individual. Peer review, through Likes, +1s, Pins, star-ratings and comments (number of comments, average length of comments, and whether or not they were positive or negative) can help identify the qualitative engagement too.

The organization should also, however, trawl the social technologies in use to see if there are conversations taking place with stakeholders that the organization is not participating in but perhaps should. Companies must monitor whether individuals should adjust the tone with which they engage with customers or fellow employees. Do employees sound professional, youthful, collegial, or helpful (as appropriate for the target audience) or do they sound patronizing, unhelpful, selfish, antagonistic, and out-of-touch?

If one of the incentives is to build engagement in to the performance appraisals of individuals, then managers should be able to conduct the review of that engagement and see for individuals if the content posted is relevant and fit-for-purpose; if it suits the message; and if it fits the organization's culture. It might be that more resources are needed to increase, for example, the number of videos posted or to monitor the comments and interactions with customers. It might be that the type of engagement needs to be adjusted, for example, to include live events (Tweets, video, or audio streaming), or that the employees need to spend a little more time simply listening. One should engage but not over-engage.

Review

The review process in the SITCER^{TM} framework (Chapter 28) also needs to be reviewed, to see if the metrics and methods of appraisal are still relevant and appropriate. It creates and needs an eternal spiral – strategize, incentivize, trust, champion, engage, review, strategize, incentivize, trust – in order to make sure that the technologies are not allowed to fail as soon as a fire needs putting out or a new project diverts attention.

If no changes are required now, great. More frequent reviews might be more preferable at the start of the implementation to make sure that things are being implemented as planned, and any issues are dealt with at the time and then incorporated into the strategy, the incentivization program, the level of trust, champions, or how to engage. Every month or even every week would be reasonable at the start of the implementation process. Once the technologies are up and running, given the frequency with which social technologies change, periodic reviews should still be at least every six months for an informal review.

When reviewing the review strategy, organizations will need to consider if they are using the right measures of success; measuring the appropriate interactions; if the metrics are still relevant to achieve what was originally intended; and whether more detailed or joined-up measures have become available since the process started that will now allow a better idea of what works and what does not. If the strategy is engaging with customers, a decision will need to be made on whether or not to employ an external agency to measure the success of that engagement. The review process, in this case, would also need to review the performance of that agency to ensure it is delivering actionable insights.

Finally…

As mentioned already in reviewing the "strategy" part of the SITCER™ framework, everyone, from leaders to managers, from marketers to knowledge sharers, and from office administrators to graduate trainees, should keep abreast of the changes in social technologies. We must review what new tools are available, what new platforms are being used, and what platforms have been overtaken and are now of no significance with the target audience. Just because something is new, it doesn't mean it has no place in an organization that "has worked perfectly well as it is for a long time already thank you very much."

Technologies are not for information systems and technology (IS&T) departments only. Social technologies are for everyone. They are not just for everyone to use but for everyone to consider using – to think about how they can possibly find benefits within their own work practices. Social technologies are the future, because they are not set in stone.

Social technologies do not rely on wires and hard drives, or on SSD cards. Social technologies do not rely on wearable computing, Wi-Fi, or even the internet. Social technologies could be tools that are useful in a specific unit within the organization, or could engage the entire planet. Social technologies are, by their nature, for everyone. Not for everyone to use – some will be closed to a sub-set or a specific group – but for everyone to appraise. If you, as a manager, as a leader, are not aware of what tools are around, you have no opportunity to explore their potential use within the organization. Worse – if you assume that new technologies are "for kids" or "for techies" or irrelevant to your organization, you are doomed to either fail in the long term or eat humble pie.

Organizations do not have to be innovative and entrepreneurial to embrace new technologies – only to ensure that they are not burying their heads in the sand and assuming that all the technology they will ever need has already been invented. It hasn't. Before this book hits the shelves, there will be new technologies available that have not been mentioned. There will be new platforms that have captured the zeitgeist. There will be new scaremongering by certain quarters that we are giving away the keys to the treasury if we allow customers, or employees, to take part in our decision-making process.

The future's bright. Just don't be blinded.

Part 4

The Future's Bright...

35

The Future of Technology

Prediction is very difficult, especially about the future.
Niels Bohr, Danish physicist (1885–1962)

New technologies don't die – they just make us feel old.
Then we get used to them. Then we wonder what people did before that technology existed.

Thomas J. Watson, from IBM, is said to have
stated in 1943: "I think there is a world market for about five computers." Whether
or not Watson said this, a brief look
at the state of computing at the time
suggests that it is not as ridiculous a
statement as at first it might seem. It was
only in 1944 that IBM designed and built the
Harvard Mark-1 (conceived by Howard Aiken from
Harvard)[1] and the era of modern computing only
started coming into its own from 1939 onwards. Much of the investment came from the military (such as the UK's "Bombe" for decrypting
Nazi coded communications, made possible with the work of Alan
Turing, amongst others) or was for academic purposes. In 1949, the
first practical stored-program computer, EDSAC, was built at Cambridge
University. This was in part thanks to funding from Lyons Tea Co. who

New technologies don't die – they just make us feel old. Then we get used to them. Then we wonder what people did before that technology existed

built the world's first computer for business applications based on the EDSAC in 1951,[2] known as LEO I (Lyons Electronic Office I). Ironically (though, again, it is disputed whether or not this was ever actually uttered), Cambridge professor Douglas Hartree is claimed to have said: "all the calculations that would ever be needed in this country could be done on the three digital computers … in Cambridge, … Teddington and … Manchester. No one else would ever need machines of their own, or would be able to afford to buy them."

So how could Watson and Hartree (and doubtless millions of others at the same time) have been so mistaken about the global demand for computers and the miniaturization that made personal computing possible and allowed many in the developed world to carry powerful computers wherever they go in the form of smartphones and tablets? Would we, in their position, have made different predictions? I suspect not.

It is worth remembering our own first experiences with certain technologies. In the 1980s, mobile phones were the preserve of the very rich and required a separate briefcase-sized battery pack to be carried around. Even when they became small enough to be handheld bricks, they were a symbol of city professionals and conspicuous consumption. I acquired my first mobile phone relatively early, in 1995, to be the company phone in a business I started with two others – whoever was on duty would have the mobile and field the calls. The university computer department I studied at in the 1980s had no personal computers, only mainframes with terminals that students could log on to. It was a rare student who had their own computer capable of word-processing their assignments. Friend geeks in the early 1980s began experimenting with computing if they were fortunate enough to be bought Sinclair ZX81s, then Sinclair Spectrums, Commodores, and BBC Micros by their parents – but few adults had access to any kind of computer in the home.

It is worth remembering how things have developed since then to help see how things might develop in the future. Innovations and new technologies often receive much attention from the press only to then be dismissed shortly afterwards (a year or two later) when the promised benefits didn't materialize – either because the promises were excessive and not based on reality, or the expected timeline to achieving those benefits was too short.

Gartner's Hype Cycle

Gartner, the technology research firm, produced the first Hype Cycle in 2007. This measured hype for different technologies (the excessive and intensive promotion by the media, the organization concerned, or even the general public of an idea, product, or service) over time. Gartner identified five stages on the Hype Cycle: (i) technology trigger; (ii) peak of inflated expectations; (iii) trough of disillusionment; (iv) slope of enlightenment; and (v) plateau of productivity. The first stage, the "technology trigger," could be compared to the "innovation" or "early adopter" stages of the diffusion process or the product life cycle (see Chapter 16) and is the typical "hockey stick" slope of sharply rising growth in hype over a new product. The technology press – by definition consisting of large numbers of early adopters who are targeted by organizations with innovations to help create word-of-mouth publicity, hype, and interest from investors or other potential business partners – are usually the ones who drive the hype such that even the general public will often know about a product or service long before it is ready to be publicly released or is ready for general consumption.

For greater detail on the Hype Cycle, readers are advised to investigate Gartner's publications, such as *Mastering the Hype Cycle: How to Choose the Right Innovation at the Right Time*.[3] However, it is worth looking at some of the Hype Cycles over the past few years to show how things have developed.

In 2006, for example, Web 2.0 (or social technologies, as we have called it for most of this text) was at the peak of inflated expectations (where the innovation reaches the mainstream press and achieves the highest level of visibility while being touted as the greatest thing since sliced bread). It is worth noting, however, that wikis and folksonomies, all part of the Web 2.0 ecosystem, were already sliding down (in an inverted hockey stick curve) from those inflated expectations into the trough of disillusionment (where everyone assumes the technology was a passing fad, fundamentally flawed with no place in business and no business model, or would never gain traction). At this point the hype and visibility of the new technology is at the lowest point since launch. The danger of a technology reaching this stage at a particular point in a start-up's life is that it would be harder to get investment to help the company survive until it reaches the "plateau of productivity." In 2007, Web 2.0 was also sliding down that slope and by 2008 it languished at the bottom of the trough with people assuming that it was simply another way to waste time.

By 2009, however, it was beginning to rise up the "slope of enlightenment" – where the press and the general public begin to see legitimate uses of the technology, the price is perhaps reduced so that the technology becomes more affordable to a wider population making it easier to achieve critical mass (see Chapter 21). There will have by now been some widely publicized and celebrated cases of how the technology has enabled a particular company to achieve a particular goal. By 2010 it didn't even figure on the chart at all – having reached the plateau of productivity where everyone understands that it is now simply another part of the way the world works and nothing to be fearful of.

Virtual is Real

Virtual Worlds, by contrast, have been languishing in the trough of disillusionment since passing the peak of inflated expectations in 2007. This explains the director of one London-based media agency, who students of mine interviewed as part of a project in 2012, saying: "If you are researching virtual worlds, you are studying history, not technology management." The students, unfortunately, had been sworn to secrecy and would not divulge the name of the interviewee, so I was unable to contact him or her personally and explain Gartner's Hype Cycle. As explained before, virtual worlds are complicated and difficult to use. There are various obstacles to their uptake and they won't reach the plateau of productivity for some years yet. But they will eventually, and the latest (at the time of writing) Hype Cycle from Gartner shows them slowly moving off the bottom of the trough of disillusionment and up the slope of enlightenment.

This prediction is based on research by KZero, as mentioned in Chapter 14, showing the number of virtual worlds currently in existence, sorted by the average age of the registered users and the numbers of regular users. For example, for the ages twenty-five and above (Figure 35.1) there are nine virtual worlds of any significance (worlds with less than a million registered users are not included). The largest of these is Second Life with an average of forty-one million regular registered users – double the number in 2009 but not experiencing the exponential growth enjoyed by newer platforms. There are twenty-two million regular registered users on the closest other world for this demographic, Utherverse.

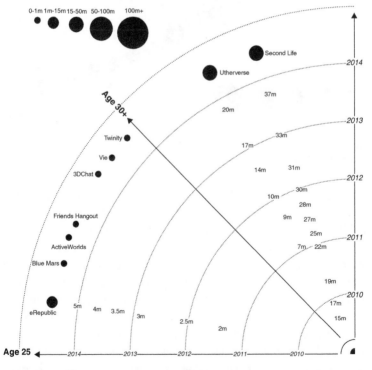

FIGURE 35.1 / Virtual World Universe Chart from 25+ courtesy of KZero

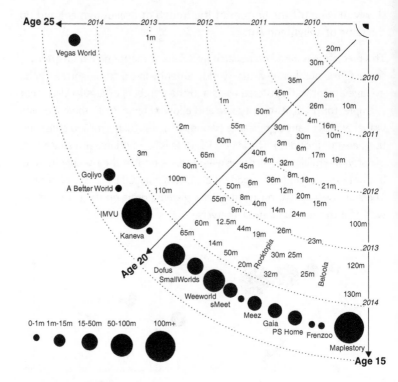

FIGURE 35.2 Virtual World Universe Chart from 15–25 years of age courtesy of KZero

Figure 35.2 shows five MUVEs for ages twenty to twenty-five with IMVU being the largest with 120 million registered users. The number suddenly increases to eleven MUVEs for the fifteen to twenty age group, with PS Home on twenty-eight million users, Gaia on thirty million, Meez on thirty-five million, Weeworld on fifty-five million (down from a high of seventy-five million two years previously), Dofus on seventy million, and Maplestory on 140 million registered users. It is worth remembering that Maplestory was only known in its native South Korea until 2010 when it grew to its current 130 million users – showing how quickly new brands and platforms can come to dominate a sector or a target audience. The thirteen to fifteen age group has thirteen virtual worlds (see Figure 35.3) with Habbo only the second largest on

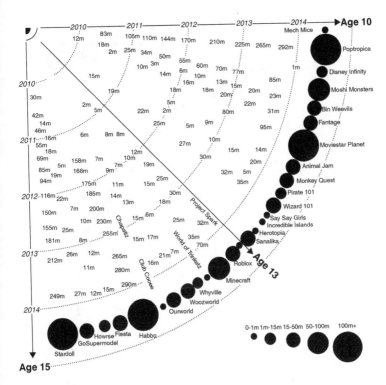

FIGURE 35.3 Virtual World Universe Chart from 10–13 years of age courtesy of KZero

295 million regular registered users and Stardoll currently most popular growing over six-fold from forty-six million registered users in 2009 to 310 million in 2014.

The ten to thirteen year olds have fifteen worlds now (Figure 35.3), down from twenty-four in 2009 as funding has dried up for some of them. Poptropica has grown with its audience over the past few years, up to 313 million users compared with eighty-three million in 2009. Moviestar planet didn't exist in 2009 (now on 182 million) and Moshi Monsters grew from twelve to ninety million users in the same time.

For eight to ten year olds (Figure 35.4) there are twenty MUVEs of size, where the big names are Neopets (up from fifty-eight million users to

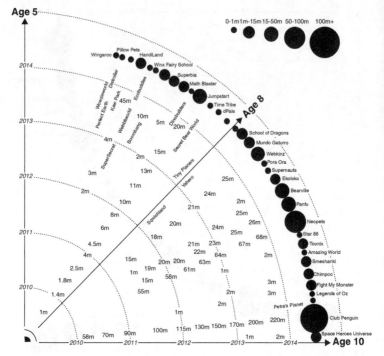

FIGURE 35.4 Virtual World Universe Chart from 5-10 years of age courtesy of KZero

seventy-five million) and Club Penguin, up from a healthy thirty-two million users in 2009 to 225 million in 214.

Finally, the early-school years of five to eight year olds have fourteen worlds to choose between with twenty-two million using Jumpstart and ten million, with an average age of six, being regular users of Boombang (also Figure 35.4).

The reason for going into such detail about the number and size of virtual worlds, knowing full-well that the information will be out-of-date by the time this book is read, is to show just how big this (virtual) universe really is.

Looking at the whole "universe" together in Figure 35.5, whilst much of the detail will be lost due to the size of the page, it is useful to see

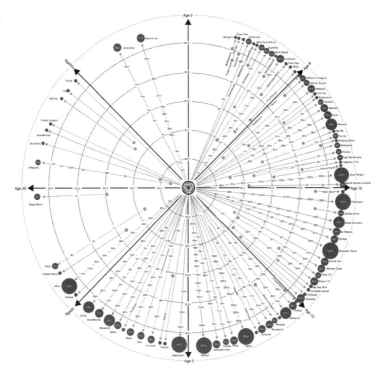

FIGURE 35.5 Virtual World Complete Universe Chart courtesy of KZero

the dominance of virtual worlds for children and teenagers compared to adults. And that is not because they are toys. Second Life has shown what is possible in a business context, the dozens of MUVEs aimed at young people demonstrate how a new generation has embraced them as a means of communicating, collaborating, and being.

These children will go through higher education in ten to fifteen years, and then into the workplace in fifteen to twenty years. They will be as comfortable with virtual worlds for all types of communication and interaction as we all are now with telephones and email, and as some of us are already with social networks and status updates. Exactly how long it will take for virtual worlds to reach the plateau of productivity is, clearly, difficult to say – but there should be no doubt that virtual worlds will be a very important channel of communication and an environment in which learning, social interaction, and business can take place.

3D Printing is a technology that has also been around for many years, first appearing in the technology trigger period in 2007. Yet, in the most recent Hype Cycle from Gartner in 2012, it is still only at the peak of inflated expectations. More and more people are beginning to understand what 3D printing can do. 3D printers are now affordable enough for the home or small office, well below $500. High-street print shops are now able to 3D print on the premises and large department stores offer customers the chance to be 3D scanned and have a small figurine of themselves created by a printer.

Houses have been created using 3D printers in China,[4] whilst a Dutch firm is constructing complex structures for housing using 3D printers.[5] The 2014 version of Gartner's Hype Cycle for Emerging Technologies shows, finally, that Enterprise 3D printing is now, slowly, rising up the slope of enlightenment, whilst Consumer 3D printing is still at the peak of inflated expectations. Virtual worlds, over ten years after launching as a technology, are still in the trough of disillusionment.

At the time of writing, virtual reality headsets (such as Oculus Rift, mentioned before) are becoming more affordable, mobile phones are able to project 3D "holographic" displays, and games controllers have developed to the stage that one can control computers with gestures alone. It can only be a (short) matter of time before the interface between the hardware, the human and the overall user experience is blended to combine a seamless, easy-to-use 3D world that will finally push virtual worlds up Gartner's slope of enlightenment to the plateau of productivity.

When Old was New

Another way of thinking about this is to take an every-day product and then remember back to when it first appeared. I often enjoy asking a classroom of twenty to thirty year-old postgraduates when various technologies were invented – and they never fail to conform to type and underestimate how long the innovations have been around.

For example, when I ask about the first smartphone, the typical answers focus on iPhone (launched in 2007) or even the BlackBerry (which came out in 1999), but IBM produced the first phone combining computing and telephone functions in the same device, the "Simon," in 1994 – two decades before writing this. It is only in the past two or three years that smartphones have achieved ubiquity.

What about tablet computers? There are many who think only of iPads and similar handheld tablets (first released in 2010) whilst some talk of the PC tablet computers that appeared with a Windows XP Tablet PC Edition operating system in 2001 or earlier attempts in the 1980s and 1990s. However, the RAND Tablet allowed users to draw, write, and select menu options on a touch-screen surface measuring ten inches by ten inches.[6] The price was prohibitive (£100,000 in today's money[7]) but the technology was first created in 1964.

The first digital audio player (where the music is stored within the device rather than on removable media such as cassettes, CDs, or MiniDiscs) was also around long before the iPod (released in 2001) and similar mp3 players, with the design and patents (although, unfortunately, no physical product) created in 1979 by Kane Kramer. The business plan for Kramer's IXI device showed how digital rights management would protect recordings against piracy, how music would be unbundled (previously sold as singles or albums), and how distribution would be through users filling their memory cards from music stores or buying pre-programmed cards. The only thing Kramer hadn't banked on was the internet and the ability to download without physically going to a shop.

The Future Won't Be What it Was

Moore's Law, named after Intel's co-founder, Gordon Moore, states that the number of transistors on a chip will double approximately every two years[8] – with the implication, later added, that costs would halve each time. Alvy Ray Smith, co-founder of Pixar, suggests that Moore's Law reflects the maximum speed with which humans can innovate.[9]

The futurist Ray Kurzweil's *Law of Accelerating Returns*,[10] however, suggests there is exponential growth in the rate of growth of technological change, such that we will experience 20,000 years of progress in the twenty-first century when compared to the hundred years of progress in the twentieth century. Furthermore, Armstrong has compared predictions from other futurists and agrees with Kurzweil that computer intelligence will exceed that of humans by around 2045.[11] At this point, Kurzweil says, when computers are able to design and build computers that are more intelligent still, it will be impossible to predict the speed of growth of technological advances.

Explore, Don't Ignore

All of this shows that we should not ignore innovations, no matter how ridiculous they might seem to us now. They might not reach critical mass for a few years yet. They might be aimed at another target audience or a different customer segmentation. Their main uses in the future might be a result of reinventions that have not yet occurred.

But it should be incumbent upon everyone, and particularly those in business, that new technologies should be explored, not ignored. They could add value to the organization, or they could help transform the business model. If ignored, of course, they might kill you.

Notes

Preface

1. For a full history of things not being what they used to be, readers are referred to Quote Investigator, (2013) "Nostalgia Is Not What It Used To Be" Available at: http://quoteinvestigator.com/2013/07/06/nostalgia-is-not/ [Accessed: 10 August 2013].

1 What are Social Technologies?

1. Adapted from the 3Cs Strategic Framework proposed by Ohmae, K. (1982) "The Mind of the Strategist" London: McGraw-Hill.
2. Wikipedia (2010) "Web 2.0" Available at: http://en.wikipedia.org/wiki/Web_2.0 [Accessed: 10 January 2010].
3. O'Reilly, T. (2005) "What is Web 2.0?" Available at: http://radar.oreilly.com/2005/09/what-is-web-20.html [Accessed: March 2008].
4. McAfee, A. (2006) "Enterprise 2.0: The Dawn of Emergent Collaboration," *MIT Sloan Management Review*, 47(3), 21–8. Available at: http://sloanreview.mit.edu/the-magazine/articles/2006/spring/47306/enterprise-the-dawn-of-emergent-collaboration/ [Accessed: 24 January 2010].
5. McAfee, A. (2009) *Enterprise 2.0: New Collaborative Tools for Your Organization's Toughest Challenges*. Boston: Harvard Business School Publishing.
6. Gartner (2013) "Glossary: Social Technologies" [Online] Available at: http://www.gartner.com/it-glossary/social-technologies [Accessed: 30 May 2014].
7. Wikipedia (2012) "Social Technology" [Online] Available at: http://en.wikipedia.org/wiki/Social_technology [Accessed: 18 January 2012].
8. Cauz, J. (2013) "Encyclopaedia Britannica's Transformation" Interviewed by Scott Berinato, [Podcast] *Harvard Business Review* IdeaCast, 7 February.

Available at: http://blogs.hbr.org/ideacast/2013/02/encyclopaedia-britannicas-
tran.html [Accessed: 9 February 2013].

2 Crowdsourcing

1. Galton, F. (1907) "Vox Populi" *Nature*, Vol. 75: 450–1 (7 March).
2. Perry-Coste, F.H. (1907) "The Ballot-Box" [Letter] *Nature*, Vol. 75: 509–10 (28 March).
3. Wikipedia (2006) "Wikipedia: Statistics" Available at: http://en.wikipedia. org/wiki/Wikipedia:Statistics [Accessed: 30 October 2011].
4. Wikipedia (2012) "Wikipedia: Size Comparisons" Available at: http:// en.wikipedia.org/wiki/Wikipedia:Size_comparisons [Accessed: 8 August 2012].
5. Giles, J. (2005) "Internet Encyclopaedias go Head to Head" *Nature*, Vol. 438: 900–1 (15 December).
6. *Encyclopædia Britannica*, Inc. (2006) "Fatally Flawed: Refuting the Recent Study on Encyclopaedic Accuracy by the Journal Nature" [Online] 21 March. Available at: http://corporate.britannica.com/britannica_nature_response. pdf [Accessed 22 November 2012].
7. *Nature* (2006), "Encyclopaedia Britannica and Nature: A Response" [Online] 23 March. Available at: http://www.nature.com/press_releases/Britannica_ response.pdf [Accessed 22 November 2012].
8. Tapscott, D. and Williams, A.D. (2006) *Wikinomics: How Mass Collaboration Changes Everything*. London: Atlantic Books.
9. Owen, L., Goldwasser, C., Choate, K., and Blitz, A. (2007) "The Power of Many: ABCs of Collaborative Innovation Throughout the Extended Enterprise" [Report from the IBM Institute for Business Value] Available at: http://www-935.ibm.com/services/us/gbs/bus/pdf/g510-6335-00-abc. pdf [Accessed: 14 November 2007].
10. *Nature* (2012) "Open Innovation Pavilion" Available at: http://www.nature. com/openinnovation/index.html [Accessed: 21 August 2012].
11. General Mills (2012) "Label friendly Yeast and Mold Inhibitors" G-Win Site [Online] Available at: https://genmills.inno-360.com/projects/e54a9dbe-b41132a47fc9da13d14540df/briefs/72037e3e4d68a9383b80247db2030 22a/ [Accessed: 1 December 2012].
12. IBM (2006) "Airbus Achieves A380 First Flight on Schedule with Help from IBM" [PDF] New York: IBM Corporation. Available at: ftp://ftp.software. ibm.com/software/solutions/pdfs/ODC00174-USEN-00.pdf [Accessed: 20 September 2007].

13. Amazon (2012) "Amazon Mechanical Turk: Welcome" Mturk.com [Online] Available at: https://www.mturk.com/mturk/welcome [Accessed: 10 January 2012].

14. Geeklist (2013) "Geeklist" [Online] Available at: https://geekli.st/home [Accessed: 7 January 2014].

15. Geeklist (2014) "Geeklist #Hack4Good 0.5 – Global!" [Online] Available at: https://geekli.st/hackathon/52c49d837689332d5f000019 [Accessed: 14 February 2014].

16. Hult Prize (2014) "Hult Prize: History" [Online] Available at: http://www.hultprize.org/en/about/history/ [Accessed: 20 February 2013].

17. Full disclosure: I work for Hult International Business School.

18. Vincent, J. (2014) "Russia Offers £65,000 Bounty to Identify Users on Anonymous Tor Network" (28 July) [The Independent Online] Available at: http://www.independent.co.uk/life-style/gadgets-and-tech/russia-offers-65000-bounty-to-identify-users-on-anonymous-tor-network-9633419.html [Accessed: 29 July 2014].

3   Crowdfunding

1. Kickstarter (2012) "Project Guidelines" [Online] Available at: http://www.kickstarter.com/help/guidelines [Accessed: 10 January 2012].

2. Indiegogo (2012) "Indiegogo: Home" [Online] Available at: http://www.indiegogo.com/ [Accessed: 15 January 2012].

3. WeFund.com (2012) "We Fund: Home" [Online] Available at: http://wefund.com/ [Accessed: 18 August 2012].

4. PleaseFund.us (2012) "PleaseFund.Us: Home" [Online] Available at: http://www.pleasefund.us/ [Accessed: 19 August 2012].

5. PeopleFund.It (2012) "People Fund It: Home" [Online] Available at: http://www.peoplefund.it/ [Accessed: 18 August 2012].

6. CrowdCube (2012) "CrowdCube: Home" [Online] Available at: http://www.crowdcube.com/ [Accessed: 19 August 2012].

7. Kiva.org (2012) "Kiva.org: Home" [Online] Available at: http://www.kiva.org/ [Accessed: 19 August 2012].

8. Kubaru.org (2012) "Kubaru: Home" [Online] Available at: http://www.kubaru.org/ [Accessed: 9 August 2012].

9. Kiva.org (2012) "About Us" [Online] Available at: http://www.kiva.org/about [Accessed: 19 August 2012].

10. Berman, J. (2014) "I Backed Oculus Rift On Kickstarter And All I Got Was This Lousy T-Shirt" 26 March [Online] Available at: http://www.huffingtonpost.com/2014/03/26/oculus-rift-kickstarter_n_5034511.html [Accessed: 29 March 2014].

4 Blogging

1. "What you see is what you get" – the types of editors one sees on most word processing software, for example, where the author sees how the final formatting will look.

2. Shirky, C. (2008) "It's not Information Overload, it's Filter Failure" 18 September. Web 2.0 Expo Available at: http://blip.tv/web2expo/web-2-0-expo-ny-clay-shirky-shirky-com-it-s-not-information-overload-it-s-filter-failure-1283699 [Accessed: 29 September 2009].

3. Twitterholic (2012) "The Twitaholic.com Top 100 Twitterholics based on Followers" [Online] Available at: http://twitaholic.com/ [Accessed: 8 November 2012 and 25 May 2014].

4. Zhao, B. et al (2011) "Serf and Turf: Crowdturfing for Fun and Profit." Santa Barbara: University of California Available at: http://arxiv.org/abs/1111.5654 [Accessed: 15 December 2011].

5. Chen, C. et al (2011) "Battling the Internet Water Army: Detection of Hidden Paid Posters" Available at: http://arxiv.org/abs/1111.4297 [Accessed 28 November 2011].

6. Technorati (2014) "Technorati Top 100 (1–25)" [Online] Available at: http://technorati.com/blogs/top100/ [Accessed: 25 May 2014].

7. Jarvis, J. (2005). "Dell Hell" [Blog post] Available at: http://www.buzzmachine.com/archives/cat_dell.html [Accessed: 10 January 2010].

8. Warner, B. and Yeomans, M. (2012) *#FAIL: The 50 Greatest Social Media Screw Ups and How to Avoid Being the Next One*. London: SMI.

9. Jarvis, J. (2005) "Dell Hell: Seller Beware" [Blog post] 1 July Available at: http://buzzmachine.com/2005/07/01/dell-hell-seller-beware/ [Accessed: 15 June 2007]

10. Webster, F.E. and Wind, Y. (1972) *Organizational Buying Behavior*. New Jersey: Pretence Hall.

11. Menchaca, L. (2006) "Real People are Here and We're Listening" Direct2Dell blog [Blog] 11 July. Available at: http://en.community.dell.com/dell-blogs/direct2dell/b/direct2dell/archive/2006/07/11/real-people-are-here-and-we-re-listening.aspx [Accessed: 27 June 2007]

12. TheInquirer.net (2006) "Dell Blames Battery for Exploding Notebook" [Online] Available at: http://www.theinquirer.net/inquirer/news/1029097/dell-blames-battery-exploding-notebook [Accessed: 17 September 2007].

13. Fried, I. and Krazit, T. (2006) "Apple Recalls 1.8 Million Batteries" 24 August [Online] Available at: http://news.cnet.com/Apple-recalls-1.8-million-batteries/2100-1041_3-6109198.html [Accessed: 30 August 2006].

14. Menchaca, L. (2010) "Dell's Next Step: The Social Media Listening Command Center" Direct2Dell blog [Blog] 8 December. Available at http://en.community.dell.com/dell-blogs/direct2dell/b/direct2dell/archive/2010/12/08/dell-s-next-step-the-social-media-listening-command-center.aspx [Accessed: 10 December 2010].

15. Menchaca, L. (2009) "Expanding Connections with Customers through Social Media" Direct2Dell blog [Blog] 8 December. Available at: http://en.community.dell.com/dell-blogs/direct2dell/b/direct2dell/archive/2009/12/08/expanding-connections-with-customers-through-social-media.aspx [Accessed: 17 January 2010].

16. Arthur, C. (2006) "What is the 1% Rule?" *The Guardian* [Online] 20 July Available at: http://www.guardian.co.uk/technology/2006/jul/20/guardianweeklytechnologysection2 [Accessed: 20 March 2008].

17. Li, C. and Bernoff, J.(2008) *Groundswell: Winning in a World Transformed by Social Technologies*. Boston: Harvard Business School Press.

18. Bernoff, J. (2010) "Social Technographics: Conversationalists get onto the Ladder" 19 January [Blog] Available at: http://forrester.typepad.com/groundswell/weekly_data_chart/ [Accessed: 10 February 2010].

19. Forrester Research (2009) "What's the Social Technographics Profile of Your Customers?" Available at: http://empowered.forrester.com/tool_consumer.html [Accessed: 15 November 2009].

20. GE (2012) "GE Reports" [Online] Available at: http://www.gereports.com/ [Accessed 20 October 2012].

21. Schaefer, M. (2011) "The 10 Best Corporate Blogs in the World" [blog] Available at: http://www.businessesgrow.com/2011/01/05/the-10-best-corporate-blogs-in-the-world/ [Accessed: 20 January 2012].

22. Disney Parks (2012) "Disney Parks Blog" [Online] Available at: http://disneyparks.disney.go.com/blog/ [Accessed 20 January 2012].

23. Southwest Airlines (2012) "Nuts About SouthWest" [Blog] Available at: http://www.blogsouthwest.com/blog/medical-transportation-grant-program-turns-miles-smiles [Accessed: 21 January 2012].

24. Langert, B. (2011) "Reflections from CSR discussions in China" AboutMcDonalds.com [Blog entry] 1 February 2011. Available at: http://community.aboutmcdonalds.com/t5/Let-s-Talk/Reflections-from-CSR-discussions-in-China/ba-p/40 [Accessed: 22 February 2011].

25. Marriott, B. (2007) "Uncharted Territory" Marriott on the Move [blog entry] 15 January Available at: http://www.blogs.marriott.com/marriott-on-the-move/2007/01/uncharted-territory.html [Accessed: 17 September 2007].

26. Halzack, S. (2008) *"Marketing Moves to the Blogosphere"* Washington Post [Online] 25 August. Available at: http://www.washingtonpost.com/wp-dyn/content/article/2008/08/24/AR2008082401517.html [Accessed: 10 August 2010].

27. Torkells, E. (2008) "Et tu, Bill Marriott?" Budget Travel [Blog entry] 10 June. Available from: http://www.budgettravel.com/blog/et-tu-bill-marriott,9912/ [Accessed: 10 July 2012].

28. Op cit.

29. Kador, J. (2011) "Chief Executive's Top Ten CEO Blogs" ChiefExecutive.net [Blog entry] 26 September. Available at: http://chiefexecutive.net/chief-executives-top-ten-ceo-blogs [Accessed: 7 August 2012].

30. Goldstein, A. (2012) "Sea Views" [Blog] Available at: http://www.answeri-troyally.com/blog/ [Accessed: 31 October 2012].

31. Colony, G. (2012) "The Counterintuitive CEO" [Blog] Available at: http://blogs.forrester.com/ceo_colony [Accessed: 31 October 2012].

32. Glocer, T. (2012) "Tom Glocer's Blog" [Blog] Available at: http://tomglocer.com/ [Accessed: 31 October 2012].

33. Roberts, K. (2012) "KR Connect" [Blog] Available at: http://krconnect.blogspot.co.uk/ [Accessed: 31 October 2012].

34. Greene, J. (2011) "Scoop: Oracle scrubs site of embarrassing Java blog" Cnet.com [Online] 22 July. Available at: http://news.cnet.com/8301-1023_3-20082151-93/scoop-oracle-scrubs-site-of-embarrassing-java-blog/ [Accessed: 30 January 2012]

35. Branson, R. (2012) "Why aren't more business leaders online?" LinkedIn.com [Blog entry] 22 October 2012. Available at: http://www.linkedin.com/today/post/article/20121019130632-204068115-why-aren-t-more-business-leaders-online?trk=mp-details-rr-rmpost [Accessed: 22 October 2012]

36. IBM (2012) "Leading through Connections" [Online] Available at: http://www-935.ibm.com/services/us/en/c-suite/ceostudy2012/ [Accessed: 22 October 2012].

37. JNJBTW.com (2007) "About JNJ BTW" [Blog] Available at: http://www.jnjbtw.com/about-jnj-btw/ [Accessed: 10 July 2008].

38. Monseau, M. (2007) "Welcome to JNJ BTW" [Blog entry] Available at: http://jnjbtw.com/2007/06/welcome-to-jnj-btw/ [Accessed: 10 January 2010].

39. Nokia (2012) "Conversations by Nokia" Nokia Conversations [Blog] Available at: http://conversations.nokia.com/ [Accessed: 20 August 2012].

40. The White House (2012) "The White House: President Barack Obama" [Blog] Available at: http://www.whitehouse.gov/blog [Accessed: 20 September 2012].

41. Gillard, J. (2012) "Blog" Prime Minister of Australia: the Hon Julia Gillard MP [Blog] Available at: http://www.pm.gov.au/blog [Accessed: 30 October 2012].

42. HM Government (2012) "News Stories" The Official Site of the British Prime Minister's Office [Online] Available at: http://www.number10.gov.uk/news-type/news-stories/ [Accessed: 20 September 2012].

43. Cabinet Office (2011) "Hundreds of Government Websites Closed" 7 October. [Online] Available at: http://www.cabinetoffice.gov.uk/news/hundreds-government-websites-closed [Accessed: 31 October 2012].

44. Cabinet Office (2012) "Social Media Guidance for Civil Servants" 17 May. [Online] Available at: http://www.cabinetoffice.gov.uk/resource-library/social-media-guidance [Accessed: 30 July 2012].

45. Lynch, C.G. (2007) "How to Use Enterprise Blogs to Streamline Project Management" CIO.com [online] 7 December. Available at: http://www.cio.com/article/163250/How_to_Use_Enterprise_Blogs_to_Streamline_Project_Management_ [Accessed: 17 July 2008].

46. IBM Global Services (2011) "From Social Media to Social CRM: What Customers Want" Available at: http://www-935.ibm.com/services/us/gbs/thoughtleadership/ibv-social-crm-whitepaper.html [Accessed: 20 January 2012].

47. Hubspot (2012) "The 2012 State of Inbound Marketing" [PDF] Available at: http://blog.hubspot.com/Portals/249/docs/ebooks/the_2012_state_of_inbound_marketing.pdf [Accessed: 31 October 2012].

48. Hubspot (2010) "The 2010 State of Inbound Marketing" [PDF] Available at: http://www.hubspot.com/Portals/53/docs/resellers/reports/state_of_inbound_marketing.pdf [Accessed: 31 October 2012].

49. Netcraft (2012) "October 2012 Web Surver Survey" 2 October. [Online] Available at: http://news.netcraft.com/archives/category/web-server-survey/ [Accessed: 20 October 2012].

50. Sullivan, D. (2007) "Google Kills Bush's Miserable Failure Search & Other Google Bombs" SearchEngineLand.com [Online] 25 January. Available at: http://searchengineland.com/google-kills-bushs-miserable-failure-search-other-google-bombs-10363 [Accessed: 20 July 2008].

51. WebProNews (2008) "Confirmed: Crusaders Google Bomb Scientology" [Online] 30 January. Available at: http://www.webpronews.com/confirmed-crusaders-google-bomb-scientology-2008-01 [Accessed: 5 July 2009].

52. Wired.com (2008) " 'Google Bomb' an Enemy" How-To Wiki [Online] Available at: http://howto.wired.com/wiki/'Google_Bomb'_an_Enemy [Accessed: 10 February 2009].

5 Microblogging

1. Lacy, S. (2008) "SXSW: Not Much to Twitter About" BusinessWeek [Online] Available at: http://www.businessweek.com/stories/2008-03-13/sxsw-not-much-to-twitter-aboutbusinessweek-business-news-stock-market-and-financial-advice [Accessed: 7 April 2008].

2. McClure, D. (2008) "The Problem with the Zuckerberg-Lacy interview @ SXSW: Sarah's not a Geek" [Blog] 9 March. Available at: http://500hats. typepad.com/500blogs/2008/03/the-problem-wit.html [Accessed: 11 March 2008].

3. Jarvis, J. (2008) "Zuckerberg Interview: What Went Wrong" [Blog] 10 March. Available at: http://buzzmachine.com/2008/03/10/zuckerberg-interview-what-went-wrong/ [Accessed: 11 March 2008].

4. Terdiman, D. (2008). "Journalist becomes the Story at Mark Zuckerberg SXSWi Keynote" Cnet [Online] 9 March. Available at: http://news.cnet.com/8301-13772_3-9889528-52.html [Accessed: 11 March 2008].

5. Thompson, B. (2008). "How Twitter makes it Real" BBCNews.com [Online] 10 March. Available at: http://news.bbc.co.uk/1/hi/technology/7287536.stm [Accessed: 11 March 2008].

6. SXSW (2010) "SXSW Keynote: Mark Zuckerberg - SXSW 2008" [Video Online] Available at: http://www.youtube.com/watch?v=-mvz9nv4x5U [Accessed 11 June 2010].

7. Google (2012) "Search query: sarah lacy mark zuckerberg interview sxsw 2008 " [Online] Available at: http://www.google.com/search?q=sarah+lacy+mark+zuckerberg+interview+sxsw+2008 [Accessed: 12 September 2012].

8. Gruenbaum, R. (2009) "Get Ambition - 'Does the arts speak digital?'" [Blog] 17 July. Available at: http://www.technowaffle.com/search/label/arts%20council [Accessed: 8 November 2012].

9. Mydans, S. (2007) "Monks' Protest Is Challenging Burmese Junta" New York Times [Online] 24 September. Available at: http://www.nytimes.com/2007/09/24/world/asia/24myanmar.html [Accessed: 12 October 2007].

10. OpenNet Initiative (2008) "Pulling the Plug: A Technical Review of the Internet Shutdown in Burma" [Online] Available at: http://opennet.net/research/bulletins/013 [Accessed: 2 January 2009].

11. Huang, C. (2011) "Facebook and Twitter key to Arab Spring uprisings: report" The National. [Online] 6 June. Available at: http://www.thenational.ae/news/uae-news/facebook-and-twitter-key-to-arab-spring-uprisings-report [Accessed: 28 August 2012].

12. Specsavers (2012) "Should Have Gone to Specsavers... #Korea pic.twitter. com/nqDSU8oR" [Microblog] 26 July. https://twitter.com/Specsavers/sta tus/228540086445297664 [Accessed: 28 July 2012].

13. Cole, K. (2011) "Millions are in uproar in #Cairo. Rumor is they heard our new spring collection is now available online at http://bit.ly/KCairo - KC" [Microblog] 3 February. Available at: http://mashable.com/2011/02/03/ kenneth-cole-egypt/ [Accessed: 5 February 2011].

14. BBC (2009) "Habitat sorry for Iran Tweeting" BBC [Online] 24 June. Available at: http://news.bbc.co.uk/1/hi/uk/8116869.stm [Accessed: 5 February 2011].

15. Lubin, G. (2012) "McDonald's Twitter Campaign Goes Horribly Wrong #McDStories" Business Insider [Online] 24 January. Available at: http:// www.businessinsider.com/mcdonalds-twitter-campaign-goes-horribly- wrong-mcdstories-2012-1 [Accessed: 10 February 2012].

16. Chowney, V. (2012) "Snickers 'hijacks' Katie Price's Twitter account for PR stunt" Econsultancy.com [Online] 22 January. Available at: http://econsul- tancy.com/us/blog/8768-snickers-hijacks-katie-price-s-twitter-account-for- pr-stunt [Accessed: 12 March 2012].

17. *The Guardian* (2012) "Media Talk Podcast: The Demise of the PCC and Rio's Sweet Tweets" Media Talk podcast [Podcast] 9 March. Available at: http:// www.guardian.co.uk/media/audio/2012/mar/09/media-talk-podcast- disney?INTCMP=SRCH [Accessed: 12 March 2012].

18. ASA (2012) "ASA Adjudication on Mars Chocolate UK Ltd" Advertising Standards Authority [Online] 7 March. Available at: http://www.asa. org.uk/Rulings/Adjudications/2012/3/Mars-Chocolate-UK-Ltd/SHP_ ADJ_185389.aspx [Accessed: 12 March 2012].

19. Pingdom (2011) "Internet 2012 in Numbers" Pingdom.com [Online]. 12 January. Available at: http://royal.pingdom.com/2011/01/12/internet- 2010-in-numbers/ [Accessed: 20 February 2012].

20. Radicati Group, Inc. (2011) "Why You Should Consider CloudBased Email Archiving" [PDF] 29 January. Available at: http://www.radicati.com/wp/ wp-content/uploads/2011/01/Why-You-Should-Consider-Cloud-Based- Email-Archiving.pdf [Accessed: 20 February 2012].

21. Radicati Group, Inc. (2012) "Email Statistics Report, 2012-2016" [PDF] 29 January. Available at: http://www.radicati.com/wp/wp-content/ uploads/2012/08/Email-Statistics-Report-2012-2016-Executive-Summary. pdf [Accessed: 30 May 2012].

22. Chui, M., Manyika, J., Bughin, J., Dobbs, R., Roxburgh, C., Sarrazin, H., Sands G., and Westergren, M. (2012) "The Social Economy: Unlocking Value and

Productivity through Social Technologies" [PDF] McKinsey Global Institute 29 January. Available at: http://www.mckinsey.com/insights/mgi/research/ technology_and_innovation/the_social_economy [Accessed: 30 May 2012].

23. BBC (2011) "Atos Boss Thierry Breton Defends his Internal Email Ban" BBC [Online] 6 December. Available from: http://www.bbc.co.uk/news/ technology-16055310 [Accessed: 20 April 2012].

24. Frum, D. (2012) "The Challenge for Cable News" CNN [Online] Available at: http://edition.cnn.com/2012/08/23/opinion/frum-cable-news/index.html [Accessed: 26 August 2012].

6   Folksonomies/Tagging

1. Vander Wal, T. (2007) "Folksonomy Coinage and Definition" [Online] 2 February. Available at: http://vanderwal.net/folksonomy.html [Accessed: 2 June 2008].

7   Wikis

1. Wikipedia (2008) "Wiki" [Online] Available at: http://en.wikipedia.org/ wiki/Wiki [Accessed: 10 March 2008].

2. Wikipedia (2012) "Wiki" [Online] Available at: http://en.wikipedia.org/ wiki/Wiki [Accessed: 22 November 2012].

3. Wikipedia (2014) "Wiki" [Online] Available at: http://en.wikipedia.org/ wiki/Wiki [Accessed: 31 December 2014].

4. Wiktionary (2012) "Wiki" [Online] Available at: http://en.wiktionary.org/ wiki/wiki [Accessed: 22 November 2012].

5. McAfee (2006) *Enterprise 2.0: How to Manage Social Technologies to Transform Your Organization*. Boston: Harvard Business School Press.

6. Gilbertson, S. (2010) "Feb. 16, 1978: Bulletin Board Goes Electronic" Wired. com [Online] Available at: http://www.wired.com/thisdayintech/2010/02/ 0216cbbs-first-bbs-bulletin-board/ [Accessed: 5 February 2012].

7. WikiMedia Foundation (2012) "Home" Wikimedia.org [Online] Available at: http://wikimediafoundation.org/wiki/Home [Accessed: 20 November 2012].

8. Wikileaks (2012) "What is Wikileaks?" Wikileaks.org [Online] Available at: http://wikileaks.org/About.html [Accessed: 20 November 2012].

9. Elmer, R., Schmitt, D., and Assange, J. (2008) "Bank Julius Baer: Grand Larceny via Grand Cayman"Wikileaks.org [Online] 29 February. Available at: http://www.wikileaks.org/wiki/Bank_Julius_Baer:_Grand_Larceny_via_ Grand_Cayman [Accessed: 20 July 2008].

10. McAfee (2009).

11. Mehling, H. (2007) "Wikis in the Enterprise Face Security, Compliance Challenges"[Online] August. Available at: http://searchcio.techtarget.com/ tip/Wikis-in-the-enterprise-face-security-compliance-challenges [Accessed: 20 January 2012].

12. Open Source Initiative, (nd) "Licenses by Name"[Online] Available at: http:// opensource.org/licenses/alphabetical [Accessed: 20 November 2012].

13. Ubuntu (2012) "List of Open Source Programs" Ubuntu Documentation [Online] 3 November. Available at: https://help.ubuntu.com/community/ ListOfOpenSourcePrograms [Accessed: 20 November 2012].

14. Musk, E. (2014) "All Our Patent Are Belong To You" 12 June [Blog] Available at: http://www.teslamotors.com/blog/all-our-patent-are-belong- you [Accessed: 16 June 2014].

8 Podcasts

1. YouTube (2015) "Statistics" [Online] Available at: http://www.youtube. com/t/press_statistics [Accessed: 1 January 2015].

2. Jacobs, H. (2014) "We Ranked YouTube's Biggest Stars By How Much Money They Make" 10 March [Online] Available at: http://www.businessinsider. com/richest-youtube-stars-2014-3?op=1 [Accessed: 16 June 2014].

3. Medich, R. (2012) "Ikea Launches YouTube Page for Assembly Instruction Videos" Fuel the future. Adweek [Online] 29 February. Available at: http:// fuelthefuture.adweek.com/trending/ikea-launches-assembly-video- youtube-page/19974/ [Accessed: 2 December 2012].

4. BBC World Service (2012) "Click" [Podcast] Available at: http://www.bbc. co.uk/podcasts/series/digitalp [Accessed: 10 January 2012].

5. Target Internet (2012) "Digital Marketing Podcast" [Podcast] Available at: http://www.targetinternet.com/tag/digital-marketing-podcast/ [Accessed: 10 January 2012].

6. Dubner, S. (2012) "Freakonomics Podcast" [Podcast] Available at: http:// www.freakonomics.com/tag/freakonomics-podcast/ [Accessed: 10 January 2012].

7. BBC (2012) "Friday Night Comedy" [Podcast] Available at: http://www.bbc.co.uk/podcasts/series/fricomedy [Accessed: 10 January 2012].

8. *Harvard Business Review* (2012) "HBR Ideacast" [Podcast] Availabe at: http://blogs.hbr.org/ideacast/ [Accessed: 10 January 2012].

9. Site Visibility (2012) "Internet Marketing Podcast" [Podcast] Available at: http://www.sitevisibility.co.uk/impodcast/ [Accessed: 10 January 2012].

10. *The Guardian* (2012) "Media Talk" [Podcast] Available at: http://www.guardian.co.uk/media/series/mediatalk [Accessed: 10 January 2012].

11. *The Guardian* (2012) "Tech Weekly" [Podcast] Available at: http://www.guardian.co.uk/technology/series/techweekly [Accessed: 10 January 2012].

12. TED Conferences (2012) "TED" [Podcast] Available at: http://www.ted.com/ [Accessed: 10 January 2012].

13. TWiT (2012) "This Week in Google" [Podcast] Available at: http://twit.tv/twig [Accessed: 10 January 2012].

14. *Wired* (2012) "Wired.co.uk Podcast" [Podcast] Available at: http://www.wired.co.uk/podcast [Accessed: 10 January 2012].

15. Zen Internet Ltd. (2015) "Zen Monthly" [Podcast] Available at: http://www.zen.co.uk/newsletters.aspx [Accessed: 1 January 2015].

16. Cisco (2012) "Perspectives Multiplied: Sally Blount on the Enduring" [Podcast] Available at: http://www.youtubecisco.com/csr [Accessed: 20 September 2012].

17. Clifford, S. (2012) "Video Prank at Domino's Taints Brand" *The New York Times* [Online] Available at: http://www.nytimes.com/2009/04/16/business/media/16dominos.html?_r=0 [Accessed: 10 January 2012].

18. Carroll, D. (2012) *United Breaks Guitars: The Power of One Voice in the Age of Social Media*. New York: Hay House.

19. Greenpeace (2010) "Sweet Success for Kit Kat Campaign: You Asked, Nestlé has Answered" [Online] Available at: http://www.greenpeace.org/international/en/news/features/Sweet-success-for-Kit-Kat-campaign/ [Accessed: 10 January 2012].

20. Ko, V. (2011) "FedEx Apologizes After Video of Driver Throwing Fragile Package Goes Viral" Time Newsfeed [Online] Available at: http://newsfeed.time.com/2011/12/23/fedex-apologizes-after-video-of-driver-throwing-fragile-package-goes-viral/ [Accessed: 10 January 2012].

9   Social Networks

1. Wikipedia (2013) "List of Social Networking Sites" [Online] Available at: http://en.wikipedia.org/wiki/List_of_social_networking_websites [Accessed: 29 December 2012].

2. Association of Virtual Worlds (2012) "Association of Virtual Worlds" [Online] Available at: http://network.associationofvirtualworlds.com/ [Accessed: 10 January 2012].

3. AODL (2012) "Art of Digital London" [Online] Available at: http://the knowledge.aodl.org.uk/index.php/Frontpage [Accessed: 29 December 2012].

4. Metcalfe, B. (2006) "Guest Blogger Bob Metcalfe: Metcalfe's Law Recurses Down the Long Tail of Social Networks" [Blog] 18 August. Available at: http://vcmike.wordpress.com/2006/08/18/metcalfe-social-networks/ [Accessed: 28 September 2006].

5. Yarrow, J. (2014) "Here's the Magic Word that Can Boost Your Post in Facebook's News Feed" 29 April [Online] Available at: http://www.businessinsider.com/facebook-news-feed-ranking-2014-4 [Accessed: 16 June 2014].

6. Rumsfeld, D. (2002) "DoD News Briefing – Secretary Rumsfeld and Gen. Myers" US Department of Defense [Online] Available at: http://www.defense.gov/transcripts/transcript.aspx?transcriptid=2636 [Accessed: 13 April 2008].

7. SocialBakers.com (2012) "Facebook Brand Statistics" [Online] Available at: http://www.socialbakers.com/facebook-pages/brands/ [Accessed: 29 December 2012].

8. Facebook.com (2012) "Dusty & Michael: Page Creators" Coca Cola Facebook page [Online] Available at: http://www.facebook.com/cocacola/app_132920893413852 [Accessed: 29 December 2012].

9. Interbrand (2012) "Best Global Brands 2012" [Online] Available at: http://www.interbrand.com/en/best-global-brands/2012/Best-Global-Brands-2012-Brand-View.aspx [Accessed: 29 December 2012].

10. FirstDirect (2012) "first direct: Facebook page" Facebook.com [Online] Available at: http://www.facebook.com/firstdirect/posts/137984746323858 [Accessed: 25 February 2012].

10 Widgets/Apps

1. Lacy, S. (2012) "Handy: Evernote Acqui-hires Digital Handwriting App Penultimate" PandoDaily.com [Online] 7 May Available at: http://pandodaily.com/2012/05/07/handy-evernote-acqui-hires-digital-handwriting-app-penultimate/ [Accessed: 30 May 2012].

2. Takahashi, D. (2012) "After 6M Paid Downloads, Mobile Hit Pocket God Wraps up with its Final, Apocalyptic Update" [Online] 19 December

Available at: http://venturebeat.com/2012/12/19/after-6m-paid-downloads-mobile-game-hit-pocket-god-wraps-up-with-its-final-apocalyptic-update/ [Accessed: 29 December 2012].

3. Ferris, T. (2012) "How to Build an App Empire: Can You Create The Next Instagram?" [Blog] Available at: http://www.fourhourworkweek.com/blog/2012/04/22/how-to-build-an-app-empire-can-you-create-the-next-instagram/ [Accessed: 12 May 2012].

4. Anderson, C. (2006) *The Long Tail: How Endless Choice is Creating Unlimited Demand*. London: Random House Business Books.

5. Anderson, C. (2009) *Free: How Today's Smartest Businesses Profit by Giving Something for Nothing*. London: Random House Business Books.

11 Internet of Things

1. Ashton, K. (2009) "That 'Internet of Things' Thing" 22 June [Online] Available at: http://www.rfidjournal.com/articles/view?4986 [Accessed: 20 June 2013].

2. Gartner (2013) "Gartner Says the Internet of Things Installed Base Will Grow to 26 Billion Units By 2020" 12 December [Press Release] Available at: http://www.gartner.com/newsroom/id/2636073 [Accessed: 17 February 2014].

13 Mashups

1. *The Guardian* (n.d.) "Free our Data" Guardian.co.uk [Online] Available at: http://www.guardian.co.uk/technology/free-our-data [Accessed: 10 October 2010].

2. Gheorghe, A. (n.d.) "The Longest Poem in the World" [Online] Available at: http://www.longestpoemintheworld.com/ [Accessed: 10 December 2012].

14 Virtual Worlds

1. Barss, P. (2010) *The Erotic Engine: How Pornography has Powered Mass Communication, from Gutenberg to Google*. Toronto: Doubleday Canada.

2. Seely Brown, J. and Thomas, D. (2006) "You Play World of Warcraft? You're Hired!" Wired.com [Online] Available at: http://www.wired.com/wired/archive/14.04/learn.html [Accessed: 8 January 2007].

3. Reeves, B., Malone, T.W., and O'Driscoll, T. (2008) "Leadership's Online Labs" 1 May. *Harvard Business Review*, R0805C-PDF-ENG.

4. Kzero.com (2013) "Digital Kids Conference Presentation" [Online] Available at: http://www.slideshare.net/slideshow/embed_code/16445109?rel=0# [Accessed: 14 February 2013].

5. SecondLife.com (2011) "The Second Life Economy in Q3 2011" [Blog] Available at: http://community.secondlife.com/t5/Featured-News/The-Second-Life-Economy-in-Q3-2011/ba-p/1166705 [Accessed: 3 September 2012].

6. Sulake.com (2012) "Habbo Hotel – Where Else?" [Online] Available at: http://secondlife.com/destination/clube-do-sexo-brasil [Accessed: 3 September 2012].

7. Mindark.com (2007) "Entropia Universe Enters China to Create the Largest Virtual World Ever" [Press Release] 30 May. Available at: http://www.mind-ark.com/press/press-releases/documents/Entropia_Universe_Enters_China.pdf [Accessed: 29 June 2007].

8. Au, W.J. (2007) "Avatar-based Workers Unite? Labor Union Protest against IBM to Enter Second Life" [Blog] Available at: http://nwn.blogs.com/nwn/2007/09/labor-union-pro.html [Accessed: 30 September 2007].

9. Mystakidis, S. (2012) "IBM Inclusive Leadership Training in Second Life T4S" [Video] Available at: http://www.youtube.com/watch?v=H4Iw8GBQfl4 [Accessed: 20 March 2012].

10. IBM (n.d.) "IBM Virtual University on Demand" [Online] Available at: http://www-304.ibm.com/easyaccess1/csipartners/contenttemplate/!!/xmlid=226820 [Accessed: 30 April 2012].

11. Gandhi, S. (2010) "IBM Dives into Second Life" IBM [Online] 19 January. Available at: http://www.ibm.com/developerworks/opensource/library/os-social-secondlife/?ca=drs- [Accessed: 27 January 2010].

12. Cisco (2010) "Next-Generation Events. Cisco Strategic Leadership Offsite" [PDF] Available at: http://www.cisco.com/web/about/ac79/docs/innov/Next-Gen_Events_Case_Study_SLO_1025.pdf [Accessed: 20 January 2011].

13. SuperDataResearch (2012) "Worldwide Virtual Goods Market Reaches $15 Billion. Monetization Still a Four Letter Word." [Online] 29 August. Available at: http://www.superdataresearch.com/blog/monetization-is-a-four-letter-word/ [Accessed: 19 September 2012].

14. OECD (2011) "Virtual Worlds: Immersive Online Platforms For Collaboration, Creativity And Learning". Paris: Organisation for Economic Cooperation and Development (OECD).

15. *The Guardian* (19 April 2010). "Sims 3 and Renault Announce Product-placement Deal." [Online] Available at: http://www.guardian.co.uk/

technology/gamesblog/2010/apr/19/sims-3-renault-ea-games [Accessed: 5 March 2012].

16. Tatar, J. (2012) "Second Life Focus Groups – Four Years Later" Gem Research Solutions [Blog] 24 October. Available at: http://www.gemresearchsolutions.com/second-life-focus-groups-four-years-later/ [Accessed: 10 January 2013].

17. NBC News (2010) "Virtual Reality at Airbus" [PhotoBlog] 21 October. Available at: http://photoblog.nbcnews.com/_news/2010/10/21/5329351-virtual-reality-at-airbus [Accessed: 10 January 2011].

18. PA Consulting (2006) "World First: PA Consulting Group the First Major Consultancy to Open for Business in the Virtual 3D World 'Second Life'" [Press Release] 24 October. Available at: http://www.paconsulting.com/introducing-pas-media-site/archive/world-first-pa-consulting-group-the-first-major-consultancy-to-open-for-business-in-the-virtual-3d-world-second-life/ [Accessed: 20 June 2007].

19. PRWeb (2009) "TSTC Takes One Small Step for Virtual Worlds, One Giant Leap for Virtual World Education" [Press Release] 18 May. Available at: http://www.prweb.com/releases/TSTC/virtual_education/prweb2419874.htm [Accessed: 15 June 2009].

20. Medical News Today (2008) "First Paramedic Course To Use Second Life" Medical News Today, 13 October 2008. Available at: http://www.medical-newstoday.com/articles/125259.php [Accessed: 13 October 2009].

21. NHS (2009) "Welcome to Second Health Hospital" Available at: http://slurl.com/secondlife/National%20Health%20Service/140/99/26 [Accessed on 13 October 2009].

22. Medical Media and Design Laboratory, (2009) "About MMDL at Imperial College London" Available at: http://medmedia.wordpress.com/ [Accessed: 13 October 2009].

23. Cook, J. (2004) "Accessing Virtual Hallucinations" Available at: http://www.ucdmc.ucdavis.edu/ais/virtualhallucinations/ [Accessed: 13 October 2009].

24. Ryan, M. (2008) "16 Ways to use Second Life in your Classroom: Pedagogical Approaches and Virtual Assignments" Available at: http://www.lancs.ac.uk/postgrad/ryanm2/SLEDcc08_ryan_paper.pdf [Accessed on: 18 August 2009].

25. Gerstein, J. (2009) Personal email and Second Life interview. Jackie Gerstein, Online Faculty for Departments of Education, Kaplan University, 2 July.

26. WorldViz (2010) "Architecture Interactive - MiniWorld Navigation in Virtual Reality" [Video] 22 July. Available at: http://www.youtube.com/watch?v=T3WOtQq5e7Q [Accessed: 29 April 2012].

27. Gosney, J. (2013) "Project: Second Life Faculty Learning Community: Exploring teaching and learning with Second Life" Available at: http://uits. iu.edu/page/bbcn [Accessed: 14 February 2013].

28. Sobkowiak, W. (2009) Personal email interview. Professor at School of English, Adam Mickiewicz University, 24 June.

29. Jankowski, M. (2010) Personal email. Co-Founder and President, Shapiro Negotiations, 11 January 2010.

30. Stafford, J. (2009) Personal email interview. R&D Coordinator, Teaching & Learning Technology, Winona State University, 23 June.

31. Facebook (2014) "Facebook to Acquire Oculus" 25 March [Press Release] Available at: http://newsroom.fb.com/news/2014/03/facebook-to-acquire-oculus/ [Accessed: 26 March 2014].

32. Northwestern University. (2008) "Real-world Behavior And Biases Show Up In Virtual World." ScienceDaily [Online] 11 Sep. Available at: http://www. eurekalert.org/pub_releases/2008-09/nu-rba090808.php [Accessed: 10 December 2012].

33. Hussain, Z. and Griffiths, M.D. (2008) "Gender Swapping and Socializing in Cyberspace: An Exploratory Study," CyberPsychology and Behavior 11: 47–53.

34. Lomanowska, A.M. and Guitton, M.J. (2012) "Virtually Naked: Virtual Environment Reveals Sex-Dependent Nature of Skin Disclosure". PLoS ONE 7(12): e51921. doi:10.1371/journal.pone.0051921 Available at: http://www.plosone.org/article/info%3Adoi%2F10.1371%2Fjournal. pone.0051921 [Accessed: 14 February 2013].

35. Linden Lab. (2011) "July Update" [Blog] 6 July. Available at: http://community.secondlife.com/t5/Featured-News/July-Update/ba-p/964435 [Accessed: 20 September 2011].

15 Gamification

1. Silverman, R.E. (2011) "Latest Game Theory: Mixing Work and Play" *Wall Street Journal* [Online] 10 October. Available at: http://online.wsj.com/article/SB10001424052970204294504576615371783795248.html [Accessed: 20 November 2011].

2. Schaeffer, C. (n.d.) "Gamification—CRM Use Cases, Rewards and Risks" [Online] Available at: http://www.crmsearch.com/crm-gamification.php [Accessed 20 November 2014].

3. Morgan, J. (2012) "The Risks of Gamification for the Enterprise" [Online] Available at: http://www.thefutureorganization.com/risks-gamification-enterprise/ [Accessed: 15 April 2012].

16   Spreading the Word

1. Tosti, G. (1897) "The Sociological Theories of Gabriel Tarde", *Political Science Quarterly* 12, 3 (September): 490–511.
2. Rogers, E.M. (2003) *Diffusion of Innovations* (5th edn). London: Simon & Schuster International.
3. Ryan, B. and Gross, N. C. (1943)"The Diffusion of Hybrid Seed Corn in Two Iowa Communities" *Rural Sociology* 8: 15–24.
4. Moore, G. A. (1991) *Crossing the Chasm: Marketing and Selling Technology Products to Mainstream Customers*. Oxford: Capstone Publishing.
5. Winograd, T. (1996) *Bringing Design to Software* (1st edn). London: Addison Wesley.
6. Ngak, C. (2012)"The 25 most common passwords of 2012"[Online] 24 October. Available at: http://www.cbsnews.com/8301-205_162-57539366/the-25-most-common-passwords-of-2012/ [Accessed: 14 February 2013].
7. Willis, J. (2007) "The Neuroscience of Joyful Education" *Educational Leadership: Engaging the Whole Child* 64 (summer). Available at: http://www.district287.org/clientuploads/287Staff/SEL/ME_PrereadingJudyWillisEdLeadArt.pdf [Accessed: 19 August 2010].
8. United Nations, (2000)"We The Peoples"[PDF] Available at: http://www.un.org/en/events/pastevents/pdfs/We_The_Peoples.pdf [Accessed: 20 August 2008].
9. Warren, C. (2014) "28 Days of Fame: the Strange, True Story of 'Flappy Bird'" 11 February [Online] Available from: http://mashable.com/2014/02/10/flappy-bird-story/ [Accessed: 12 February 2014]
10. Rogers, E.M. (2003) *Diffusion of Innovations* (5th edn). London: Simon & Schuster International.
11. Levitt, T. (1965) "Exploit the Product Life Cycle" *Harvard Business Review*, November–December: 81–94.

17   Deaf to the Word

1. Rogers, E. M. and Shoemaker, F. F. (1972) *Communication of Innovations: A Cross-Cultural Approach* (2nd edn). New York: Free Press.

18 Some are More Equal than Others

1. ITU (2014) "ITU_Key_2005-2014_ICT_data" [Excel] Available at: http://www.itu.int/en/ITU-D/Statistics/Documents/statistics/2014/ITU_Key_2005-2014_ICT_data.xls [Accessed: 4 January 2014].
2. ITU (2013) "The World in 2013" [PDF] Available at: http://www.itu.int/ITU-D/ict/facts/material/ICTFactsFigures2013.pdf [Accessed: 20 March 2013].

19 Deciding to Do Something

1. Rogers, E.M. (2003) *Diffusion of Innovations* (5th edn). London: Simon & Schuster International.
2. Moore, G.A. (1991) *Crossing the Chasm: Marketing and Selling Technology Products to Mainstream Customers*. Oxford: Capstone Publishing.
3. Shirky, C. (2008) *Here Comes EveryBody: The Power of Organising without Organizations*. London: Penguin Books.
4. Hamel, G. (2007) *The Future of Management*. Boston: Harvard Business School Press.
5. Ward, J. and Peppard, J. (2002) *Strategic Planning for Information Systems* (3rd edn). Chichester: John Wiley & Sons.
6. Parsons, J. (1983) "Information Technology – A New Competitive Weapon" *Sloan Management Review*, 25(1): 3–14.
7. Ray-Couquard, I., Philip, T., Lehman, M., Fervers, B., Farsi, F., and Chauvin, F. (1997) "Impact of a Clinical Guidelines Program for Breast and Colon Cancer in a French Cancer Center" *JAMA* 278(19): 1591–5.
8. BBC (2006) "Blogging 'Set to Peak Next Year'" [Website: 14 December 2006] Available at: http://news.bbc.co.uk/1/hi/6178611.stm [Accessed: 11 September 2010].

20 What's Marketing Got to Do with it?

1. Moore, G.A. (1991) *Crossing the Chasm: Marketing and Selling Technology Products to Mainstream Customers*. Oxford: Capstone Publishing.
2. Rosen, E. (2000) *The Anatomy of Buzz: How to Create Word-of-Mouth Marketing*. New York: Doubleday.

3. Li, C. and Bernoff, J. (2008) *Groundswell: Winning in a World Transformed by Social Technologies*. Boston: Harvard Business School Press.

4. Forrester Research Inc. (2009) "What's The Social Technographics Profile Of Your Customers?" [Online interactive tool] Available at: http://www.forrester.com/Groundswell/profile_tool.html [Accessed: 18 September 2009].

21   Critical Mass

1. Markus, M.L. (1987) "Toward a 'Critical Mass' Theory of Interactive Media Universal Access, Interdependence and Diffusion" *Communication Research* 14 (5): 491–511.

2. Gladwell, M. (2000) *The Tipping Point: How Little Things Can Make a Big Difference*. London: Abacus.

3. Crepeau, N.M. (2009) "Facebook Usage: How Often Do Different Types of Users Access Facebook?" [Blogpost at Coherent Social Media: 12 August 2009] Available at: http://nmc.itdevworks.com/index.php/2009/08/facebook-usage-how-often-do-different-types-of-users-access-facebook/ [Accessed: 16 September 2010].

4. Shirky, C. (2008) *Here Comes EveryBody: The Power of Organising without Organizations*. London: Penguin Books.

5. Dunbar, P.R. (2004) *Grooming, Gossip and the Evolution of Language* (2ndedn). London: Faber and Faber.

6. Bennett, D. (2013) "The Dunbar Number, From the Guru of Social Networks" BusinessWeek.com [Online] 10 January. Available at: http://www.businessweek.com/articles/2013-01-10/the-dunbar-number-from-the-guru-of-social-networks [Accessed: 20 March 2013].

7. IBM (n.d.) "Welcome to the IBM Jam Events Page" [Online] Available at: https://www.collaborationjam.com/ [Accessed: 1 April 2013].

22   Innovations in Organizations

1. Mahler, A. and Rogers, E. M. (1999) "The Diffusion of interactive Communication Innovations and the Critical Mass: The Adoption of Telecommunications Services by German Banks" *Telecommunications Policy*, 23: 719–40.

2. MOD (n.d.) "Social Media Guidance for UK Armed Forces and MOD personnel" Defence Social Media Hub – (BETA) [Online] Available at: http://www.blogs.mod.uk/social-media-guidelines.html [Accessed: 20 March 2013].

3. Zaltman, G., Duncan, R., and Holbek, J. (1973) *Innovations and Organizations*. London: John Wiley & Sons.

23 All Change Please

1. Eason, K. (1988) *Information Technology and Organizational Change*. London: Taylor & Francis.

2. Fischer, U. and Orasanu, J. (1999) " Cultural Diversity And Crew Communication" [PDF] Available at: http://lmc.gatech.edu/~fischer/AIAA99.pdf [Accessed: 2 June 2010].

3. Hofstede, D.G. (1984) *Culture's Consequences: International Differences in Work-Related Values* (Abridged edn). California: Sage Publications, Inc.

4. Mulder, M., Veen, P., Rodenburg, C., Frenken, J. and Tielens, H. (1972) "The Power Distance Reduction Hypothesis on a Level of Reality" *Journal of Experimental Social Psychology* 9(2): 87–96.

5. Jones, G. and Goffee, R. (2003) *The Character Of A Corporation: How Your Company's Culture Can Make or Break Your Business* (2nd edn). London: Profile Business.

6. Burke, W.W. and Litwin, G.H. (1992) "A Causal Model of Organizational Performance and Change" *Journal of Management* 18(3): 523–45.

7. Tapscott, D. and Williams, A.D. (2006) *Wikinomics: How Mass Collaboration Changes Everything*. London: Atlantic Books.

8. Owen, L., Goldwasser, C., Choate, K. and Blitz, A. (2007) "The Power of Many: ABCs of Collaborative Innovation Throughout the Extended Enterprise" [Report from the IBM Institute for Business Value] Available at: http://www-935.ibm.com/services/us/gbs/bus/pdf/g510-6335-00-abc.pdf [Accessed: 14 November 2007].

24 Management Choices

1. McLoughlin, I. and Clark, J. (1988) *Technological Change at Work*. Milton Keynes: Open University Press.

26 Findings from the Research

1. McKinsey (2009) "How Companies are Benefiting from Web 2.0: McKinsey Global Survey Results" *McKinsey Quarterly*, September. Available at: https://www.mckinseyquarterly.com/Business_Technology/BT_Strategy/ How_companies_are_benefiting_from_Web_20_McKinsey_Global_ Survey_Results_2432 [Accessed: 20 June 2010].

2. McKinsey (2013) "Business and Web 2.0: An Interactive Feature" [Online Interactive Tool] Available at: http://www.mckinsey.com/tools/ Wrappers/Wrapper.aspx?sid={D582D6EB-2CC7-45F0-8BD5- 49464985E816}&pid={52FA595C-7E8B-401F-9FEF-3E4096867DBC} [Accessed: 10 April 2013].

3. Prochaska, J., Norcross, J., and DiClemente, C. (1994) *Changing for Good* (pp. 40–56). New York: Avon Books.

4. Linkenbach, J. and Perkins, H.W. "Most of Us Prevent Drinking and Driving: A Successful Social Norms Campaign to Reduce Impaired Driving among Young Adults in Western Montana." Conference presentation at The National Conference on the Social Norms Model, July 25.

5. Fishbein, M. and Ajzen, I. (1975) *Belief, Attitude, Intention, and Behavior: An Introduction to Theory and Research*. Reading, MA: Addison-Wesley.

6. Saporito, R. (1988) "Uncovering Mars' Unknown Empire – They are America's richest family, who got to be worth $12.5 billion by selling sweets and sustenance to man and beast. But their cult of secrecy is costing them dearly." [Online] 26 September. Available at: http://money.cnn.com/maga- zines/fortune/fortune_archive/1988/09/26/71053/ [Accessed: 10 April 2010].

7. Miller, N.E. and Dollard, J. (1941) *Social Learning and Imitation*. New Haven: Yale University Press.

8. Thaler, R.H. and Sunstein, C.R. (2009) *Nudge: Improving Decisions About Health, Wealth and Happiness*. London: Penguin Books.

9. Duhigg, C. (2012) *The Power of Habit: Why We Do What We Do, and How to Change*. London: William Heinemann.

10. Kotler, P. and Lee, N.R. (2008) *Social Marketing: Influencing Behaviors for Good* (3rd edn). Thousand Oaks, CA: Sage Publications, Inc.

11. Kaushik, A. (2007) *Web Analytics: An Hour a Day* (Pap/Cdr. Edn). Chichester: John Wiley & Sons.

12. Solis, B. (2010) "*The Maturation of Social Media ROI*" [Blog] Available at: http://mashable.com/2010/01/26/maturation-social-media-roi/ [Accessed: 21 November 2010].

13. Williams, K. (2009) "Dell Hell: The Impact of Social Media on Corporate Communication" [Case Study] https://learningspaces.njit.edu/elliot/content/dell-hell-impact-social-media-corporate-communication [Accessed: 20 June 2010].

14. McAfee, A. (2009) *Enterprise 2.0: New Collaborative Tools for Your Organization's Toughest Challenges*. Boston: Harvard Business School Publishing.

15. Qualman, E. (2009) *Socialnomics: How Social Media Transforms the Way We Live and Do Business* (1st edn). Chichester: John Wiley & Sons.

16. McKinsey (2009) "How companies are benefiting from Web 2.0: McKinsey Global Survey Results", *McKinsey Quarterly*, September. Available at: https://www.mckinseyquarterly.com/Business_Technology/BT_Strategy/How_companies_are_benefiting_from_Web_20_McKinsey_Global_Survey_Results_2432 [Accessed: 20 June 2010].

17. Kaplan, R.S. and Norton, D.P. (2004) *Strategy Maps: Converting Intangible Assets into Tangible Outcomes*. Boston: Harvard Business School Press.

27 Obstacles and Excuses

1. Greenwald, G., MacAskill, E., and Poitras, L. (2013) "Edward Snowden: The Whistleblower Behind the NSA Surveillance Revelations" *The Guardian* [Online] Available at: http://www.theguardian.com/world/2013/jun/09/edward-snowden-nsa-whistleblower-surveillance [Accessed: 13 June 2013].

2. McAfee, A. (2009) *Enterprise 2.0: New Collaborative Tools for Your Organization's Toughest Challenges*. Boston: Harvard Business School Publishing.

29 Strategize

1. Kahneman, D. (2011) *Thinking, Fast and Slow*. London: Penguin Books.

2. Kaushik, A. (2007) *Web Analytics: An Hour a Day* (Pap/Cdr. edn). Chichester: John Wiley & Sons.

30 Incentivize

1. Maslow, A.H.(1943) "A Theory of Human Motivation" [Online] Available at: http://www.researchhistory.org/2012/06/16/maslows-hierarchy-of-needs/ [Accessed: 20 June 2014]. Originally Published in *Psychological Review*, 50: 370–96.

31 Trust

1. Government Digital Service (2014) "Countersigning Passport Applications and Photos" [Online] Available at: https://www.gov.uk/countersigning-passport-applications [Accessed: 20 April 2014].

2. Ipsos MORI (2013) "Trust in Professions" [Online] Available at: http://www.ipsos-mori.com/researchpublications/researcharchive/15/Trust-in-Professions.aspx?view=wide [Accessed: 20 April 2014].

3. Information Commissioner's Office. 2014 "Bring your Own Device (BYOD)" [PDF] Available at: http://ico.org.uk/for_organisations/data_protection/topic_guides/online/~/media/documents/library/Data_Protection/Practical_application/ico_bring_your_own_device_byod_guidance.ashx [Accessed: 20 April 2014].

4. Tjan, A.K. (2010) "Four Lessons on Culture and Customer Service from Zappos CEO, Tony Hsieh" 14 July [Online] Available at: https://hbr.org/2010/07/four-lessons-on-culture-and-cu/ [Accessed: 3 August 2010].

5. SMI-Online (2014) "Social Media in the Military & Defence Sector" [Online] Available at: http://www.smi-online.co.uk/defence/uk/conference/social-media-within-the-military-and-defence-sector/ [Accessed: 20 April 2014].

6. Harding, L. (2014) "How Edward Snowden went from loyal NSA contractor to whistleblower" [The Guardian Online] Available at: http://www.theguardian.com/world/2014/feb/01/edward-snowden-intelligence-leak-nsa-contractor-extract [Accessed: 1 February 2014].

35 The Future of Technology

1. Computer History Museum (n.d.) "Timeline of Computer History" [Online] Available at: http://www.computerhistory.org/timeline/?category=cmptr [Accessed: 2 April 2013].

2. Centre for Computer History, (n.d.) "1951 LEO I Computer Became Operational" [Online] Available at: http://www.computinghistory.org.uk/det/6162/LEO-I-computer-became-operational/ [Accessed: 2 April 2013].

3. Fenn, J. and Raskino, M. (2008) *Mastering the Hype Cycle: How to Choose the Right Innovation at the Right Time*. Boston: Harvard Business School Press.

4. Levy, K. (2014) "A Chinese Company 3-D Printed 10 Houses In A Day" [Online] Available at: http://www.businessinsider.com/a-chinese-company-3d-printed-10-houses-in-a-day-2014-4?utm_content=buffer83be1 [Accessed: 14 April 2014].

5. Wainwright, O. (2014) "Work Begins on the World's First 3D-printed House" 28 March [Online] Available at: http://www.theguardian.com/artanddesign/architecture-design-blog/2014/mar/28/work-begins-on-the-worlds-first-3d-printed-house [Accessed: 28 March 2014].

6. Davis, M. and Ellis, T.O. (1964) "The RAND Tablet: A Man-Machine Graphical Communications Device" RAND Corporation [PDF: RM-4122-ARPA] Available at: http://www.rand.org/content/dam/rand/pubs/research_memoranda/2005/RM4122.pdf [Accessed: 18 April 2013].

7. ComputerHistory.org (n.d.) "Rand Tablet" [Online] Available at: http://www.computerhistory.org/VirtualVisibleStorage/artifact_main.php?tax_id=04.06.01.00 [Accessed: 19 April 2013].

8. Intel (n.d.) "Moore's Law and Intel Innovation" [Online] Available at: http://www.intel.co.uk/content/www/us/en/history/museum-gordon-moore-law.html [Accessed: 19 April 2013].

9. Smith, A.R. (2013) "How Pixar Used Moore's Law to Predict the Future" Wired.com [Online] 17 April. Available at: http://www.wired.com/opinion/2013/04/how-pixar-used-moores-law-to-predict-the-future/ [Accessed: 19 April 2013].

10. Kurzweil, R. (2001) "The Law of Accelerating Returns" 7 March. [Online] Available at: http://www.kurzweilai.net/the-law-of-accelerating-returns [Accessed: 2 April 2007].

11. Armstrong, S. (2012) "How We're Predicting AI" Singularity Summit Presentation [Video] 14 October. Available at: http://fora.tv/2012/10/14/Stuart_Armstrong_How_Were_Predicting_AI [Accessed: 10 January 2013].

Index

Printed and bound by CPI Group (UK) Ltd, Croydon, CR0 4YY